SO-ABD-326

Predator
Caller's
Companion

Predator Caller's Companion

GERRY BLAIR

WINCHESTER PRESS
Tulsa, Oklahoma

Copyright © 1981 by Gerry Blair
All rights reserved

Library of Congress Cataloging in Publication Data
Blair, Gerry.
  Predator caller's companion.

  Includes index.
  1. Game calling (Hunting)   2. Predatory
animals.   I. Title.
SK281.5.B53   799.2   81-497
ISBN 0-87691-336-2   AACR1

Published by Winchester Press
1421 South Sheridan Road
P. O. Box 1260
Tulsa, Oklahoma 74101

Book design by Quentin Fiore

Printed in the United States of America

1 2 3 4 5   85 84 83 82 81

Contents

Foreword

You will find a thrill to predator calling you won't find on other hunts. Most hunters go afield and move about an animal's territory hoping for a chance encounter. The hunter is moving and the quarry is still, which stacks the deck in favor of the critter. The roles are reversed when a predator call is used; the hunter hides and the animal moves to him. This gives the hunter the edge needed to take smart predators like the coyote, fox and bobcat. Some hunters use the call to take hard-to-hunt trophy animals such as mountain lion and black bear. Others use the call to bring deer and javelina to handshaking distance. At one time or another every critter that walks or flies will respond to a call. I have called about everything except a fish, and one of these days I'm sure I will see a rainbow trout come flopping up out of a mountain stream to check on the racket.

Predators are the critters that respond most often to calling. They eat meat and the distress cry of a prey animal means groceries. Each of the predators has his own style of response: The bobcat and mountain lion may take more than an hour before suddenly materializing thirty feet out; a virgin coyote will come at full speed; the javelina comes with a great gnashing of teeth and rock rolling; the great horned owl comes silently, floating out of the darkness to brush a cap bill with a gentle wingtip.

Calling critters is an exciting sport, and high fur prices have made it profitable as well. Many hunters make good money in season skinning and selling fur.

Every predator called and shot by a hunter means more game for next season's hunt. Wildlife professionals in Arizona have waged a five-year battle to prevent coyote predation from exterminating a historic antelope herd; at this point the coyote is winning. In another part of the state a wildlife biologist is conducting a mountain lion study. He estimates that lions take a hundred thousand deer a year in Arizona, which is five times the legal hunter harvest.

If wild meat is in short supply the critters turn enthusiastically to domestic animals. Some sheepmen have gone out of the business because of coyote predation, and cattle growers feed a good part of their calf crop to mountain lions. Every predator called and killed reduces this predation. It is also one less critter for the U. S. Fish and Wildlife Service to trap.

I have been a hardcore caller for five years. I start calling them when the first frost hits the high country and stop when the fur degrades in early spring. I call all day every day; I probably have crowded more calling experience into those five years than most hunters get in a lifetime.

Most of my calls have been for coyote since I spend most of my time in coyote country. I have also called bobcat, gray fox, red fox, raccoon, bear, mountain lion and javelina.

Most calling books seem to have a fatal weakness; they reflect the experience of only one caller. Much of the time the author's calling expertise does not extend much past the county line. There is a world of difference between calling coyote in Arizona and red fox in Ohio. I wanted to make this book as complete as possible; not just another book by a hunter who knows something about calling coyote in Arizona, in Ohio, or in any other singular area. To accomplish this, I contacted expert callers in other parts of the country and asked them to provide a "second opinion" that would supplement my own knowledge. You will be getting advice from men whose accumulated calling experience totals more than a hundred years. These men did not have a book such as *Predator Caller's Companion* to teach them the tricks of the trade—they learned the hard way.

Here are some of the folks you will meet as you read the book:

Murry Burnham is a legend in predator calling circles. He has more than thirty years of calling experience and may be the best all around caller alive today. Murry lives in central Texas where he night hunts for fox, cats and coyote. He shares his technique in the chapter on night calling.

Major Boddicker is a professional caller from LaPorte, Colorado. He has designed and marketed a predator call. Major has hunted red fox in South Dakota and Colorado and has called and shot more than a thousand reds.

George Oakey is a two-time Arizona State Champion Predator Caller. He has hunted all over Arizona from the low desert to the high mountains. George has called and shot more than a thousand bobcat, coyote and gray fox. He discusses technique and the early days of the sport.

Tom Morton is a cat caller and has called in every state west of the Mississippi River. He won the World Predator Calling Championship in 1967. Tom has called and shot hundreds of bobcat. He has also bagged twelve mountain lions with the predator call. He discusses cat-calling technique.

Dick Beeler won the World Predator Calling Championship in 1963 and 1964. He has called hundreds of javelina, maybe as many as a thousand. Dick tells you how to scout for javelina, how to bring them close enough to smell their breath, and how to take them with bow or handgun. Dick runs his own guide service out of Payson, Arizona.

Riney Maxwell is another professional guide. He takes clients into the rugged Blue Mountain Range that straddles the Arizona-New Mexico border. Riney uses a tube call to bring black bear out of the Blue's steep canyons. He has called 24 bear in the past five years and his hunters have taken sixteen.

Mike Mell is another guide. He is best known as a bighorn sheep guide but is also a talented caller. He has fifteen years' experience calling Arizona gray fox. He is also a skilled bear hunter. Mike discusses technique for calling both fox and bear.

Ed Sceery is a professional predator caller from Santa Fe, New Mexico. He has called more than two thousand coyote. He is the author of *Professional Predator Calling* published by Spearman Publishing Company in 1979. He also markets a profesional call which took him five years to develop. Ed offers a second opinion on calling coyote.

You will also get expert advice on varmint guns and loads. **Bill Ruger** of the Sturm, Ruger Company suggests possible choices for varmint guns. **Joyce Hornady** of the Hornady Manufacturing Company does the same and gives you the loads that have worked for him. **Fred Huntington**, designer of the RCBS line of reloading equipment, discusses loads and calibers. **Bruce Hodgdon** of the Hodgdon Powder Company explains why he would choose the .17 caliber for fur hunting.

This book is full of know-how and excitement. It will tell you about the animals, how to call them, what to shoot them with, and what to do with them when they are on the ground. It will make you a better hunter and send you home with more game. I really don't see how any serious hunter can do without this book.

PREDATOR
CALLER'S
COMPANION

1

The First Callers

Calling is an art that has been practiced by hunters for hundreds of years. In an article published in the October 1917 issue of *Sunset Magazine*, author Saxton Pope tells of an interview with an Indian named Ishi. The Indian was discovered wandering the California coast when he was barely a teenager. Ishi told Pope that his tribe had lured game to bow range by squeaking through their lips and this skill had been passed from generation to generation for centuries. Pope went on a hunt with the Indian and watched him perform. Ishi placed two fingers across his lips and sucked. The high pitched squeak resembled the distress cry of a mouse or a baby rabbit. Ishi called a jackrabbit and a bobcat on the first stand. Pope shot four arrows at the cat before it spooked. On the next eleven stands Ishi called critters five times. The two men sighted squirrels, coyotes, rabbits, wildcats and bear.

The Indians of the Southwest also had this skill. I have talked to Indians from three separate tribes who told me their fathers and grandfathers called game by holding a short piece of grass or leaf in front of their mouths and blowing, which produced a high-pitched scream. That technique is still used today.

Other writers have wondered why Indians would want to call coyotes, bobcat and fox. To me the answer is simple: They called them to supplement their meager diet of juniper berries, cactus fruits, and the grubs and lizards they dug from rotten logs. Aboriginal man was not as fussy about his groceries as we are. In addition the call served to bring more traditional fare such as rabbits, deer and javelina.

The predator call as we know it was developed more than fifty years ago. Morton Burnham was a hunter who discovered he could call fox, coyote, bobcat and wolves by making the same lip squeak used by Ishi. He once called and killed two dozen fox in an afternoon hunt. Morton passed the skill to his sons, Winston and Murry, and they designed a reeded tube that was later marketed as the first of the Burnham line of calls.

Other calls were being developed at about the same time. Some manufacturers offered dying rabbit squealers and as the sport gained popularity other tubes appeared. Jack Cain and Lew Mossinger of Goodyear, Arizona, developed a gravelly toned call that was the prototype for the present Circe line of predator calls. The Circe call had the range to carry across the vast southwest prairie and attract the far ranging coyote. The hoarse screams of the Circe were deadly on western critters. It was a new sound. They were easily convinced that a big western jackrabbit was about to meet his Maker. The critters came at a dead run to dispose of the corpse.

Southwestern Indians have called animals for centuries. Their lip squeaks probably brought critters such as these desert bighorn sheep. *Photo Gerry Blair.*

Predator calls resemble the distress cry of prey animals. This jackrabbit lets loose with a hoarse gravelly scream when he is hurt or scared, a sound that means groceries to predators. *Photo Gerry Blair.*

Most of the early calls were hardwood tubes constructed around a metal reed. Wood was later replaced with a hard plastic because it has a tendency to warp with temperature and humidity changes. This warping can often cause the reed to lose its tone. Plastic can be produced faster and sold to the consumer for considerably less.

Some callers were sorry to see the wood tubes go. They felt the wood gave a purer tone than the plastic. Most present call manufacturers offer the tubes in either wood or plastic with the wood costing a bit more. I have both wood and plastic in my assortment of calls, and to my tin ear they sound the same.

Calling Contests

Better calls and more callers resulted in the formation of calling clubs in many areas. The Arizona Varmint Callers Association was formed in 1956, but after four or five meetings the club all but failed. It was reorganized the next year with Lucky Wade as president and George Oakey as vice-president. That same year a calling contest was held. It was a platform affair where the callers blew to three judges a hundred yards out. Oakey won that first Arizona State Championship.

George Oakey with a cat and a pair of full-furred northern Arizona coyote. These three critters were taken from a single stand. *Photo courtesy George Oakey.*

Another field-calling contest was held the following year. The contest began about mid-October and ended in late February. Two-man teams went afield during the winter to call and kill predators. They saved the tails and turned them in at monthly club meetings. Fox tails were worth five points, coyote tails seven points and bobcat tails twenty points. The handsome bobcat pelts, worth several hundred dollars on today's market, were worthless then. George Oakey and Del Western won the contest. I talked to George recently to learn the calling conditions then.

> Del had a friend who lived on the Papago Indian Reservation and he got us permits to hunt there. God, there were a lot of coyotes there. They came to the call like grapes in bunches. We sometimes had gangs of five and six running around the blind. I shot a .250-3000 and Del shot a .257 Roberts. We didn't save the hides then as they weren't worth skinning. We considered ourselves lucky if we got half the coyotes we called. I guess we would have done better with a shotgun but I enjoyed rifle shooting too much to give it up.
>
> Most of the Papago is flat as a table top—typical low desert with the usual cactus, mesquite trees along the wash banks, and Palo Verde trees on the scattered ridges. It was perfect country for winter calling; cool temperatures, very little wind, and too many predators. We would set up the portable blinds backed up to one of the trees. I was blowing a Circe call and it really worked on those uneducated critters. We wouldn't shoot until we were sure of getting one or two.

One weekend we sighted fifty-seven coyotes. I don't remember how many we took home but most of the time our take was less than half of what we saw. A good day's hunting might produce ten or twelve coyotes, a couple of gray fox and three or four cats. Gas was cheap then and we would run out to the desert whenever we had a little time. You didn't have to go as far then as there weren't as many callers, and no trappers at all. There were a lot of predators.

I think that the most important part of predator calling is picking the country. I don't believe that the way you blow the call is very important unless the coyotes have been called a lot and are educated. I went hunting once with a man who had a bad stutter. When he blew the call it sounded like a stuttering rabbit in trouble. We were calling the San Carlos (another Indian reservation) and must have been in virgin country. That stuttering rabbit had coyotes running all over.

George doesn't remember how many tails he and Del turned in to win the first place trophy. A couple of years later, in 1961, Del Western and Bennie Murry teamed up to take the trophy. In eighteen weeks of calling they took 264 coyotes, eight bobcats and five fox. During that same period of time they called and sighted 495 coyotes, ten bobcats and six fox.

The calling contests helped the sport to grow. The publicity and the competition attracted new people and call manufacturers were motivated to develop new and better calls.

This tassel-eared squirrel could not resist author's close-in call. *Photo Gerry Blair.*

5

Why They Come

Any animal might respond to a given call for a number of reasons, the major one of which usually is food. Most prey animals scream when they are under attack either out of fear or to warn others of danger, or both. A predator knows that such screams mean that another predator has cornered a victim and he then will come charging in, hoping at least to share in the meal, or perhaps take it away from the first predator for himself.

Many predators, I believe, come to the call because of an instinct to defend their territory. Most adult predators have territories marked by feces, urine and scratches. If they get the idea that a coyote from across the canyon is doing a bit of poaching they come running with neck hair raised and teeth bared to protect what is theirs. Some of the critters fetched by a call, however, are not hungry and are not intent on defending a territory. A jackrabbit, for example, sometimes will come to the sound of a dying rabbit's scream, more out of curiosity, it seems, than anything else.

Some predator calls imitate the sound of young predators in distress. These young coyote squeal when threatened, which brings mom and pop on the run. *Photo Duane Rubink, U.S. Fish & Wildlife Service.*

Some Come Running

All critters do not have the same degree of intelligence and most of the young tend to lack experience as well. Some of these young critters come running and may try to crawl into the blind with you. Sam Dudley of Phoenix, one of the pioneers of the sport, had a young coyote do exactly that. Sam was well hidden in a small depression when the critter decided Sam was a potential victim. Sam and the critter rolled out of the blind and tumbled down a slight incline. Sam finally got the business end of his shotgun in the coyote's direction and the situation was resolved.

Older coyotes sometimes come in fast, particularly early in the calling year. They may have been called the past season but the passage of time has dulled their recollection of the trickery. I was calling the slope of a juniper push one fall morning when I sighted two hard-running coyotes coming from a half mile away. I stopped calling to watch the race. The critters came neck and neck most of the way, each extending himself so as to be the first to the imagined victim. Seventy seconds passed from the time I sighted them until the winner ran up the barrel of my full-choked twelve. The autoloader took the loser while he was trying to figure out why his buddy was kicking in the dirt.

Coyotes will often run in groups early in the fall. By that time, den mates have left home and they may stick together for several weeks. When they come as a gang they come fast. A competition seems to build to see who gets there first. I have had five coyotes come to a stand a number of times and at one stand I sighted seven. I made the stand at the timbered edge of a juniper push and was well hidden in the dead arms of a stringbark juniper. I had the .22-250 topped with a 6X Weaver. The critters were all over me before I knew what was happening. I put the scope on a hardcharging silver about twenty feet out. He looked as big as a buffalo through the scope and I *knew* I couldn't miss. I was wrong. In the end, I had emptied the five-shot Ruger and had never touched a hair.

Predator Paranoia

If a coyote answers the call and escapes with his life he is a disappointed but wiser critter. He is likely to develop a paranoid personality when it comes to eating rabbit. He may come to the call again but you can bet he won't come running. Some will come to the call slowly, making frequent stops to size up the country ahead. If the coyote is upwind of the call he will circle a hundred yards out to get downwind. If he gets behind you, and no masking scent is used, it is goodby critter. If I am well hidden and have a dependable masking scent I will not shoot one of these critters until I feel his nose on the back of my boot. Otherwise I will take my chance when the crafty critter starts the circle.

A fox becomes call smart slower than a coyote. This is particularly true of the gray. This is probably for two reasons: A fox comes to the call differently than a coyote. He is the small kid on the block and has to stop a little ways out to make sure there is nothing eating the rabbit that is likely to be dangerous. When the fox is convinced there is no danger he is determined to have the rabbit. This persistence lets very few fox escape.

The second reason fox are slow learners has to do with their size. As the third largest predator using the area he must be persistent in his hunting habits to survive. If he gave up a rabbit every time he got fooled, he would soon starve.

Unlike the coyote and the fox, the cat family never seems to learn. I am convinced that a bobcat or a mountain lion will come to the call every time they hear it. I don't think the cat is smart enough to associate the call with the hunter. If he thinks about it at all he probably cusses his luck for blundering into a hunter every time he sets out for a rabbit supper.

Game Animal Response

Many game animals come to a predator call mainly, I think, because they are curious. They may come because they feel one of their own is being attacked and they want to help if it's a friend and laugh if it's an enemy. Deer come most often in the spring and early summer when the fawns are about. I once called a meadow at the edge of a juniper push and sighted a coyote working his way to me through the tall grass. The critter was cagey and never offered a decent shot. I made the Burnham tube cry piteously but the coyote stayed in the weeds. I finally brought him out in the open by squeaking through my lips. He stepped out of the grass thirty feet out, took one look to my left, and turned to run. I did the dirty deed with the .22-250 and swung quickly left to cover the critter that had spooked the educated coyote. I was almost overrun by a herd of twenty mule deer. They had snuck in the back door while I was working that stubborn coyote out of the grass.

Javelina are the biggest suckers in the world. If I could learn to talk peccary I know damn well I could make a million bucks selling them the Grand Canyon. Their eagerness to come to the call can be great—if you are hunting javelina. It can be a pain in the neck if you are calling for fur. I called a rugged piece of Arizona real estate called Bloody Basic one winter and the desert pigs were so much

8

of a problem I had to pack up and leave. Sounders of hogs came to almost every stand. They come in hard, kicking rocks, huffing and snapping their tusks. Most of the desert predators have a healthy respect for a herd of adult javelina and make it a point to be low key when the pigs are in the area. Many pig hunters use the predator call to get close to the hogs. It is a deadly technique, particularly for bow hunters and those using other primitive weapons that demand close shots. Predator calling for pigs will be covered in detail in a later chapter.

Domestic livestock will also come to the call. I have called cattle, horses and goats. On one stand, believe it or not, I called in a buffalo. I was calling the Raymond Ranch east of Flagstaff where the state maintains a herd of about a hundred head that are allowed to roam free on twenty-six sections of land. I had made a stand under an alligator juniper, and three minutes into the call I heard the approach of a heavy animal. The critter was kicking rocks, grunting and growling, and sounding downright ferocious. I climbed as high into the juniper as I could and tried to look friendly. The bull patrolled the base of the tree for more than an hour, blowing through his nose, growling and making an amazing variety of hostile sounds. Eventually, he left.

I once called a bull buffalo—I hope it is my last. This ornery critter kept me treed for over an hour. *Photo Gerry Blair.*

Most of the flying predators come to the call. Red-tail hawks are common customers in the West. *Photo Gerry Blair.*

I have also had a few anxious moments with ranch dogs. I avoid calling near ranch buildings if I know the country but, in new country, a ranchhouse can be within call range but out of sight. The dogs usually come to the call as fast as a virgin coyote and they are usually mean. I have never been forced to shoot one to save my hide, but I have found it necessary on several occassions to use a dead juniper limb to earn a bit of respect.

Other Volunteers

Most flying predators will come to a call the first time they hear it. Crows and ravens are the most common in this part of the country. But they are smart critters and will wise up fast if they are fooled a time or two. If I go into an area to call and get quick response from these black bandits I am encouraged, because this means very little calling has taken place here or the crows would have been educated.

Circling crows also add to the stand. I once saw a coyote coming to the call by watching the circles of a group of interested raven. It was a windy day and the coyote may have had trouble locating the sound. I saw him stop frequently to eyeball the ravens and I guessed he was estimating the center of their circles and was homing on that. Whatever his problem was, I solved it with one pill from the barrel of the .22-250.

Jays and magpies also come to the call. They usually make a lot of racket and light in gangs in nearby trees and bushes. Their noise also adds to the call. The screams of the call and the chatter of the birds is a combination that will bring the smartest critter.

Eagles come to investigate a rabbit squeal but seldom stay long. Most of the time they circle a hundred yards up, surveying the ground below. When their keen eyesight reveals the fraud they soar away. Once or twice I have had eagles land in nearby trees. I have had my best luck with goldens, perhaps because there are more of them here in Arizona than there are the bald.

Hawks are not as smart as eagles. I have had redtails light in the bush that hid me. I have had them sit on limbs a few feet from my greased-up face and stare at me hungrily with their big yellow eyes. The accipiters are mostly smaller than the buteos and seem particularly susceptible to the call. They come best to a high-pitched squeak which resembles a mouse in trouble. I have had a pair of shinned hawks light on a limb five feet from my face and spend almost two minutes looking me over.

Owls also come close. They come mostly at night but will show up with alarming frequency at dawn and dusk calls. It can be downright unsettling to have one of the great horned owls brush your nose with a silent wingtip.

The fur-bearing predators come most eagerly to the call. In the West and Southwest you are most likely to see a coyote come galloping to the rabbit. Eastern callers will probably see more red fox than anything else. Southern callers, particularly those who hunt at night, will likely learn a lot about the nocturnal habits of the raccoon. All callers will have surprises. They will see bobcat on a fairly regular basis. Lion and bear will appear if they are in the area. Gray fox, ringtails, coati mundi and badger also come. That is one of the fringe benefits of calling; you never know what to expect. Sometimes, you may get no response to the call, but if a critter does come you never know if it will be badger or bear. At one time or another, I have called everything from a dickey bird to a game warden.

Sparrow hawks and other small falcons come best to the lip squeak. This handsome fellow lit on a limb 5 feet from my head and didn't leave until he heard the click of the shutter. *Photo Gerry Blair.*

2

Predator Calls

Mouth Calls

Even the most inexperienced caller can fool a coyote, a fox or a bobcat once in a while. Any of the tube calls on the market will make a sound that will fetch a critter of some kind. I went hunting a few years back with a young biology major from the local university who had never been on a predator hunt. I asked him to read the instruction sheet packed with a Circe call and gave him no further advice. I picked the calling stands, choosing locations that my experience and intuition told me had critters. He brought in a pair of hungry coyotes on the first stand. We made nine other stands that day and sighted customers on five of the nine. We went home with three coyotes and a bobcat.

The novice, who did all of the calling, went home convinced he was the world's fastest learner. The next weekend, however, he went hunting with a college buddy and came home complaining that they never even sighted a hair. Blowing the tube is not the most important element in predator calling. The best blower in the world can't blow up a critter if there are none around to hear the music.

To be consistently successful a caller has to learn a lot about the habits of the critters he hunts. He also needs to know what the varmints eat, where they sleep and the kind of country that best fits their hunting methods. By setting up his stand in prime critter habitat the hunter has a good chance of success.

I have used most of the tube calls on the market at one time or another. Every one will call critters if they are used in accordance with the maker's recommendations. I have found that each of the calls have strong and weak points. All of the calls do not work equally well on all critters. A change in location might also change a call's effectiveness. A loud, long-range call that works great on prairie coyotes might do a lousy job on the coyotes that live in the brushy can-

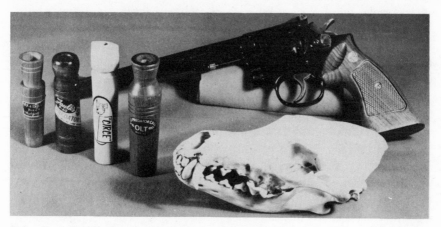

Four tube calls. The Circe is the only call with a fitted mouthpiece. *Photo Gerry Blair.*

yons. I have listed the calls I have had experience with, and I have made notations on their effectiveness. They are listed in alphabetical order.

Burnham Brothers

Murry and Winston Burnham may be the best known names in the call manufacturing business. Their dad, Morton Burnham, was an accomplished lip squeaker and he taught both boys the technique. The lip squeak works fine in brushy country but does not have enough range to call critters from great distances. Murry and Winston experimented until they had developed a reeded tube that approximated the death cry of a rabbit. They still do business from the Burnham Brothers store in Marble Falls, Texas.

The Burnhams market tube calls in wood and plastic. In my opinion, the best is the walnut tube. It has a scream that is a bit higher pitched than some of the other tubes, a sound that works especially well on cat and gray fox. The WF-4 is a small call that fits easily in my shirt pocket. The high, pure tone allows a great range of whines, whimpers and squeals. I have used my present call for three years and have had no trouble with the reed. It is a good call to use in heavy brush or in country with a lot of shallow canyons.

The Burnham firm also sells a pair of close-in calls. These are pocketknife-sized and -shaped calls that are played like a harmonica. The S-4 Mini-Squeal has a plastic reed that produces a high-pitched whine. One end of the plastic extends from the holder. A hunter can tighten the reed by pulling on this tag end. The tighter the reed is stretched the higher the tone produced. With practice you can make squeals that resemble a baby rabbit, a baby fox, bird distress cries, a kitten or a puppy. All of the sounds will fetch critters. This is basically a short-range call. I use it in heavy brush for the original series of calls. If I do not attract a customer in a couple of minutes I go to one of the tubes and produce some screams that will interest the coyotes on the far side of the mountain. The call is also good if you have a critter sighted who is bashful about coming close enough for the shot. The little squealer will fetch them out of the brush in a hurry.

A recent addition to the Burnham line is the Coon Call. It is a plastic tube containing a metal reed. If the call is blown in the standard manner a high-pitched moan is produced. The trick to blowing it correctly is to flutter your tongue while you are blowing. The call will emit a high-pitched trill, a sound that will remind brother coon of a water bird. It took me about two hours of practice to perform this complicated maneuver. I am a slow learner and it might take you much less. The sound is unique among calls.

In addition to the calls, the Burnhams market a full line of hunter products. Everything from camo tape to telescope sights. The Burnhams are one of the few sources of skunk essence, often used as a masking scent. They sell electronic calls in eight track and cassette and offer taped distress calls of rabbits, birds, fox, chickens and goats.

Circe

The Circe calls are popular in the West and Southwest. They are manufactured in Goodyear, Arizona, by Jack Cain. Cain is one of the calling pioneers who became interested in making a better call. He and Lew Mossinger started the Circe line in the early fifties. The most familiar of the Circe line is the light green plastic tube that can be reeded for either jackrabbit or cottontail. The Circe Professional Model has three reeds—one jackrabbit, one cottontail rabbit and a high-pitched squealer. The correct reed is selected by rotating one end of the tube until the correct alignment is obtained. The Circe close call is a rubber bulb with a reeded air outlet. When the bulb is squeezed a high-pitched squeak is produced. Most call models are offered in either plastic or walnut. The wood calls are more expensive.

My favorite Circe call is the plastic tube reeded for the cottontail rabbit. I feel that this slightly less gravelly reed works best for me on coyote, fox and bobcat. If I am embarking on a lion or bear hunt, I will choose the jackrabbit model. The hoarse, gravelly tone is closer to the death cry of a deer or antelope and is more likely to attract the big predators. They may be reluctant to walk a mile for a rabbit but would have no hesitation to cover the distance for a big piece of meat such as a young deer.

I feel that I get more volume from the Circe calls than from any of the other tubes. Volume can be important if you are calling high prairie or sagebrush flats where the critters may be a mile or more away.

Another advantage of the Circe is the fitted mouthpiece. Their tubes have a mouthpiece tapered to fit the mouth. This can be important on a two- or three-day hunt where an uncomfortable fit might cause you to blow your lip.

Since the reeds in my Circe calls will often change tone, I carry a reed replacement kit on every hunt. I change the reed at the first sour note.

I have to say that I don't like the tube with the three reeds. It has been my experience that a caller never has time to make the change when he is involved in a stand. It makes more sense to carry two or three separately reeded calls. I wrap tape around one of the calls so it can be selected by touch. That way I don't have to take my eyes away from the hunt.

Circe offers a 45 rpm instruction record. They also market calling tapes in cassette and eight track. The instruction sheet packed with each Circe call is, in my opinion, the most complete offered by any manufacturer.

Crit'r Call

This unique call is marketed by Rocky Mountain Wildlife Products of LaPorte, Colorado. Major Boddicker, a good hunter and trapper, is the designer. The call body is bright red (predators are color blind) and is about three inches long. Both body and reed are plastic. The caller can make a variety of sounds by placing the exposed reed into the mouth and varying the air pressure. A skillful caller can make a cottontail or jackrabbit scream. He can also make a fawn squall, a javelina distress call, a mouse squeak and a coyote pup squeak. The Crit'r Call is undoubtedly the most versatile of the tube calls. However, it is more difficult to master than most of the other tubes, but many callers feel that the added time needed to master the Crit'r Call pays off in a wider variety of sound and an increased bag at the hunt's end. I have found that the Crit'r Call will attract game from areas that have been heavily called with other tubes. The new sound, I guess, does the job.

Another asset of the Crit'r Call is durability. The reed is made of plastic; under normal use it should last a lifetime.

Faulks

Faulks predator calls are manufactured in Lake Charles, Louisiana. I have their P-60. It is a wood tube containing a metal reed. The cry is on the high side and seems capable of doing the tricks I expect of a high-pitched call. The volume of the Faulks call is not as great as the Circe nor does it have the gravelly scream that makes the Circe so effective. I would like the call better if it had a fitted mouthpiece. This might not be a defect to an occasional hunter.

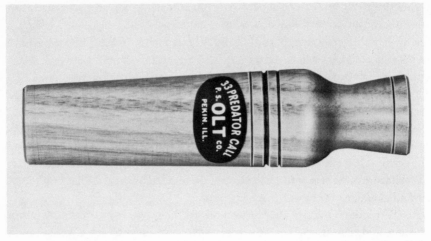

Olt Model 33 predator call. I used a knife on mine to reshape the mouthpiece. *Photo P. S. Olt Company.*

Olt

The P. S. Olt Company is another second generation concern. The business was founded by Phillip S. Olt more than seventy-five years ago and is now run by Arthur and James Olt.

Most of the calls marketed by the P. S. Olt Company are designed to attract ducks and geese. This was the original interest of the elder Olt when he founded the company and remains the mainstay of its business to this day.

Olt markets four models of predator calls. The most familiar is the T-20, a hard rubber tube with a soft plastic reed, which seems more durable than many of the metal reeds and holds its tone well. The tone is medium-high and works well on all land predators.

Olt also offers a metal-reeded call in a walnut tube. I like the looks and sound of the call but find the round mouthpiece a bit uncomfortable for extended calling trips. With a sharp pocketknife, I reshape the mouthpiece to get a tapered fit. A few minutes work with fine sandpaper finishes the job. I do not feel the Olt call has the same volume that a Circe does. It is a good, durable call though and will give more trouble-free service than the temperamental Circes. The sound of the Olt is unique and can be used effectively in country that has been heavily hunted with other calls. Olt also makes a coon caller and a close-in call. The short-range call is the harmonica type with a stationary plastic reed. The tone is a bit coarser than the Burnham Mini-Squeal.

Weems

Wayne Weems was another pioneer in the predator call field. His Fort Worth, Texas, business developed at about the same time as the Burnhams'. Weems sells tube-type calls in wood and plastic. His dual tone model is the most popular call for all-around calling. It has a straight voice tone plus a high-pitched calling reed for close critters. The second reed is mounted at right angles to the barrel. Both reeds can be blown simultaneously or each can be blown separately. When both reeds are blown, the noise produced is a varmint-fetching harmony. My Weems call seems to work particularly well in brushy country where volume is not critical. The dual tone call works well on bobcat and fox.

I have been told that the Weems family is no longer active in the manufacture and marketing of the calls. I do know the company has moved its mail order sales to Fort Smith, Arkansas. Repeated letters to the company seeking information have gone unanswered.

There are other tube-type calls on the market. I have not tried them and will make no attempt to evaluate them. It should be noted that every predator call on the market must have a following to remain in business. All will call critters if they are used properly. Most experienced callers agree that stand selection, calling technique and camouflage are more important than the call used.

Close-Range Calling

Close-range calls come in two basic designs. Circe makes a rubber bulb that has a reed at an air outlet. Squeezing the bulb produces a high-pitched mouse-like squeak. It is a deadly sound for all predators if they are close enough to hear it. If there is no wind and the country is fairly open the squeak can be heard by a keen-eared predator for several hundred yards. Many callers tape or glue the bulb to the offside of their gunstock. It can then be squeezed when the gun is in shooting position.

Circe also makes a tube call they market as the Squealer. It is not a close-range call in the strictest sense as it can be blown to carry a quarter of a mile. The tone is extremely high pitched and works wery well on cats and gray fox. I like the Squealer for calling heavy brush. Its high tone makes it easy to manipulate and a wide variety of heartrending sounds can be produced. It does not have the range of a standard tube but certainly is effective as a backup call.

The second type of close-range call is what I call the harmonica type. It is pocketknife-shaped and -sized. Two pieces of hard plastic sandwich a thin, plastic reed. Blowing into the call produces a series of low, agonizing whines.

Harmonica-type close-in call. This call can be held in the mouth and sounded even while the gun is in shooting position. *Photo P. S. Olt Company.*

The calls can also be sucked to produce a slightly different sound. This type of call can be held in the mouth and blown without using the hands, leaving them free for shooting. Both Olt and Burnham market this type of call. The Burnham is a bit higher pitched and may have an advantage over the Olt because one end of the reed has been left exposed. The caller can pull on the exposed end, tighten the reed, and produce a variable pitch tone.

Burnham sells a harmonica-type call that is not strictly a close-in call. It is named the Mini-Squeal and it can duplicate the distress calls of several animals. With practice, the call can produce the sound of a gray fox pup in distress, a killer sound for coyotes. The call works best for me in heavy cover and it is effective on both cat and fox.

A serious caller should not limit himself to one call. I never go hunting with less than three. I take the prime call (which will vary depending on the game and country I will be hunting), a backup call (in the event my prime call poops out on me) and a close-in call to convince the reluctant customers. With these three calls I can make every sound I need to fool even the smartest critter.

Kissing the Close Ones

An alternative to the close-range call is a technique used by Ishi the Indian. Wet the back of your hand and suck on the wet spot to get a high-pitched squeak. With some practice you will be able to make the squeak without using your hand; just suck air in through your pursed lips. This leaves the hands free for the important job of shooting. The call is low volume but on a still day it can be heard by an interested coyote a couple of hundred yards away.

Another variation of the lip squeak is the use of a piece of coarse grass or a leaf section. Make a slit in the center of the three-inch section of grass and hold the grass firmly between your thumbs. Place your lips over your thumbs and blow vigorously. The high-pitched squeal will bring coyote, fox and bobcat from several hundred yards.

The lip squeak, or mouth squeak, as it is sometimes called, will attract any critter that will come to a conventional call. I have used this technique to good advantage on a number of occasions. A couple of years ago, I was using the Burnham tube to interest a big Arizona bobcat. The cat came out of a thick stand of junipers that surrounded a waterhole and came well until he was two hundred yards out. Then he stopped and refused to budge, even though I blew so expertly on the tube that I had blood leaking from every note. I didn't have a close-range call with me that day and my twelve magnum was certainly not up to a two-hundred-yard shot. Things looked grim until I thought to try the lip squeak. The cat came to me like he was on a leash. His progress was slow but he never stopped

Predator calls on quail hunts can be productive. This prime gray fox was fooled by a series of lip squeaks. The birdshot was replaced by #3 buck. *Photo Gerry Blair.*

working my way. It took me five minutes of "kissing" and cost me a bad case of lover's lip, but I got the big tom in to forty yards and did the dirty deed with a load of No. 4 buck.

On another hunt I was after desert quail in late winter when I sighted a big red dog coyote. It was one of the few times I had gone afield without a couple of calls tied around my neck. So I had to resort to lip squeaking. I slipped the No. 6 birdshot from my 20-gauge Silver Snipe and substituted a pair of magnum No. 3 buck. I kissed that coyote so close I was almost afraid to shoot, fearing the load would cut him in two at that close range. I gambled and won. The pelt damage was minimal and I repaired it with a needle and thread. The prime winter coyote pelt paid for my quail trip.

Electronic Calls

An electronic call is a battery-powered device that plays a tape or a record of animal distress calls. It is a fairly recent innovation in predator calling. Johnny Stewart of Waco, Texas, and the Burnham Brothers make good units and offer a good selection of tapes. The calls are powered by "D" size batteries and may be obtained in either eight track or cassette. Most of the tapes are recorded screams of actual critters. A live rabbit or bird is handheld with his mouth close to the tape recorder microphone. Any wild critter is naturally scared to be this close to a human and will cooperate by producing a series of heartrending screams.

One disadvantage to the electronic calls is the price. A cassette call from either Stewart or Burnham will lighten the wallet to the tune of a couple of hundred bucks. Another drawback is weight. Many callers do a lot of walking, and these units, with their dozen "D" batteries, soon tire the arms. Set-up and take-down is time consuming as well and will reduce the number of stands made during the hunt. Battery purchase and replacement also can be expensive.

The tape and record players also have obvious advantages. They make amateur callers into instant experts as far as the quality of the sound is concerned. The calls transmitted are actual animal distress calls and will attract the most wary predator. There are a variety of tapes available so that the caller can vary the sound, in much the same way as a fisherman will try different lures. A critter who has been fooled once will not eagerly respond to that same sound for a while. He may come eagerly, however, to a new sound. The electronic call lets the hunter experiment with different sounds until a winner is found.

The most simple electronic call available to the hunter — and the least expensive — is the cassette tape player. Many hunters take the player afield and

Electronic calls sometimes get lazy when temperatures drop so carry a back-up tube call just in case. If calling is poor, use a fresh snowfall to scout for future calling stands. *Photo Gerry Blair.*

have good luck. One disadvantage to this simple setup is volume. Most of these units are low power and the sound produced will be considerably less than a good tube call. Another drawback is speaker quality. The speaker used in most cassette players is a mid-range speaker that might not accurately reproduce the high-pitched screams of the prey animal. One last criticism: The player must either be placed near the hunter so that he can control the volume or placed a distance away. If it is close, the critter will come in on top of the hunter. If the player is placed a distance away so that the critter's attention is directed away from the hunter, the hunter has no control over volume or any cassette player malfunctions.

Some hunters buy an auxiliary speaker for their players, usually one that is balanced for the high-pitched screams of the dying rabbit. By adding a bit of wire the hunter is able to place the speaker some distance away. This diverts the critter's attention but keeps the player close for adjustments. The quality of the sound produced will improve but the volume will remain quite low.

Volume can be increased, however, by adding an amplifier between the cassette player and the speaker. But when the amplifier is added it is also necessary to add a power source to make it work. A unit constructed in this manner will do almost everything a factory electronic call will do and the cost will be considerably less. I built my unit by buying a speaker and a ten-watt amplifier. The speaker is an eight-watt power horn that leans to the high side of the sound range. I used two six-volt lantern batteries wired in parallel as a power source. This feeds twelve volts into the amplifier and keeps it happy. I have fifty feet of electrical wire attached to the speaker, which lets me place the speaker (and the screams) at a distance so the charging critters will not be likely to see me skulking in the brush. Keeping the speaker off by itself has one other advantage: It is easier on my ears.

I have found it a good practice to carry a hand call or two when I am using the electronic call. The batteries may go dead in the call at a critical moment, or a wire might come loose. If the electronic call gets sick, it is a simple matter to grab the tube and finish the business at hand.

Cold temperatures also may be a disadvantage to battery-powered units. Last winter in the northern part of Arizona, we had more than two hundred inches of snow. When I made the first stand of the day the thermometer often read below zero. The batteries that power the cassette player and the amplifier, it should be noted, do not like to go to work when it is that cold. A tube call is a good back-up on any hunt.

One further comment on electronic calls—they may not be legal in all states. Check with your local game department before going afield.

3

Stand Selection

Stand selection is a critical element in successful predator calling. No critters can come if there are none to hear the call. There are a number of sources to help you find territory where predators are likely to be found.

Expert Advice

The field men assigned to the local game department office may be the best source of information. They are out in the woods frequently and have an opportunity to discover concentrations of predators. I have a number of friends in the Arizona Game and Fish Department who have been very helpful in supplying information on predator habitat. To have a friend, I have found, one must be a friend. I make it a point to be one hundred percent law-abiding. I also report to the rangers any information I may encounter indicating unlawful activities. At times this will pay off in more than one way. I had completed a fifteen-minute stand for coyote one winter day and had nothing but a cold rear to show for my effort. On the hike back to the truck I found a spot of fresh frozen blood. I followed the dim blood trail for several hundred yards and found the front half of a three-point mule deer at the trail's end. I spent several minutes on the poach site looking for evidence that might reveal the identity of the butchers. I was startled to catch a glimpse of movement and see an anxious coyote hotfooting my way. The critter may have been coming late to the call or he may have been headed for the deer carcass for a bite of lunch. The .22-250 put him down with authority and I skinned a coyote that I would have otherwise missed. I relayed information on the poaching to the game department. There was not enough

Local wardens can be a source of information on predator concentrations. This Arizona Game Ranger inspects burro damage to a desert tree. *Photo Gerry Blair.*

evidence to trace a suspect but the department increased its patrol of the area. Two weeks later three men were arrested for poaching.

Agents of the Animal Damage Control Section of the U. S. Fish and Wildlife Service can pinpoint crowds of coyote for the hunter. They are charged by law to respond to complaints of animal damage and that usually translates to coyote control. These men are usually happy to share their information with a citizen who wants to help them do their job. Again, cooperation is a two-way street. I am sometimes asked by these government trappers to give them a hand in controlling coyote numbers in problem areas. I did just that last year when some of the trappers spent the early part of the summer removing fawn-eating coyotes from Anderson Mesa in Northern Arizona. I spent almost a week on the mesa calling coyotes and giving instruction on calling technique.

Ranchers can also be helpful in locating good predator country. If I am scouting new country I make it a point to contact the area ranchers. I introduce myself and usually present a business card that contains my name and address. I tell the rancher I am after predators and describe the technique I will use. They are almost always interested and will offer good information on predator

Fish and wildlife trappers can pinpoint coyote populations in their area. This trapper for the Arizona Game Department eartags a trapped coyote. *Photo Gerry Blair.*

25

numbers and concentrations. I have had several offer to accompany me on a personal tour of the ranch to point out the hotspots. I usually make a call or two while they are along and have made some fast friends. Always ask the rancher what he does with his dead livestock. Most of the time the carcasses will be towed to a central point a mile or so from the ranch headquarters. Coyote will congregate around these carcasses and will remain in the area until only hair and stink remain. Even then they will return occasionally to roll in the stinking hide.

Buzzard Bait

I always keep one eye on the sky when I hunt. Flying carrion eaters, such as buzzards, crows and ravens will tip me off to the presence of a ripe carcass. Much of the time I surprise a coyote or two munching on the remains. If no coyotes are visible you can bet they are not far away. I was hunting with a friend one day when I spotted circling ravens a half mile off a dirt road. The country was flat and treeless—there was no place to hide. I asked my friend to drive the truck a mile or so down the road and come back for me in thirty minutes. When he left I walked to the carcass and hid on the upwind side by lying flat on my back in the short grass and blowing the jackrabbit-reeded Circe tube at the midmorning sun. About three minutes into the call I raised up to look a hardcharging coyote in the eye. He turned tail and ran but a 52-grain hollowpoint stopped him. I laid back down and began baying at the sky again. Four minutes later I raised up and discovered another coyote three hundred yards out. This one was standing with his front feet on the top strand of a barbwire fence straining to get a better look. The flat shooting .22-250 did what it was supposed to do, and I walked back to the truck with a coyote dangling from each shoulder.

Calling information can be obtained from unexpected sources. I was returning from an all-day hunt when I was stopped by a highway patrolman. A passing vehicle had thrown a piece of gravel into one of my headlights and I was requested to have it repaired. In our conversation I mentioned I was a coyote hunter and the patrolman spent several minutes drawing me a map of the areas he had seen coyotes and fox cross the road. I followed his advice on the next hunt and had a very successful day.

Tracks

Tracks will also reveal the presence of predators in an area. Take a drive through your intended hunting country after a light snow and make a note of the track concentrations. If there is no snow, check the soft dirt along sand washes or gullies. Watch for offal and scratches. Usually fox and coyote have small territories, and a couple of trips into an area should shed light on their hunting patterns.

Howl Patterns

Coyotes can often be scouted by making a note of howl patterns. Visit the hunting area at night and make a map of the distance and direction of howls. Burnham Brothers offers an excellent tape containing coyote howls that really sets the critters to singing. Some hunters (I am not one of them) can make a coyote howl with their mouth that does the same job. Coyote howls are not fully understood by game biologists. The howls probably are used to reinforce territorial boundaries, but they also may be an invitation for other coyotes to come and share in a large food source such as a beef carcass. Sometimes I think the coyote howls for the same reason some people talk to themselves—they just enjoy the sound of their own voice.

A visit to coyote country at dawn and dusk will often pinpoint coyote locations by howl patterns. *Photo Duane Rubink, U.S. Fish & Wildlife Service.*

The Stand

The hunter must pick a calling stand that stacks the odds in his favor. Cover is needed to hide the hunter from the incoming predator, but there should not be too much cover or the critter will be hidden and a shot will be difficult. The best predator country has either trees or brush. I usually pick the shady side of a tree if possible. The shade reduces visibility for the incoming varmint and makes a sun flash from the scope glass less likely. A downed tree also makes a good hiding place. I lay prone behind it if possible with only the upper half of my head visible, and I use the trunk for a rifle rest. I once made a stand in the middle of a grassy flat where the only cover was a downed juniper. My first series of calls brought two eager coyotes from a hidden depression almost half a mile distant. The two hungry critters staged a race to be the first to the treat. One was the clear winner and had a fifty-yard lead on his pal when he hit the finish line. I was using a shotgun and did not want to take the leader until the trailer was within range. I waited a second too long. The first coyote was only a bound away when I raised the gun to take the far coyote. He went down but the close one bounded over the tree and over me. I wasn't able to turn in time for a shot and the critter never broke stride as he disappeared into the grass. I didn't get that coyote and he didn't get the rabbit, but we both left with a tale that will thrill our grandkids.

Calling the Wind

The wind can be a good friend or a bad enemy to a predator caller. Too much wind can ruin a hunt, and a variable wind can be almost as bad. A day with little, or no, breeze is best. I position myself so that my main area of vision is upwind, and most of the time, the critter will appear from the anticipated route. Masking scents, which will be covered in the next chapter, can offset most of the damage done by an unreliable wind.

Showdown at Sunset

Many calls are made at sunrise and a few are made at sunset. At sunrise stands, in particular, the hunter must take the rising sun into consideration. I once hit a juniper push at the crack of dawn and did everything right in drawing in a coyote. The problem that developed, however, was the rising sun. It broke the horizon just as the critter loped into rifle range. I could see nothing through the scope but sun flare. I tried a desperation shot as the curious coyote pranced by at thirty yards. I missed, of course, and never got a second chance. The critter ran away directly into the sun. If possible place the sun in the critter's eyes instead of your own. Sun squint will be his problem and not yours. If you must call into the sun because of other considerations, try to move back into any available shade.

Mobility

Pick a stand that gives you plenty of room in which to move. The customer may come at an awkward angle which makes it necesary to move to get the shot. There may be more than one critter and you need to move to make the second shot.

I was calling at the edge of a juniper push one morning and had made myself a nest in the low limbs of a juniper. I was well hidden, had good vision, the sun was at my back and I was staring upwind. I called in two coyotes at that stand but never fired a shot. The first came from an unexpected angle. I could

Stay in the shade on all calls. It will make you hard to see and will keep the sun out of your eyes. *Photo Gerry Blair.*

see him but I knew if I changed position to shoot he would spook. I let him run behind me hoping he would come out the other side and give me a chance. He didn't. The second coyote came from about the same angle a minute later. I fought my way out of the limbs, but by the time I was free for a shot, the coyote was long gone. I left the stand with nothing but sad memories. Those memories were erased two weeks later though, when I went back to the same spot, picked a more open stand, and left with a pair of coyotes swinging from my shoulders.

Shooting Opportunity

I try to pick a stand that offers an open area that the critters must cross to get to the rabbit. The more open the area, the better chance of putting fifty-two grains of lead where it will do the most good. If there is a tree or large bush you can bet the critter will use it to his advantage. I was set up in a prairie that contained a few low-growing junipers. The area directly ahead was clear except for a juniper tree about the size of a small car. A big silver coyote came to the call using the tree to hide his advance. He took one step around the tree, took a quick look at the two-hundred-pound rabbit, and made a hasty retreat.

Pick a stand where the critters must cross an open area to get to the rabbit. It will make them easier to see and easier to shoot. *Photo Duane Rubink, U.S. Fish & Wildlife Service.*

The Comforts of Home

Pick a stand that offers as many of the comforts of home as possible. You may need to sit perfectly still for ten or fifteen minutes, and you will need all the comfort you can get. Try to pick a spot that is free from thorns, spines and scratchy leaves. Many rotten logs which may be otherwise attractive often are crawling with a variety of insects. Pick dry ground if possible. It is hard to shoot straight if you are wet or otherwise uncomfortable. I carry a foam rubber cushion on my hunts and consider it a necessity. If you are comfortable, you are able to sit still longer, and this pays off in less critters spooked by a squirming hunter. Some hunters may prefer a stool or a lightweight folding chair. Whatever you use the main purpose is to put something between you and the ground.

While on the subject of comfort it might be well to discuss the correct position to assume at the start of the call. Many beginning hunters sit with legs crossed beneath them in what I call the yoga position. This may be comfortable for a minute or two, but if the legs soon go to sleep, this position can become quite unbearable. The best sitting position I have found is with my backside firmly planted on the cushion and my legs drawn up so that the knees offer a handy support for the rifle. This is a position you can live with for fifteen minutes. It will also increase rifle accuracy.

I have made stands standing, kneeling and lying on my belly. The hunter must let the landscape features dictate the best position. The prone position, I have found, is great for rifle accuracy at a standing target, but it has two serious flaws—vision usually is reduced and it is a terrible position for a moving shot if the critter refuses to pose.

Sighting Game

If you have chosen the stand carefully you should have little trouble in locating incoming customers. They are usually running and can be detected easily. Educated coyotes, educated fox and all bobcats are hard to see. These are the sneakers who move slowly and use every bit of available cover. The problem is compounded if the calling area offers cover in the way of trees, brush or tall grass. In such situations, a caller can increase his odds by two techniques.

The first minute or two on each stand should be spent checking for ghosts—small bushes, clumps of grass and shadows that might look like varmints to a pair of straining eyeballs. Knowing where the ghosts are, the hunter won't be raising the scope during the stand to identify them. Less movement means less spooked critters.

The second technique is to be alert to birds and other critters in the area. I was playing the dying rabbit blues from a rock rim in central Arizona one morning, hoping to attract a bobcat from the brushy canyon below. Fifteen minutes of music attracted no applause so I was considering ending the call since an early morning wind had come up. Before I could get up, a flock of pinion jays began a noisy chatter two hundred yards down canyon. I put away the tube and went to the mouth moaner. I worked that moaner for a full twenty minutes before I saw a flash of fur in the underbrush fifty yards below. Through the six-power I could see a suspicious eye peering around a manzanita bush. I was almost sure it belonged to a bobcat. I centered the duplex on the eye, held my breath and stroked. I walked into the brush to find a one-eyed, stone dead bobcat. I mumbled a thanks to the jays and went home a richer man.

On another hunt I was calling standing junipers with my twelve magnum. A herd of cattle was grazing in the area when I started the call. As cattle usually do, they looked me over carefully when I blew the first few notes. It didn't take them long to go back to supper. Five minutes later, one of the heifers turned her head sharply to stare intently behind me. I worked around my hiding tree and flushed out a pair of coyotes that had come in the back door. I dumped one with the magnum and peppered the rear of the second. A third shot took the survivor when he was forty yards out. I thanked bossy for snitching on the two sneakers and promised to bring her an apple on the next trip out.

Cats can be hard to spot; they are sneakers and use every scrap of cover to hide their approach. *Photo Gerry Blair.*

4

Calling Camouflage

To most hunters camouflage is the brown and green leaf-patterned fatigues used by many military forces. While a hunter in this get-up might be tough to see in a shadowy undergrowth he would stand out like a sore thumb against a snowbank. The point is, a smart hunter will pick clothes to match the type of country he hunts. But there is more to proper camouflage than changing your appearance. Almost all animals depend on their sense of smell and hearing as well as sight. It does little good to disguise against one of the senses and ignore the other two. This chapter will deal with camouflage for all three senses.

The Color-blind Coyote

According to wildlife biologists, the coyote and other predators are colorblind, but the hunter should not be too concerned with this. He should be concerned more with the tonal intensity of the clothing than with the color. If a coyote or other critter sees only in blacks, whites and shades in between, he will lock in on contrast rather than color. An extreme example would be a black cat against white snow. He is obviously very visible. A medium red fox standing against a grey background, on the other hand, might be almost invisible to the predator. He sees the contrast in the colors rather than the colors themselves.

On most of my hunts I wear a deep green pair of trousers which blend almost exactly with the shade of the junipers where I spend most of my time. I probably would wear a camouflage jumpsuit if I could find one for heavyweights, but every one I have tried shrinks after the first washing and I have a tough time getting into them. I wear a medium-green work shirt, a camouflage sweatshirt

This hunter is well camouflaged—even his hands and gun are hidden. He is not likely to lose a critter because of sloppy camo. *Photo by Gerry Blair.*

and cap. A headnet or facepaint tops off my hunting wardrobe. Sometimes, if it is cold, I will wear gloves.

If I am hunting prairie country, I wear a set of work khakis. In sagebrush I go back to the leaf-design outfit. Calling snowy flats, however, has caused me problems. The best outfit I have found is the white painter's denims found in most department stores. Night hunters, naturally, will want to stick with dark clothing.

Gloves

Gloves of some kind are needed to disguise the white of the hands as well as provide warmth in frigid weather. One note of warning about gloves however: They often can cause problems with your aim. The trigger on my Ruger is set at a hair over three pounds and it is as crisp as overdone bacon. I bought a handsome pair of gloves when I first started calling and promptly missed eight coyotes in a row. To make matters worse I had a hunting buddy along that day who felt obligated to share the experience with all of my friends. I was about to give up varmint calling when I realized that my worse-than-usual marksmanship started when I began wearing the gloves. I took them off and hit eight of the next ten critters I called. I still wear the gloves, but I have slit the trigger finger from tip to web. When I am ready to shoot, out pops the old finger, warm and ready to work.

One more comment about gloves. If you are using a tube call you will find that it is difficult to blow with gloved hands. The hands cup below the tube to serve as a sounding chamber. The gloves tend to absorb part of the sound and drastically reduce volume. If I am hand calling, I do it barehanded and put up with the icicles.

Masks and Makeup

The hunter must do something to disguise the bright whiteness of his face. Often he must turn his head to discover incoming customers. This movement, coupled with whiteness, spooks a lot of predators. I have used both camo paint and headnets, and I have decided that either will do a passable job. Both have defects, but until something better comes along, a serious hunter has only these two choices. I am serious enough about my hunting that I grow a beard in the winter and let my hair grow long in back to help camouflage the skin.

The first headnet I used was a bag type with no eyeholes and a drawstring that pulled up around the throat. I could see through the netting but I felt my vision was reduced. The net bothered me, particularly when it came time to aim through the scope. I cut eyeholes through the net to solve the problem. I could see much better but had trouble keeping the holes lined up with my eyes. I soon discarded the net in favor of camo paint.

Facepaint does not impair vision the way a headnet does but it's messy to use. I put up with the mess and use the grease. *Photo Gerry Blair.*

The camouflage paint cured the vision problem but I found that it was a bit messy and had a tendency to come off on the gun stock every time I put it to my shoulder. It also was time consuming to paint up two or three times a day. The painted face sometimes has a surprising effect on people encountered during the hunt. I was driving a rough backcountry road between stands on one hunt when I met two cowboys chousing a small herd of whitefaces. I stopped the truck to keep from spooking the cattle and one of the cowpokes moved his horse in close for a better look. We talked for several minutes and he seemed uncomfortable the whole time. Finally he could stand it no longer. "Pardon me for saying so, feller," he drawled, "but you are the queerest-looking human I ever saw."

Recently I have discovered a new type of facemask that does an excellent job. It is marketed by Penn's Woods of Delmont, Pennsylvania, and consists of a camo net attached to an eyeglass frame. The frame fits across the ears and keeps the eyeholes aligned. There is a Velcro fastener on the back to keep the mask taut. The same company also markets an excellent camo face cream. The three-tube set I bought has black, brown and green creams. Best of all, it is treated with a scent neutralizer.

The musk of the spotted skunk (civet) does the best job as a masker. I may use a mounted specimen like this one as a sight decoy. *Photo Gerry Blair.*

Masking Scents

When called, most critters will approach from downwind. Upwind varmints—especially those who have been burned with a predator call before—may circle downwind to taste the air before committing themselves. These customers will be lost if the caller does not use a masking scent. If you are one of those people who just have to bathe once a week, do it with an unscented soap. Skip the deodorant and aftershave lotion; pass on the scented hair oil. Don't smoke. Burning nicotine stinks up your clothes and your hair. The odor will remain with you all day and most predators will avoid you like a reformed three-pack-a-day man.

No serious hunter should go afield without some form of masking scent. I have used most of them at one time or another, but I think that skunk gunk is the best. You can get the real item straight from the skunk if you have a friend who is a trapper or if you trap yourself. While I prefer the fluid from the spotted skunk (sometimes called civet), the fluid from the striped, hooded or hognosed skunk will do about as well.

Skunk scent is available commercially, but many hunters prefer to extract the fluid themselves. The first step is to catch skunk, which should be no problem as they are plentiful in most parts of the country, as well as totally trap dumb. When you have caught one, kill it by shooting it with a .22 caliber CB short. Place the bullet just behind the front leg. The low velocity bullet will have little shocking power and should not cause the skunk to evacuate, but it will take the critter several minutes to pass on. When you are sure he is dead put on a pair of rubber gloves which can be found in most variety stores. Remove the skunk from the trap and locate the two marble sized glands on each side of the anal vent. Hold a small jar to the gland opening and squeeze gently. The fluid will be amber colored. One skunk should deliver plenty to last a season or two. Pour a few drops of the fluid into a jar containing cotton balls and keep it capped tightly until you are ready to use it. Out on the stand open the jar and set the essence of skunk downwind so you will not insult your sensitive sinus glands during the hunt. Use a jar with a plastic lid. Metal will not last long as the skunk juice soon rusts it away.

If, however, you are not into skunk milking, the scent can be bought from one or two suppliers. Burnham Brothers is one. The other is Skunk Skreen of College Station, Texas.

There are other alternatives to the skunk fluid if none is available. They are not as good as the skunk, in my opinion, but they are better than nothing. Buy liquid garlic at the grocery store and put a drop or two on each heel before each stand. Pine oil—which can be found at any well-equipped archery supply—can also be used. As a last resort rub a raw onion briskly on your shoes.

Hiding Other Equipment

Any item taken to the stand must also be camouflaged. I have camo-painted an old suitcase in which I carry my electronic call. I used a solid coat of flat green for the first application. When it was dry I cut random leaf patterns from wide masking tape and stuck it to the case. The second coat was a flat brown. When it was dry, I peeled off the tape. I have to be truthful and say that finished product was not pretty; you might even say it was ugly. No matter. By the time a customer gets close enough to be struck by the ugliness, it is too late.

Make it a point to take off all jewelry before a hunt. Rings and bola ties are light reflectors and will spook the critters. I use a brown canvas band on my watch. If you now have a metal expansion band, or worse, a silver and turquoise band, leave it home when you go hunting. Other potential light reflectors are belt buckles and eyeglass frames. There are very few natural substances in nature that will reflect light, and wary predators will spook with little provocation.

Hiding the Gun

The hunter's gun may be his worst enemy afield. The highly polished surfaces of the metal and wood can cost the hunter a number of coyotes during the course of a season. If the rifle carries a telescopic sight the problem is compounded because the glass will reflect light as well.

The stock of the gun presents the least problem to the hunter, yet most of the Remington line of rifles and shotguns leave the factory equipped with an almost mirror finish that can spell trouble to the predator caller. Take fine steel wool or sandpaper and work the finish slowly until the high sheen disappears. A little effort will produce a finish that closely resembles the expensive hand-rubbed treatment found on many custom guns. This will solve ninety percent of the problem. If further camouflage is desired the stock may be camo taped or camo painted using browns, greens and blacks in a flat paint. Winchester guns also come with the glossy finish and also may need some help from the sandpaper. Rugers have the more sensible semi-gloss finish.

The metal parts of the gun present more of a challenge. I have read different instructions for camo painting the metal but have never been able to force

This camo taped rifle will not spook a crafty critter. The untaped bi-pod is non-reflective. *Photo Gerry Blair.*

myself to take the paintbrush to these parts. A more sensible response, in my opinion, is a chemical treatment. Most competent gunsmiths offer a bluing service that will reduce the reflective potential of the gun. It is usually called a hunter's finish and consists of bluing without the high polish. It is a better finish than the factory finish but not as good as the Parkerized finish found on most military firearms, which is my favorite. It cuts reflection to near zero and does not make it as ugly as a coat of paint would. Philadelphia Ordinance, of Horsham, Pennsylvania, is one company that offers the Parkerization process and there may be others.

A non-permanent camouflage for the metal is the camo tape. It can be applied quickly and is inexpensive. The occasional hunter will find that the tape will fill needs at a moderate price, but those who do a lot of hunting will find that the tape is not durable. I have tried it and found that I needed a new tape job about half way through the season.

There is nothing the hunter can do about the glass in the scope that I know of. The best way to handle this is to keep the scope aimed skyward until it is time to do business.

Sound Camouflage

Predators hunt using all of their senses. We have discussed sight and smell and offered suggestions to neutralize those senses. The third important hunting tool that a predator uses is his highly developed hearing. His good hearing, as a matter of fact, is what allows him to respond to that rabbit squeal more than a mile away. He also can hear unnatural sounds at such distances. A hunter can minimize his chance of failure by paying strict attention to potentially alarming noises.

When driving to the calling area, I make it a point to leave the radio off. Even in winter, with the windows shut, a keen-eared coyote can snap on a Willie Nelson song from a surprising distance. I also maintain the vehicle so that squeaks and rattles are kept to a minimum. Nothing is loaded in the bed of the truck that might roll and produce noise.

I also make it a point to maintain absolute silence walking to a stand. If you have a calling companion, have a serious talk with him before the hunt starts. Explain that all predators have a highly developed sense of hearing and that they will spook out of the country if silence is broken. Advise him that the purpose of the hunt is to call predators and that no predators will co-operate if he slams the door of the truck, laughs or otherwise exercises his vocal cords. As a clincher, tell him if he inadvertently laughs, coughs or sneezes you will take the stout end of a juniper limb and thrash him until he whines like a whipped hound. That should do it.

I once hunted with a companion who was a compulsive hummer. He was most apt to hum when he was nervous and he always seemed nervous on a predator hunt. I had two eager coyotes coming at one stand and my musician friend hummed them clear out of the country. Coughers, sneezers and nose blowers are just as bad. If you must include them in your circle of friends don't ask them to go hunting.

The rule of silence should also be observed while walking out. I took a neighbor to the junipers to hunt coyote one fall day and we took two hard-charging critters. We were packing them back to the truck when my excited companion began reliving the action. His voice spooked a big bobcat coming in the back door. I had one tough shot at two hundred yards. To my friend's surprise—and my own—I put the cat down with the .22-250. Most of the time, shots at spooked critters have a less happy ending.

5

Rifles and Loads

I shot my first called coyote with a hand-loaded .30 caliber. I was after deer on the Arizona North Kaibab when the yodel dog sang from a ridge a quarter mile upwind. I blew an amateurish squall through my brand new Burnham tube and two minutes later, I had the panting critter out front begging for the rabbit. The 165-grain spitzer, encouraged by 58 grains of 4831, put his lights out fast. When the dust cleared I discovered the deer load had left very little dignity to the corpse. I decided there must be a better way.

The years of experience since I downed that first coyote have convinced me of one cold hard fact: There is no perfect gun for all facets of varmint shooting. The best a hunter can hope for is a gun that will do the job he wants most of the time. In order to make an intelligent choice, the needs of each job must be analyzed.

Accuracy

The primary consideration of any varmint rifle, obviously, is accuracy. No gun will kill them if you can't hit them. While most modern centerfires have enough built-in accuracy to take deer-sized game at reasonable ranges, there is a world of difference in connecting with a two hundred pound deer and a 10 pound fox. Don't misunderstand. I'm not maligning old Betsy or old Blue eyes. I know that any reasonably good shot can hit a fox once in a while with the deer gun. What I am saying is if you get serious about predator calling you will want to connect with some regularity. At fifty bucks a pelt for grays and half that again for reds, your pocketbook will not forgive many misses.

Knock-down Power

Any gun will kill almost any animal if the shot placement is precise. A friend of mine sighted a medium-sized mountain lion while running a trap line. His only firearm was a .22 caliber revolver loaded with shorts. He showed poor judgment, I think, when he coaxed the cat in close with a Burnham squeaker and put one of the shorts between the cat's eyes. The lion dropped as if he had been zapped with an elephant gun. Another time a different friend took a 100-yard chance at a running coyote with a rifle loaded with CCI's .22 stinger. The coyote folded at the crack of the gun as if he had been poleaxed. The little 32-grainer had dodged between two ribs to explode in the coyote's vitals. The point is, both of these critters were killed with guns that would not ordinarily do a clean job. Just because Joe down the street claims he once killed an elk with his .222, do not assume that the .222 is a good elk gun. Joe may have made a lucky shot, he may have encountered an elk that was about ready to die anyway, or he may be lying.

A good varmint gun must have enough muscle to put the critter down with no backtalk. Most predators are tough for their size and will absorb a lot of punishment. Use a gun that will put them down fast and anchor them to the spot. A scared coyote can cover a quarter of a mile in thirty seconds; he may die from the wound but it does the caller little good if he can't find the body. Even a fox or a cat can disappear in a hurry if they get into the brush and have a chance to hole up. Do yourself a favor and use enough gun.

Range

Your shooting range is also important to consider when choosing the right caliber. If you are mainly a night hunter, as Murry Burnham is, your shots will likely be at about fifty yards. Murry is one of the best critter callers in the country and is *el jefe* of the Burnham Brothers firm. He uses a .222 loaded down to minimize pelt damage. He uses 14 grains of 4227 behind a 45-grain Sierra soft-point. The load does a great job close in, putting the critters to the ground with almost no pelt damage. The load, it should be pointed out, is strictly a short-range load. Past a hundred yards the soft-point looses zip fast. Both accuracy and knock-down power suffer. That is not a disadvantage at night as shots are usually in the thirty-yard range.

At the other end of the scale, a friend in Northern Arizona uses a .25-06 for his coyotes. Dennis Hall is a cowboy with the Babbitt spread and is a good

Most serious hunters reload to get the most out of their guns. I like the Hodgdon H380 powder for .224 loads. *Photo Gerry Blair.*

coyote caller. He is also a talented hand loader. Most of the shots Dennis is offered are several hundred yards away. His range is the rolling prairie that lies between the San Francisco Mountains and the western edge of the Navajo Indian Reservation. The wind has been known to blow across these open areas and Dennis needs a gun that is long-range and has wind-bucking capabilities. He fills his .25-06 case with a 117 Sierra boattail and pushes it with 54.9 grains of 4831. A CCI 250, or magnum, primer is used. The load chronographs at 3,250 muzzle.

Avoiding Holey Hides

A hunter should not become so carried away with knock-down power that he forgets to protect the hides. Fur prices during the past decade have reached an all-time high. These premium prices are paid for furs in undamaged condition. This criterion further restricts the hunter's choice of rifles. Most serious callers choose one of the flat-shooting .22 centerfires. A few will use the .17 caliber Mighty Mouse, and a few will go to the heavy side with .243's, .244's and the .25's.

There are two basic techniques for converting any centerfire into a pelt-saving gun. One is the load-down technique used by Murry Burnham for his .222. The second is to load up—maybe a grain or two under maximum—to produce a bullet blowup inside the critter. This usually prevents an exit hole. This load-them-hot philosophy seems to work great on coyote, fair on bobcat and poor on fox. The fox is a slender-bodied animal and usually the hot load is exiting the off-side when it explodes, creating a very messy situation. Individual calibers and suggested loads for each will be covered further along in this chapter.

Rimfire Rifles

I have done the dirty deed to fox, bobcat and coyote using the .22 long rifle rimfire. I have never challenged a mountain lion with this little pea shooter, as a rash friend did, but I am confident that if the critter was close enough and I had a clear shot at his thin-boned skull the little .22 would do the trick. The trouble is that all shots are not offered under perfect conditions. Although I have killed a number of critters with the rimfire I have also wounded more than a few. It bothers me that I was not able to deliver that quick and painless death that all creatures deserve. For that reason I refuse to shoot another large predator with the double deuce.

When the superfast .22's were introduced, I was sure that this added muscle would move the cartridge up into decent predator ballistics. CCI marketed their .22 Stinger; Remington and Winchester quickly followed with the Yellowjacket and the X-pediter. I headed afield with a 10-22 Ruger decorated with a four-power glass in a one-inch tube. In my pocket was a box of the supersonic stingers. A handsome gray fox came to my call out of a chaparral canyon and posed atop a rock fifty yards out. I put the cross hairs just behind his front leg and squeezed off. The critter fell backward off the rock and immediately set up a heartrending screaming. I didn't walk up on the wounded critter because I was sure he would slip off into the brush at my approach. I decided to tough it out, hoping he would offer a second shot if he moved from behind the rock. I had endured several minutes of the fox's screaming when I was startled to see a very large coyote come bounding into view. Shortly after the coyote disappeared behind the rock the screaming stopped. I used the call to bring the coyote out of the brush and then scared him off. If the load wouldn't kill a fox, it wouldn't kill a coyote. I retrieved the fox and used the rest of the shells for target practice. The shot, I discovered, had hit a rib close to the point of aim and had exploded. Most of the tissue damage was superficial.

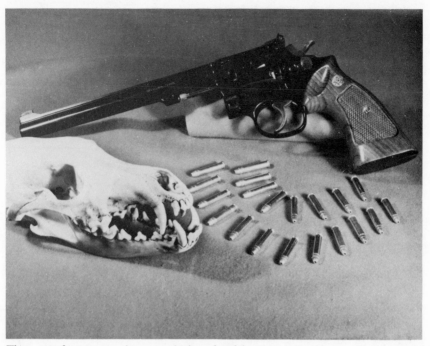

The .22 rimfire magnum does a good job on fox if the range is not extreme. A scope would improve accuracy. *Photo Gerry Blair.*

Rimfire Magnums

The .22 rimfire magnum has a longer case than the .22 long rifle cartridge, which means more powder behind the slug. The 40-grain bullet is used for both the solid point and the hollowpoint loads. The extra powder pushes the little pill at more than 2,000 fps muzzle. That is considerably faster than the 1,255 fps developed by the standard .22 long rifle and somewhat faster than the 1,640 fps logged by the stingers. The muzzle energy for the mag is 355 foot-pounds, plenty to put down fox-sized critters at a moderate range.

At 2,000 fps the mag is not affected much by a moderate crosswind. I use my scope-sighted 700 H&R autoloader on grays and usually get a solid kill. I use the gun often in brushy country (fox habitat) where the shots are apt to be less than sixty yards. My gun comes equipped with a five-shot clip. I also have a ten-shot clip made by the manufacturer. The ability to squeeze off five or ten quick shots at a close-in critter is a definite asset, particularly if you are not the best shot in the world.

I am not convinced that the .22 mag is enough gun for bobcat or coyote. I tested the caliber on trapped coyote last winter to test its effectiveness, using a S&W Model 48 Revolver with an 8⅜-inch barrel. I got spotty results. One lung-shot male fought the trap for almost a minute before he succumbed. A coyote with a yen to travel can cover a lot of ground in a minute. I shoot my coyotes now with a centerfire or with a buckshot-loaded shotgun.

.17 Remington

The .17 Remington is a good short- and a fair mid-range varmint caliber. Remington first marketed the little speedster in 1971. It is the smallest centerfire cartridge commercially manufactured. The main recommendation for the .17 is high speed. A hot-loaded 25-grainer can be pushed at more than 4,000 fps. This fast-moving midget will deliver spectacular blowups on small varmints. It is flat shooting, dropping a hair more than five inches at three hundred yards with a two-hundred-yard sight-in. The bullet will explode in the chest cavity of a coyote or bobcat and will not usually exit. Fox hunters should load down to the lowest accurate velocity if they shoot a lot of fox. I consider it a decent gun out to about two hundred yards.

Now for the bad news. The small bullet won't buck much of a headwind and it does not have the long-range accuracy of the .224 centerfires, nor does it have the punch needed to consistently knock out big western coyotes with anything but a perfect shot. The reloader is mostly limited to one bullet weight. Barnes Bullet Company does offer a 20-grainer if you want to move down a bit. The .17 is also tricky to load for. On the top end a slight increase in powder can produce massive pressure problems. Two more criticisms and I will quit nagging about the poor little .17. If you want to keep pinpoint accuracy you need to carry a wire brush on your hunts. After a half box of shells, the small bore fouls and needs to be scrubbed to restore accuracy. The tiny case neck also presents problems. It stretches at every shot, as every case does, but on the .17 the cases need to be trimmed after every firing.

Most .17 owners know that the .17 needs a Remington 7½ or a CCI BR-4 primer. If the cases are re-formed from either a .223 or a .222 mag, the case capacity is reduced. A coyote or bobcat load for the .17 might be 25 grains of H-380 loaded in a .17 case in good condition. This should push the bullet at about 3,751 fps muzzle. With a two-hundred-yard sight-in the bullet should drop about six inches at three hundred yards.

Again, a note of caution: The .17 is supersensitive to powder variations. A half grain overload can produce dangerous presures and case-head expansion.

.22 Hornet

The Hornet was the first standard American cartridge made for varmints. Savage made a bolt-action chambered for the Hornet in 1932. Winchester followed a year later with the Model 54, and it wasn't long before the caliber was available in a wide range of actions and models. But the Hornet fell on hard times in the late forties. A crowd of factory and wildcat calibers appeared and the Hornet became just another face in the crowd. Ballistically, it was left in the dust by newcomers such as the .222.

I still like the Hornet and so do a lot of other shooters. If wind is not a factor, the Hornet will be accurate out to 200 yards. It produces a milder report than some other varmint calibers and can be used in areas where noise might be a problem. Most bullet manufacturers offer a good selection for the Hornet. I like the 45-grain because it seems to deliver better accuracy.

Earl Etter, Sr. likes the .17 caliber for Idaho coyotes. The 25-grain bullet gives him consistent kills at 200 yards on called coyote and bobcat. Pelt damage is almost non-existent. *Photo courtesy Hornady Bullets.*

47

.222 Remington

The deuce, in my opinion, is the most accurate and effective medium-range varmint caliber currently available. When Remington introduced the .222 in the early 1950's, benchrest shooters were overjoyed. The flat shooting centerfire was an overnight success, mainly because of its outstanding accuracy. Most of the time a factory-produced gun straight from the dealer's shelf can deliver one-inch groups at a hundred yards. Under two hundred yards, the caliber may be the most accurate of the .22 centerfires. The deuce soon became a favorite of benchrest shooters and many new records were established. A check with the record book will reveal that the .222 still holds most of the benchrest honors.

If I could be sure that all of my varmint shots would be less than two hundred yards or so, and that all would be on windless days, I would nominate the .222 as the most effective and accurate varmint rifle. If no such warranty could be given, I would opt for something with a bit more muscle.

Ray Parent is a Law Enforcement Specialist for the Arizona Game and Fish Department. Ray has two loads he has developed for his deuce, either of which would be a good choice for the hunter who wants speed. The first load is 23 grains of H-380 ignited by a Winchester Western primer. The bullet is a 55-grain Speer spitzer that develops about 2,900 fps muzzle. The second load is 23 grains of BLC2 behind a 52-grain Sierra hollowpoint. Winchester Western case and primer are used. This load will chronograph about 3,100 fps muzzle. Either of the loads will do a good job on a large-bodied varmint such as a coyote or bobcat. To avoid a mess, however, the hunter must put the bullet into the chest cavity where it can blow up without doing much pelt damage.

.223 Remington

The .223 is almost ballistically identical to the .222 Remington Magnum. The case is a bit shorter than the mag and holds a hair less powder, and it is a good mid-range varmint caliber delivering accuracy and punch out to about 250 yards.

The .223 made its appearance in the late 1950's. It was developed for the army and was standardized as the 5.56mm Ball Cartridge M193 in 1964. At about the same time, Remington presented it commercially as the .223. Although the cartridge is named the .223 it is in reality a .224 diameter bullet. Commercially marketed guns deliver good accuracy, but most of the military-type autoloaders do not have the built-in accuracy for varmint hunting. A strong asset of the .223 is the availability of once-fired military brass. The case capacity of the military brass is approximately that of commercial brass and no special allowance is required. My Model 77 Ruger groups best using 50- and 52-grain match hollow-points.

.222 Remington Magnum

The .222 Remington Magnum has a twenty percent greater case size than the .222 and is about five percent larger than the .223. The caliber was announced by Remington in 1958 after they tried unsuccessfully to sell it as a military cartridge. The performance of the mag deuce is about halfway between the standard .222 and the .22-250. A shooter can expect about seventy-five yards more from his mag over the standard .222. The mag will deliver the same pinpoint accuracy of the .222.

The mag has never enjoyed the popularity of the standard .222 and probably never will. Although the magnum is ballistically superior to the standard and seems to be just as accurate, the eight-year lead in the development of the standard .222 has made it more popular.

A good coyote load for the .222 magnum would be 26 grains of BLC2 behind a 50-grain Speer spitzer. Use the CCI #450 Magnum primer. This load should develop about 3,250 fps muzzle and 2,300 fps at two hundred yards. With a two-hundred-yard sight-in, the load will drop a bit more than eight inches at three hundred yards.

.22-250

The .22-250 is probably the most popular varmint cartridge ever developed, starting out about fifty years ago as a wildcat. The cartridge is nothing more than a necked-down .250 Savage with a slight increase in shoulder angle. The .224-diameter bullet left the barrel at speeds considerably above the old 250-3000 and delivered astounding accuracy. It is surprising, considering the long history of the .22-250, that no major gun manufacturer offered a factory rifle for the cartridge until 1965. The .22-250 had outdistanced the popular .220 Swift years before.

Browning produced the first factory gun chambered for the .22-250, and since that time most of the major gun manufacturers have offered one or more rifles chambered for the old .22 Varminteer. The .22-250 enjoyed a brief popularity with the benchrest crowd. When it was found that it could not deliver the tack-driving accuracy of the .222 and the .222 magnum, it was all but abandoned. The cartridge is strictly a long-range load used for all types of varmints. Effective range of the cartridge is well in excess of three hundred yards. I have done the dirty deed to hundreds of varmints with my Model 77 Ruger in the five years I have had the rifle. I stay away from the top end of the reloading table and to this point have had no trouble losing the thingamajigs in the barrel that encourage the bullet to go straight.

Ray Parent, who was mentioned in the section dealing with the .222, also shoots a .22-250. A few years back he was on a varmint expedition in the junipers north of Ashfork, Arizona, when he was presented a chance at a heavy-bodied mountain lion. Ray took the critter with one shot. His load was 38 grains of H-380 behind a 52-grain Sierra hollowpoint. The load probably delivered about 3,600 fps muzzle. That is one advantage of the .22-250. It has the muscle to take critters much bigger-bodied than average varmints. A big Arizona lion might scale out near two hundred pounds. I would have no reservations in siccing the .22-250 on one. I used the gun recently on a bear that had a live weight of over 250 pounds. The little 70-grainer did a fine job of bringing him down.

Ray Parent took this Arizona mountain lion with a scope sighted .22-250. The 52-grain Sierra hollowpoint delivered a one-shot kill on the 100 pound cat. *Photo Wes Martin, Arizona Game and Fish Department.*

Cases for the .22-250 can be formed from the .30-06, .308 or the .250 Savage, but I do not recommend it. The walls on these reformed cases are thicker than those on a factory .22-250 case, which means that the internal capacity is reduced. A load that may perform well in a factory case may develop dangerous pressures in a reformed case. The .22-250 is available in a good range of factory loads and empty cases are readily available.

I use Hodgson's H-380 powder almost exclusively in my .22-250 loads. This spherical powder is fine-grained and runs through the powder measure like syrup. I weigh about every tenth load to insure accuracy but seldom find an error. I push the Speer 52-grain hollowpoint with 36.5 grains of H-380 and ignite the slow burning powder with a CCI-250 magnum primer. The load, I figure, develops about 3,400 fps muzzle and delivers about 675 foot-pounds of energy at two hundred yards. The three-hundred-yard drop from a two-hundred-yard sight-in will be about seven inches. The 52-grainer, I have found, delivers the best accuracy in my rifle.

While on the subject of accuracy, I might comment on my method of sighting-in a varmint rifle. Most shots are taken with a cold barrel so I sight my rifle to be most accurate from a cold gun. Many times shooters will fine-tune their gun with a series of shots and the end result will be a gun that shoots best from a hot barrel. There is not much difference, I admit, but there is enough so that a shot at a long-range critter might miss.

All bullet trajectories, as almost everyone knows, describe an arc from the rifle barrel to the target. The pill leaves the barrel below the line of sight, meets the line of sight a short distance out, and drops below the line of sight as it gains range. My gun is sighted to hit the point of aim at twenty-five yards. This puts me about a half inch high at fifty yards, a bit less than two inches high at one hundred yards, an inch and a half high at two hundred yards and three inches low at three hundred yards. When I was new to varmint shooting I taped a chart to my gunstock to remind me of bullet performance at varying ranges. I have since become familiar enough with the load so that the chart is no longer necessary.

There is no significant difference between the .22-250 and the .220 Swift. When the two cartridges are loaded to comparable pressures, the ballistic performance is almost identical. This is not surprising as the .22-250 case has nearly the same capacity as the .220 Swift. The advantages listed for the .22-250 would, of course, apply equally to the Swift. The main disadvantage of the Swift, as I see it, is the lack of a wide range of factory loads available for the caliber, as well as a lack of factory guns.

Larger Calibers

In the days before high fur prices, many talented predator callers used
.243's, .257's and .25-06's. Most of them were not after fur and often were disappointed if it did not rain coyote hair for a week after each shot. All of these guns
can be loaded so that they do an adequate job for the varmint hunter who does
not want to totally destroy the pelt. When down-loading, use the lighter bullets
and load them to travel around 3,000 fps muzzle. A chest shot with such a load
should do a fair job on a coyote or maybe even a bobcat. Obviously, fox and
coon shot with one of these heavyweights will resemble a jigsaw puzzle with a
few of the parts missing. But if you are serious about varmint calling, and wish to
save the fur, invest in one of the flat-shooting .22 centerfires. My best advice would
be a .222, a .222 magnum or a .22-250.

Heavy Barrels

As a general rule, guns with heavy – or varmint – barrels shoot more accurately than do the lighter-barreled sporters. The main advantage to the heavy
barrels, as I see it, is the reduction of barrel whip when the gun heats up after the
third or fourth fast shot. This is important to the long-range shooter aiming for
prairie dogs at five hundred yards. My varmint rifle has a sporter barrel. The
miniscule gain in accuracy with the heavier barrels is not worth packing that extra pound or two of iron afield. Most of my shots, as previously noted, are cold-barrel shots where the extra metal would not be a significant advantage.

Centerfire Cartridges

There are three main disadvantages to using factory loads for serious predator hunting. Obviously, the shooter is limited to what the factory offers, and
while this may satisfy the needs of many shooters, it is not likely to give optimum
performance with your particular gun. Most of the factory-loaded varmint cartridges offer less than a half-dozen different bullet-powder combinations. A handloader, in the .22-250 for example, has a choice of literally dozens of powder-bullet combos: He can choose a soft point, a hollow point or a full metal jacket
in six different bullet weights; he can propel the pill with an equal variety of powders; he can choose between a standard and a magnum primer. He can, in short,
tailor the load exactly to fit his own particular needs and his own particular gun.

The second disadvantage of factory loads is cost. A box of twenty center-fires for most of the varmint calibers will almost destroy a ten-dollar bill. Factory loads for my .22-250 cost a little less than fifty cents for every time I pull the trigger. Handloads, using the empty brass, cost a bit less than ten cents a round. I get a better product, I feel, for about one-fifth the cost. Considering that I shoot several hundred rounds in a season it is obvious that I save a lot of bucks.

Bullet Design

Rifle bullets are offered in three main types. The spitzer, or spire point bullet, is a conically shaped, pointed bullet with a portion of the lead exposed at the end of the jacketing. The soft lead deforms when it meets resistance which causes the jacketed portion of the bullet to mushroom.

The hollowpoint bullet is just what the name implies. A cavity is left at the point of the bullet and as this cavity fills with flesh the bullet expands or blows up. The full-metal-jacket bullet has neither the soft point nor the hollow point and normally will not expand to a noticeable degree.

I have had good results shooting varmints with both spitzer and hollow-pointed bullets. My best luck with the spitzers came when using the type marketed by Hornaday in the SX line. The SX bullets have thinner jackets than normal spire-point bullets, penetrate less and blow up quicker. Shooting the SX bullets from the .22-250 under a full head of steam might cause jacket rupture which can lead to keyholing and inaccuracy. Loaded at moderate velocities, the bullets deliver good accuracy and will normally blow up in the body cavity of a coyote without undesirable fur damage.

I tried the 55-grain Hornaday SX in front of 33.5 grains of 4320. Ignition was provided by CCI-200 primers which gave me about 3,400 fps muzzle, I figured. The load did a fine job on coyotes. I shot one gray fox with the load and had no problems. The fox was shot in the chest, however, and had the bullet not travelled the long axis of the critter, it would have likely produced unacceptable damage.

I like Speer's hollowpoint bullet. It has a larger opening than many others and seems to blow up a bit better. My best accuracy comes from the 52-grainer in their match hollowpoint.

I have had poor luck with the full-metal-jacket bullets and have abandoned them altogether. Obviously they deliver the least pelt damage of the three styles, but unfortunately they do not always put the critter down immediately and anchor him to the spot. I have had coyotes run a quarter of a mile before succumbing to a good hit. In timber or brush the critter will likely never be found. I want a load

53

that will put a critter down hard even with a poor shot. The hot loaded spitzers or hollowpoints do just that, and although a second shot may be necessary, the critter sticks around until the job is finished.

This opinion, I might point out, is not universally shared among varmint hunters. Ed Sceery, a talented caller from Santa Fe, New Mexico, takes large numbers of fur bearers every year using a .22-250 with full-metal-jacketed 55-grainers. Ed goes for the chest and reports no problems on lost animals.

Rifle Sights

I am convinced that a telescopic sight is mandatory for the predator hunter who hopes to bring home fur. I have shot most of the open sights and most of the peeps, and I am well aware that a good shot can make consistent hits at moderate ranges. Predators, unfortunately, do not always present good opportunities for a clear shot. They often are running and are at great distances. A coyote at three hundred yards can be completely hidden by the front sight on a semi-buckhorn or by the post on a peep. The best choice, I think, is a fixed power scope like the 6X Weaver on my Ruger. I know a number of callers who choose a variable power scope, usually in the 3X to 9X range. I have no quarrel with the variable, but I find that I usually don't have the time to take advantage of the variable feature. Most of the time I don't know the range I will be shooting until just before time to pull the trigger. The six-power feels right to me. It is strong enough to expose a sneaking fox or bobcat that is almost blended into a brushy hillside, and it has enough light-gathering ability to make twilight shots.

Most of the time telescope sights are offered in five reticles. The cross hair, the dual X, the post and cross hair, the rangefinder and the dot. My choice is the dual X. It has a fairly thick cross hair for most of the sight. Near the center it narrows down to a very fine cross hair. The coarse cross hair makes it easy to get on critters fast, even in poor light. The fine center hairs allow me to see the critter without his being hid by the coarse hairs.

I occasionally have problems on close shots with the six-power. Every once in a while a critter will surprise me by appearing out of nowhere twenty feet out. I have missed more than a few of these because they were so close that they appeared blurred in the scope. They also look as big as a buffalo and I am convinced that I cannot miss. Instead of picking a spot, I point-shoot at the entire critter and give him a free pass.

Rifle Accessories

Every rifle I own has quick-detach sling swivels. If the rifle does not come so equipped, I spend the first night of ownership attaching them. Varmint hunting, the way I do it, often involves considerable walking, usually when loaded down with other equipment. It is unhandy and tiring to hand-carry a rifle.

Another accessory I have found helpful is a bipod. The one I own was made by Harris Manufacturing and attaches to the front sling swivel stud on the rifle. When it is in place the sling can also be attached. The bipod allows me that extra bit of steadiness that sometimes means the difference between a hit and a miss. I have made good hits on standing predators at three hundred yards using the bipod. If the gun is to be shot offhand on a running critter the bipod does not interfere. I am convinced that the bipod permits me to skin a couple dozen extra critters each season.

Some Second Opinions

The correct caliber and the correct load for fur hunting is a topic that is sure to start a heated discussion around varmint callers. I have given you my own opinion on the subject. Later in the book you will receive advice from other experts, each an expert on a particular type of critter. I thought it would be interesting to talk to a few of the pioneers in the development of guns, bullets, powders and reloading equipment. Joyce Hornady, Bill Ruger, Fred Huntington and Bruce Hodgdon took time from their busy schedules to discuss their favorite calibers and loads for varmints.

Joyce Hornady

I have shot a few coyotes, mostly in connection with other hunts. I might not have gone into the bullet business at all if it was not for the Nebraska prairie dogs. When bullets became scarce during World War II we found it necessary to make our own and I have been making bullets since then.

I started varmint hunting with a .30-06 Enfield, shooting mostly 93-grain Luger pistol bullets that I bought for ninety cents a hundred. I moved up to the Lindell Chukker and this is the one I was using when I started making bullets. The Chukker is a bit like the Donaldson Wasp but is slightly shorter and is on a single shot Stevens 44½ action. We were shooting mostly 45- or 50-grain bullets. I later owned a .222 and ended up shooting 60-grain bullets. They didn't drift as much in our Nebraska

Joyce Hornady took this fine Kodiak in 1958 with one shot from a 300 Weatherby. Joyce likes the .17 caliber for close range shots at furbearers and would choose the .22-250 in open country. *Photo courtesy Joyce Hornady.*

wind. I have shot a lot of varmints with the Winchester .243. Mine was a featherweight and was accurate after I free-floated the barrel. I started with 70-grain bullets. After a lot of shooting and some throat erosion I moved up to 100-grainers. The longer bullet gave me a better accuracy. Any rifle is a good rifle if it is accurate. I don't find the heavier calibers as much fun to shoot. For my money the 6mm is as heavy as I care to go for varmints.

I shot a bear on Kodiak Island in 1958, using a .300 Weatherby loaded with our 220-grain round-nose bullet. The Weatherby certainly has capacity enough to handle heavy bullets and I figured the 220-grain should be a bear killer. The bear was quartering and I shot him at about two hundred yards through the left shoulder. The bullet was recovered back in the right hip. The one shot did the job.

If I was hunting fur bearers for a living in my part of the country I would certainly be calling them and for that purpose I would use the .17 caliber. It is deadly at short range and would do less pelt damage than the larger calibers. For long-range, open-country hunting I would use the .22-250 with our 60-grain bullet. I use the 60-grain because it does not drift as much as the lighter bullets. It is not quite as fast but has been most successful for me.

Bill Ruger

I hunted years ago with an old-timer in Alberta who is famous as a lion hunter. We were hunting sheep once and he had his dogs with him as usual. His only firearm was a very rough H&R .22 caliber revolver. I mention this to show that there is a lot of flexibility in the selection of firearms. This man was a pro.

In your country, or any country where a hunter will be shooting at fairly long range, I should think that a medium-power, high-velocity rifle would be my choice. The rifle that would be okay for bear would be different than the one needed for smaller animals. If one rifle had to do it all I would be looking at the 6mm or 7mm, the .243 or the Remington 7mm based on the .308 case. If the bear and the lion are not in the picture then I think a well-placed shot with a .22 Hornet or a .223 Remington would do the job, particularly if the range is within a hundred yards.

I don't want to forget the .357 mag and the .44 mag. They are great killers out to about a hundred yards and probably don't do as much pelt damage as some high-velocity cartridges might.

Fred Huntington

I think the old "Varminter" .22-250 is a hard one to beat for varmints. It was my first and why I got away from it no one knows. It had good accuracy and had good flat-shooting qualities. It was easy on barrels too, if you were not addicted to 20-shot strings. It would load with almost any

Fred Huntington with a 9 foot, yellow mane Zambia lion. Fred likes the .22-250 for coyote-sized critters. *Photo courtesy Fred Huntington.*

combination and shoot good groups up to about 3,350 or 3,400 fps. Some people claimed they got higher velocities but I never did with good accuracy. My pet load was 32½ grains of 4320 with a 50- to 54-grain bullet.

I think the .220 Swift is a good caliber for varmints too. This gun shot excellent groups, even better than the Varminter when loaded for around 3,500-3,600 fps. When I say "better," I mean it shot flatter and had more velocity. The Swift got a bad name from being loaded up to 4,200 fps and it was not accurate at that speed. My favorite load for the .220 was 35½ grains of 3031 behind a 55-grain bullet. Muzzle velocity was about 3,550 fps. I killed many a rock chuck at 300 to 450 yards when the wind was down.

For small critters where you want to save the fur, you might be better off with a .222 mag loaded with about 27 grains of 4895. This is a DuPont late-type powder. I would use a 50-grain Speer bullet. If I had trouble on pelt damage, I would lighten the bullet, maybe to 48 or 45 grains. Each hunter would have to test his own gun to get the exact load for accuracy and minimal pelt damage.

Bruce Hodgdon

If I was calling heavy brush, I would use a 12-gauge shotgun loaded with No. 4 buck. This would get through the brush and not damage the hide. In open country, I prefer a .220 Swift using 55-grain bullets. On close targets, the bullet will blow up and will not exit. At long range there will not be much blowup and the exit hole will be small. I also like the .243. I use H-380 powder behind a Hornaday or Speer bullet. The 80-grainers do not cause much pelt damage on a coyote.

I once shot a silver fox at over a hundred yards with a 110-grain .30-06. The bullet didn't expand and the exit hole was small. Another time I shot a red at 150 yards. The critter was facing me and I put the 50-grainer straight into his chest using a .219 Wasp. There was no exit hole and no pelt damage.

6

Shotguns

One of the most successful varmint hunters of all times used a shotgun exclusively. Morton Burnham of Marble Falls, Texas, called countless critters by making squealing sounds with his mouth. He brought fox, coyote and bobcat in close and serviced them with a 12-gauge loaded with No. 4 birdshot. He seldom missed, according to his son Murry.

The late Sam Dudley was another caller who preferred the smoothbore for varmint hunting. Sam was four times the world champion varmint caller. He often hunted the desert around his central Arizona home accompanied by a sway-backed 20-gauge named Singing Sally. Sam and Sally sung many a critter to sleep.

If a caller did everything perfect, a shotgun would be all the gun ever needed to do in a critter. Most of the time the predator is called under less than perfect conditions and the shotgun may present certain liabilities. I use a shotgun on many hunts, however, simply because it puts more fur on the stretcher—in certain country—than a rifle.

The main advantage to the scattergun is the speed with which the hunter can point and shoot—notice I didn't say aim. I have my best luck shotgunning critters when I point it instinctively. The shotgun, by its nature, does not require the same degree of skill needed for a rifle. This is another advantage on predator hunts as the action is usually fast and at a fairly short range. The shotgun also offers a fast second and third shot, if one is needed, to anchor a cripple or to swing on a fast disappearing double. The shotgun is also a fur saver. There may be a lot of small holes in the hide from a shotgun hunt, but they are usually too small to be of consequence to a fur buyer.

If I am hunting brushy or timbered country where the shooting range is likely to be less than fifty yards I usually carry a shotgun. The scattergun is particularly effective early in the calling season when the critters are naive and eager. I make a number of doubles every season with the shotgun and once in a while luck into a triple. I can only recollect a half dozen times scoring a double with the rifle and have never chalked up a triple. I also miss less often with the shotgun.

Shotgun Liabilities

The main disadvantage to the shotgun is its limited range. It is designed as a short-range weapon and the hunter likely will have to pass on some shots that are out of range or that are at marginal range. This can be particularly frustrating if the bashful critter is a bobcat that is worth a lot of bucks. When I first tried the shotgun for critters I coaxed a big bobcat from a brush canyon just off the Navajo Indian Reservation. For some reason the big bobbie stopped about seventy yards out and sat down to think about the rabbit supper. I screamed, squeaked and sucked until I had trombone lips and never budged that cat a foot closer. Eventually he tired of the game and slipped back into the canyon as silently as he had come. I cussed the shotgun every step of the way home from that trip and swore that I would never venture afield again without the long-range capability offered by a .22 centerfire. I lied, of course, and took the shotgun the very next time I called thick cover.

Cripples are another curse of the shotgunner. The pattern of the shot is not predictable, of course, and the shooter will sometimes dust a critter and let him run off. If they bleed after being shot with a .22-250 they usually die. Shotgun cripples can be minimized if the shooter will practice shot selection. Know the range of your gun and your load and do not be tempted to chance shots that are doubtful.

The best shotgun for critter hunting, in my opinion, is the gun which shoots the greatest load of shot the greatest distance. Following that line of thought, the 10-gauge magnum in the 3½-inch shell would be my first choice. I would also insist on an autoloader. I want a gun that will give me more than one shot at a critter. The Ithaca Mag 10 should be an excellent varmint gun. The 3½-inch autoloader will throw more than two inches of shot at a crafty critter. Sure kill range should approach sixty yards. The big mag has a couple of disadvantages. It costs a potful of bucks; a hunter who does not have a fabulous season might find it takes most of his season's fur to pay for the gun. The gun is also heavy. I suppose it has to be to handle that much shell, but a person could get terribly tired packing a dozen pounds of shotgun afield. The big mag costs more to shoot, and it is also a highly specialized gun. Unlike a 12 or a 20, it cannot be taken comfortably afield for an afternoon's try at birds or rabbits. It might be more gun than most hunters want.

12-Gauge

The 12-gauge is enough gun, in my opinion, to handle most calling chores. I like the three-inch magnum as it increases the sure kill range about ten yards. The magnum will shoot the standard 2¾-inch shell as well as the three inch and offers the shooter a good selection of mag and standard loads.

Many gun manufacturers offer a 12 autoloader and a good percentage make the gun in a three-inch chamber. I have shot Winchester, Browning and Remington autoloaders and like them all. My varmint shotgun is a Model 1100 Remington magnum. The gun is slightly heavier than the standard model, but is not unnecessarily uncomfortable to carry. As with my rifles, I have attached quick-detach sling swivels so that the gun may be carried on the shoulder. The gun is full choke to keep the string together until it travels the thiry-five or so yards that is the average shot.

Loads for Predators

The correct load for predators is the one that patterns best in your particular gun and that does the job for you in the country you hunt. Before I took my 1100 afield, I took it to the range and ran pattern tests with various loads of buckshot. I used buckshot because our range here in the Southwest tends to be on the long side and I wanted the extra carrying power of the heavier shot. I shot everything from oo buck through No. 4 buck and varied the distance from twenty yards to fifty-five yards. My target was coyote-sized and cut from a newspaper. I found the No. 4 buck gave the best results from my gun, using three-inch Peters mags. The shells carried 41 of the .24-inch diameter shot pushed by 4½ drams of powder. The target was riddled with shot at the closer ranges but the pattern started to thin out at forty yards. At fifty-five yards, about one-fourth of the shot hit the target; enough, I figured, to do the job on a coyote.

I bagged three coyotes the first time I took the gun to the brush. I was still in the truck having a last cup of coffee from the thermos and waiting for shooting light when I heard a coyote sing out on a ridge above. I walked to the ridge top in the half-light of false dawn and found a hidey hole under a scrubby Palo Verde tree. Three coyotes charged me before I took the Burnham tube from my mouth after the first series. I let the first one run by as he was too close to shoot when I saw him. I took the second one straight in the chest at about forty feet and swung to the last one as he scratched gravel on a sharp turn; the mag dumped him on top of his brother. The first of the eager trio had dropped off into a steep sandwash. If he had turned down the wash he probably would have escaped; he didn't though, and he paid the price. He climbed out of the wash, and when he was about forty yards straight across from me I spent the last shell in the magnum.

I do not advise hunting critters with any gauge lighter than a 12. I have killed a number of coyotes and fox with a 20-gauge and a few with a 16. In every instance, however, I was hunting birds or rabbits and took the critters as a bonus. One evening, I was hunting Gambel quail along a brushy wash when I heard a fox sound-off somewhere in the brush. While he finished his nightsong I slipped the pair of 7½'s out of the barrels of my Silver Snipe and substituted a mean-looking pair of No. 3 buck in three-inch mag. An Olt squealer brought him in fast and the little 20 over-and-under folded him neatly at twenty-five yards. I make it a practice to carry a few buckshot loads with me whenever I go after any shotgun game. A prime fox or coyote can really add zest to a small game hunt.

The Remington-Peters folks offer a number of buckshot loads for the standard and the three-inch 12. Three loads are marketed for the magnum: the No. 4 buck described above containing 41 pellets; a No. 1 buck with 24 pellets; and a oo buck with 15 pellets. For the standard 12, there is a oo buck with 9 pellets, an o buck with 12 pellets, a No. 1 buck with 16 pellets and a No. 4 with 27 pellets. R&P also offers a shell they label their standard magnum. It is available in a oo buck with 12 pellets and a No. 1 buck with 24 pellets. There is one buckshot load available for the 16, a No. 1 buck with 12 pellets, and one load for the 20, a No. 3 buck with 20 pellets.

Birdshot and Buckshot

Not every varmint caller will agree that buckshot is the correct load for critters. Some very good hunters who favor the shotgun use birdshot, but buckshot works best for me. If I spend most of my time hunting the small-bodied fox, I would likely re-think my position, but hunting big western coyotes is a different matter. Some of these critters will top thirty-five pounds. When they are moving at top speed they require a load with knockdown authority. Buckshot, in my opinion, does that job better than birdshot.

Shotgun Stands

Calling to the shotgun is different than calling to the rifle. On shotgun stands, the hunter must have the animal closer than fifty yards if he is to deliver a clean kill. This will not be much of a problem with young, eager critters that have never heard the call, but it can be a difficult task on an old and educated varmint. These critters will come to the call slowly and will be alert for any small clue that might spell danger. Shotgunners must hide more carefully than the rifle hunters and they must be more discreet in their movements because of this distance factor. I never make any movement once I sight an incoming customer. If I am using the mouth call I will let it fall to the end of the lanyard as soon as I sight the critter. Any further calling is done with the lip squeak. Many hunters I have known will find it impossible to resist the temptation to shift their position slightly when the game is sighted. They are hoping, I suppose, for a bit better shooting angle when the critter gets close, but most of the time the customer will see the movement and never come close. Remain completely still once the critter is sighted until he is close enough for a clear shot. At that point raise the shotgun and shoot in one fluid motion.

Shooting Doubles

Scoring doubles on critters is no easy task, but it can be done if the hunter keeps his wits about him. Rule number one requires that the caller not shoot until both critters are within shotgun range. If one of the customers is considerably ahead of the other, try to stop him in close with a lip squeak. He will usually stop long enough for the trailer to catch up. When shooting, take the varmint that is the farthest away with the first round. This will give you a better chance on the second customer, because you can be sure that the second shot will be a running shot. Try to decide ahead of time which way the second varmint will run, and make sure that the first target is down and out before turning your attention to the second.

I was calling a brushy Northern Arizona hillside one spring when I summoned two coyotes. Both came at a fast run toward my hiding bush. They came at me so fast that I was not able to get a shot while they were approaching. The two eager critters split my bush and zoomed by at handshaking distance. I shot at the critter to my left and saw him tumble. I swung quickly to my right and got one tough shot at the second as he departed, but he didn't go down. I swung back left and discovered that the first coyote had enjoyed a miraculous recovery. Thus, I left the stand with zero coyotes instead of two.

Masking Scent

While masking scent is a good technique for any hunter, it is absolutely necessary for the shotgunner. I do not mean to imply that hunters without masking scent will not get a critter once in a while, but they do not, in my opinion, get as many critters as they would with the scent. When working at close range, as shotgunners must, a keen-nosed varmint will pick up ambient scent even if there is no unfriendly wind. In short, use the scent and increase the bag.

Magazine Capacity

The Federal Migratory Treaty Act limits the magazine capacity of shotguns to no more than two. If you use your gun for both varmint hunting and waterfowl be sure to install the magazine plug when hunting migratory birds. Some state laws also limit magazine capacity to two shells for the taking of any wildlife. The hunter should check the laws in his state to learn the restrictions on magazine capacity. If there are no limits, I would suggest removing the magazine plug and loading as many rounds as the magazine accepts.

Pistols and Primitives

I have killed a few critters with a handgun, bagged one with a black powder gun, and almost got a coyote with a bow and arrow. I have had a couple eager beavers come in over the years that I probably could have finished off with a rock. Primitive-weapons hunters occasionally can take an animal if they are good hunters and are willing to work at it. If your purpose in hunting is to answer the challenge of a primitive hunt, go to it.

I hunt for two reasons: One is the excitement of the hunt; the other is to put fur on the stretcher. I hunt during the season and depend on my fur check for extra cash; therefore, the best two guns for my purposes are the centerfire rifle and the shotgun.

7

Night Calling

Night calling for predators is exciting. The critters loom up out of the night and come much closer than on daytime hunts. The suspense is increased as the animal is usually visible only as a set of glowing eyeballs when first sighted. The tension builds as the eyes disappear and the critter works closer to the call.

Most predators are more easily called at night. The raccoon and the bobcat are primarily night hunters and will respond readily to the call. Experienced night hunters tell me that they will sight ten bobcat on night stands for every one they sight on daylight stands. Part of this can be explained because of the light-reflecting qualities of the bobcat eyes. Those two big moons give them away whenever the light hits. Daytime cats in the exact same position may go unnoticed because of their superb camouflage.

Another reason night hunters see more cats is the cat nature. He is hunting at night and will be in the more open meadows and prairies, places the hunter is apt to call. The cats come because they feel safe in the dark. That same darkness also hides the hunter, though, and makes it unlikely he will be discovered.

Many states have laws which ban night hunting. Other states may not actually outlaw night hunting but will place difficult restrictions on the hunter. My home state of Arizona permits the hunting of raccoon at night, but the taking of all other wildlife is prohibited.

Night hunting, where it is permitted, has a number of disadvantages. The darkness hides the game as it approaches. Incoming customers are sometimes never seen until they get so close they spook out of the country. Shooting is more difficult unless the critters are at very close range. Moreover, shooting a high-power rifle at night can be dangerous. The hunter knows only what is within a fifty-yard circle; he has no knowledge of livestock, parked cars or buildings that may be a few hundred feet away.

In spite of the disadvantages, night hunting can be more productive than day hunting for most predators. The one exception is the coyote. He seems to hunt both day and night and will respond equally well at either time. He is light shy, however, and usually will spook the first time a bright light hits him in the eyeballs. Other predators are easier at night. The raccoon is a sucker for night calls. Both bobcat and fox spend more time hunting at night and therefore respond to the call eagerly. The bobcat, in particular, seems unafraid of the light.

The Burnham Technique

Most of my calling has been in daylight with only a few night trips for raccoon. Other night trips have been made to call and photograph the customers. I feel this limited experience does not qualify me to give advice to anyone on night calling, so to make this chapter on night calling more informative, I contacted Murry Burnham of the well-known Burnham Brothers firm in Marble Falls, Texas, for advice. Murry graciously agreed to share the knowledge he has gained from more than thirty years of night calling. Excerpts from an interview with Murry Burnham follow:

GERRY BLAIR: Is night calling better than day calling?

MURRY BURNHAM: Yes. Fox hunt mostly at night; so do bobcat. The raccoon is mostly a night hunter and is easy to call at night. But coyotes feed day and night and might be easier to hunt in the day.

G.B.: Why are coyotes hard to hunt at night?

M.B.: Coyotes are a different ballgame. They are quicker than the other animals. You have to be in open country to get coyotes at night; stay away from brush or trees. The best nighttime coyote country is open country with short brush or no brush at all. Call open country that you can't call in the daylight because you often can't hide your vehicle. The darkness hides you and your truck.

G.B.: Do you move away from the truck on night calls?

M.B.: No. I call from the bed of the truck at night. I have a stand built right on the truck bed.

G.B.: How does the wind affect the night caller?

M.B.: If you are in good country you don't have to worry about the wind too much anyway. If the wind is blowing, call into it and call more frequently; the call won't carry as far in the wind. I call every half a mile if the wind is blowing.

G.B.: Can you call raccoons in the daytime?

M.B.: You can call coons in the day but you have to get into the creekbeds and bluffs where they stay. Heavy brush along a creek might be good. The coons won't come very far to the call during the day.

G.B.: Is it hard to call ringtails at night?

M.B.: Ringtails will come to the call at night but won't come far. They are small and short-legged and don't range very far. Look for them in brushy canyons and the creekbeds. They are also around rocky ledges. They come best to the high-pitched squeaking calls of something that would be small enough for them to eat.

G.B.: How about skunks?

M.B.: Skunks will come occasionally but you can't depend on them.

G.B.: Are snakes a problem at night?

M.B.: Rattlesnakes can be a problem if you walk away from the truck to pick up a critter. Most snakes den in the winter but they can be a problem in the spring and summer.

G.B.: Is the dark of the moon good for calling?

M.B.: It is real good. You can hunt by moonlight but you have to use cover and hide just as you do in the daytime. If you stand out in the open, the critters will spot you even with the light shining toward them.

Murry Burnham with fur from a good night's hunt. Murry does most of his night calling from the stand built in the bed of this truck. The rifle is a .222. *Photo Murry Burnham.*

Raccoons will come during the day but come more often at night. Burnham's new trilling bird distress call brings coon up close. *Photo Gerry Blair.*

G.B.: What weather conditions affect calling success?

M.B.: The first clear day after a storm is always good, as is the last clear day before a storm. Foggy calling is good in the daytime but is no good at night; the fog breaks up the light and you can't see the critters.

G.B.: How many callers are needed to make a night calling stand?

M.B.: Two callers are ideal; one using a spotlight while the other does the shooting.

G.B.: How do you handle the light?

M.B.: Keep the main beam of the light pointed up and try to spot their eyes with the soft outer ring of light. When they are close enough to shoot, you will be able to pick up their eyes. I like to use a red spotlight. If you are afoot, the scope light works quite well, especially if you are going to shoot closer than fifty yards.

G.B.: Is a rifle or a shotgun best for night hunting?

M.B.: I like the rifle. I use a down-loaded .222 if I am trying to save the hides. I load the cartridges down to less than 2,000 fps muzzle velocity and get very little pelt damage, even on fox.

G.B.: Will the critters come as close to the truck as they do to a hunter on foot?

M.B.: No. They won't come as close to the truck.

G.B.: Is the red fox harder to call than the gray?

M.B.: The reds may be a little tougher because they have a greater territory, like a coyote. And you don't find concentrations of the reds like you do grays. Calling a red is more like calling a coyote.

G.B.: How important is it to scout for calling locations?

M.B.: I scout all of my night stands in the daytime. I usually spend more time scouting than I do calling. Certain areas will always produce but you have to rest them in between.

G.B.: Is it a good idea to use a masking scent?

M.B.: I use skunk as a masking scent. Sometimes I will kill a rabbit and use it, but I really don't think there is anything that will work a hundred percent on a coyote. I have seen a few coyotes that weren't afraid of human scent but they were coyotes that had never smelled a man before.

G.B.: How do bobcats come to a call at night?

M.B.: If you happen to set up close to them they will come at a high run or a fast trot. As a general rule they come slow. That's just cat nature. Cats are pretty dumb; if they are shot at and missed they will usually stick around. If they have been shot at a time or two before, though, they scram in a hurry. When they make up their mind to leave, nothing is going to stop them. I have run off fox and called them back for another chance, but not a bobcat.

Ringtails are a short-legged animal not built to travel great distances. You must set up in creek beds and near brushy water holes to get them consistently. Ringtails will come to the call most often at night. *Photo Gerry Blair.*

G.B.: How does a coyote come at night?

M.B.: A coyote comes good at night. You have to see them a long way off so you can pick up on him pretty far out. When he turns sideways, that's when you got to do it. You have to take your shot if he gives you that much time.

G.B.: How do raccoons come at night?

M.B.: Coons will come as close as you will let them. You could make a loud noise and scare them off, I guess, but they will crawl in your lap if you stay quiet.

G.B.: When is the time to shoot a night-called critter?

M.B.: You shoot a cat when he stops and won't budge. You have all the time in the world with a cat. Shoot at a fox when you have your first good chance; they will not hold well for the light. They hold better with the red light, so try to have a red or orange filter over the shooting light. A coyote will not hold still very long with either light. When they turn sideways you only have a couple seconds.

G.B.: How long do you call a stand before moving on?

M.B.: Twelve minutes on a stand will get ninety percent of the fox. Thirty minutes will get most cats. Coons take about twenty minutes. Give coyotes twenty minutes at night, a little more than you would in the daytime. I have seen a lot of coyotes show up after twenty minutes, even on day stands.

G.B.: Can you take more than one critter from a single stand?

M.B.: I shot five fox one night from the same stand. Another time we sighted six fox, a coyote and two cats at the same stand. Two different times I called up a dozen coyotes from the same stand. That was in the daytime, though, not at night.

Keep calling after you have a fox on the ground. Five of the seven fox were taken by Murry Burnham from one stand. He used a .222 with handloads designed not for high velocity (unneeded in this situation) but for accuracy and gentleness on the pelts. *Photo Murry Burnham.*

G.B.: How do eyes differ at night?

M.B.: Sometimes it's hard to tell. Coyote eyes will usually be higher off the ground. Fox eyes will be lower and less green, more reddish. When the fox is trotting the eyes will wobble. Bobcat have big round eyes, like a moon. The color will depend on the brilliance of the light. If the light is red the eyes will look red. A coyote's eyes are a little like a deer, a little on the green side. Coon eyes are on the red side and so are javelina. The javelina are a dull red and you will only see one eye at a time. This depends on the light, of course. From a white light, the dimmer the light the redder the eyes.

G.B.: What light do you like for shooting?

M.B.: If it is one person depending on himself the scope light is the best. He doesn't have to do anything but flip the switch and the light points with the gun. It's fast.

G.B.: Are owls a problem at night?

M.B.: That's the only thing I am afraid of. They've taken lots of people's hats right off their heads. You don't hear them and don't see them, just feel the wind off their wings. It's the great horned owl, mostly, but others come too.

G.B.: How did your dad, Morton Burnham, call?

M.B.: He used his mouth. Dad never got into making calls. I believe the varmints could hear his mouth call a mile though. It was loud. I can call that way too. There are all kinds of little squeaks you can make with your mouth. My dad shot and killed twenty-three gray fox in one afternoon. Another time he called and killed 105 fox in five and a half hours. There was kind of a fox explosion in the area. He was a good hunter.

The Red Light

The red light is probably invisible to most predators. They are color blind and will see the color red as black. However, they seem to sense the red light if it is strong which is likely a reaction to the intensity of the light rather than its actual color. The Burnhams got the idea for a red hunting light after a visit to a New York zoo. The night critters on display were illuminated by a red light in the daytime so that visitors could see them; the critters thought it was dark and moved around. During the night, a white light was turned on and the predators thought it was daylight and went to bed.

Shooting visibility appears to be decreased somewhat with the red light. Eyes can be spotted a couple of hundred yards away but the critter has to be much closer before he can be positively identified – fifty yards is about average. It is critical that all night shooters know the identity of their target. A farmer's prize bull wouldn't look too good on the living room wall. Usually there is no problem with identification if the animal is within fifty yards.

Red lights may be constructed in a number of ways. A piece of red cellophane sandwiched between two pieces of clear glass works well. Some hunters use a red-tinted lens. This seems to decrease the light output of their unit, however, and is not recommended. Another option is to paint the inside of a clear lens with a red felt marker.

Night Calling Tips

If you use a white spotting light, never point it directly toward an animal until you are ready to shoot. Keep the light high and avoid any object between the light and the critter. These obstructions create shadows that can spook your target. Callers also will find a standard two-cell flashlight a convenient accessory at night. The light can be used walking to and from stands and to locate downed game. If every member of the calling party has his own light the search for downed critters will be shortened.

Calling locations scouted during the day should be marked with plastic pennants. This will make them easier to find and recognize after dark.

Archers hunting at night should place a small piece of reflectorized tape on each arrow. This will make the arrow easier to locate if it does not hit its target.

Other things that might improve your night calling: Drive to night calling locations using dim lights or only parking lights—this will disturb the animals less and will shorten the time you need for your eyes to adjust to the dark; check your vehicle and remove any object that may roll around and create noise.

8

The Coyote

The coyote is a mammal with an average adult weight of twenty to thirty pounds for males and a bit less than that for females, but the weight will vary. Some coyotes in the northwest mountains scale forty pounds or more. The largest coyote I have encountered registered thirty-five pounds. He was a big red male that came to the call in the company of two smaller coyotes. He was smart and stayed in a thick patch of oak about seventy yards out while he decided if he wanted rabbit. A 52-grainer from my .22-250 cut through the leaves and twigs to find his ribs. His two friends slipped off into the chapparal like twin ghosts. The big red was the most foul-smelling coyote I have ever met. He smelled strongly of urine and I suspect he had spent the past few minutes rolling in a carrion carcass. The slug had done very little damage to the pelt and there was almost no blood. I washed the critter anyway to take out the stink. The fur buyer, I figured, would pay a better price if he didn't have to hold his nose as he reached for his wallet.

Predators, as a rule, are among the smartest critters around, and the coyote is probably the smartest of the predators. He has eyes that can spot a mouse at a hundred yards on a moonlit night. His hearing is so acute he can hear a feather fall. He can smell a piece of meat, or a hunter, a quarter of a mile away, and his brain can gather and retain information.

Color variation among coyotes is not uncommon. Two coyotes from the same litter may show extremes in color. A coyote may be a brown, a deep roan red or a silver, and most have a black-tipped tail but every year I see a few with white-tips.

Fur buyers have segregated coyote pelts into a number of classes. A pale Montana is usually the top of the line. These northern coyotes are large, have a very fine fur and usually show that pale silver color that is currently in the most

The coyote in the center is the largest I have shot. I didn't weigh him but I estimate the big red at 40 pounds. *Photo Gerry Blair.*

74

demand. At the other end of the scale is the Southwestern. This coyote has a reddish brown coat. The hide is more hairlike than furlike, and often shows sparse guard hair.

Most coyotes are night hunters. Like most other predators they hunt when they are likely to have the most success. In that way, they spend the minimum amount of energy for each bite of food. This may not be important in the spring and summer when food is plentiful, but it can mean the difference between life and death in the winter when many of the critters walk a thin line between survival and starvation. If the coyote is hungry he will hunt night and day. He eats the groceries that are the easiest to come by. If his belly is empty he will eat and obtain nourishment from an astonishing variety of material. Near populated areas, the coyote will rob garbage cans and dumps. Any pet dog or cat that crosses his path is likely to get a quick look at the inside of a coyote stomach. He will visit gardens to partake of watermelon, cantaloupe, vegetables and grass. He will also eat grasshoppers and other insects. Near lakes and rivers the coyote will patrol the banks for dead fish. He is not much of a fisherman himself although he will take a live one if he can corner it in shallow water.

The coyote also has a taste for reptiles. He is surprised occasionally when one of the snakes bites back, but even this does not discourage him from eating rattlesnakes. He appears to have an immunity to the poison and seldom dies from the venom. In the southwest deserts, the abundant reptile community is an important element in his diet. Young and adult birds will also be taken; he will eat the eggs from the nests of ground nesters if he has a chance.

Large and small mammals are the coyote's main course. He eats mice, rats, ground squirrels, prairie dogs, gophers and rabbits. He is an efficient hunter of the young of most big game animals. Many wildlife biologists list the coyote as the most important predator of antelope fawns. The evidence is not as conclusive on the young of deer and elk but it is certain that the coyote likely harvests more deer each year than the documented take of hunters. Most of these big game coyote victims are the young, and are sought out and eaten within hours—or days—of their birth. Wildlife biologists who have spent the past five years documenting the interaction between the coyote and the antelope in Northern Arizona have convincing data showing that coyotes take ninety percent of the fawn crop yearly.

Although the primary big game prey of coyotes is the young, the efficient predators can take adult big game under certain conditions. Adults are often killed during periods of deep snow. The coyote moves across the crusted snow rapidly and the heavier prey sinks through the crust. The winter-weakened animal is usually easy pickings for the hungry coyote.

Mating

Coyotes mate in early spring, usually in February. It may be a bit earlier in the warmer states and a bit later up north. Two months after mating the pups are born. The litter will average four to six pups and may run as high as twelve. The pups are born in a den prepared by the female. The den may be in a small natural cavern, a gap in slide rock areas, under buildings, in a dugout under a large boulder or under the roots of a large tree. In the Southwest where natural denning sites are not plentiful, the coyote will dig a bowl-shaped opening into the soft bank of a sand wash.

The young pups are cared for by the mother while the male takes care of the hunting and brings food. Often the male will return to the den with a belly full of jackrabbit which will be regurgitated for the pups. As the pups get older the food is more likely to be brought back uneaten. At times a tolerated female will assist the mother with the young. The helper most likely will be a pup from last year's litter. As the young coyotes become able to travel they will accompany the adults on the hunt. They have only a few short months of summer to learn the hunting skills they will need to survive the winter. If they do not learn well, they will not survive.

Only one breeding female is allowed in each territory. Non-breeding females may spend their entire lives without having a pup. They must wait their turn to breed, and they may inherit a breeding territory from a breeder who dies. The killing of a breeding female usually does not make a serious impact on coyote numbers. One or more substitute females are waiting in the wings to take her

Coyote mate for life or until one of the pair dies. The den is likely to be in a dug out area in heavy brush. *Photo Gerry Blair.*

Coyote pups stay close to the den until they are about two months old. This den was dug in a brushy thicket. *Photo Duane Rubink, U.S. Fish & Wildlife Service.*

place. At times the taking of a breeder may actually result in an increase in breeders. If it is a good year for food, two of the young females may split the territory and there will be two breeders where there was once only one.

The coyote family remains a unit in the home territory throughout the summer. They will often separate into hunting units for individual forays but will keep in contact through yips and howls. When the leaves begin to turn in the fall the unit will dissolve. The pups will still participate in group hunts for rabbits and other game occasionally, but they will be on their own for the most part. As winter arrives and the hunting gets tough, the youngsters will be invited to leave. If they are hesitant the parents deliver a series of painful nips to the youngsters to encourage them on their way. They leave and by the next year are no more welcome back to Daddy's territory than any other coyote.

Most mated coyotes will remain together as a pair until one dies. When that happens, the survivor will find a new mate. The newlyweds will defend the territory with the same enthusiasm as the old pair. Most other coyotes will respect these territorial boundaries; those who do not will be in for a fight. Some coyotes are allowed in the territory as tolerated guests. These may be young from the previous litter. The tolerated coyotes will be constantly reminded of their inferior status. They will be nipped about the hips by the landowners. They must demonstrate their low station in life by assuming a submissive posture to the boss coyote. This consists of lying on the back with tail beween the legs, legs in the air,

Coyotes howl to mark territorial boundaries and to communicate. This summer coyote shows degrading fur in the form of hip rubs and back singing. *Photo U.S. Fish & Wildlife Service.*

avoidance of eye contact and often a pitiful whining. If the visitors threaten to deplete the food supply of the area, the territorial coyotes will attack them repeatedly until they either leave or are killed.

The territorial boundaries of the coyote are established by howl-points and scent-posts. In late fall and winter when tolerated coyotes are forced to leave territories, a continual movement of young coyotes develops. These critters are like a man with no country. They must either take up residence in marginal habitat that nobody else wants or wander quickly through established territories. This movement can be used to good advantage by the caller. The youngsters usually do not know the country they are passing through which makes them inefficient hunters. They are always hungry, it seems, and they are an eager respondent to a varmint call. If a pair of home-range coyotes are taken by a caller, he can be sure that a couple of wanderers will soon move in to claim the territory. A territory that offers food and cover will always house coyotes and can be revisited time and again. The area should be rested between hunts, however, to allow a new couple to establish residence. The homesteading will likely take place within a few weeks of the vacancy sign.

The size of the home territory of a breeding pair will vary, the area determined by the type of country and the availability of food. A study of radio-collared coyotes in northern Arizona indicates a typical range of 8.1 square miles. The studies also indicate that the coyote will move seasonally; the winter and summer ranges might be in different parts of the total range.

Now might be a good time to clarify a point in coyote behavior. I have studied a number of papers written by wildlife professionals wherein they report on the activities of animals within a specific study area. These professionals, who should know better, often write on the animal behavior in the study area as if it were the gospel truth for every animal of that particular species anywhere in the world. One publication that I came across stated that the primary diet of the coyote was the jackrabbit and that he would turn to other food only if there were a scarcity of rabbits. That may have been true for his limited study area in Idaho where there were tons of rabbits per square mile, but it certainly is not true, however, for my home territory of northern Arizona. Here most coyotes feed on juniper berries in the winter, antelope fawn in the spring, and mice and voles through the summer. There is a danger, I feel, in extrapolating data from one area to another. If, in my writing, I seem to be saying that northern Arizona coyotes are typical of coyotes everywhere, forgive me. Coyotes, like people, are often individualists. They will modify their behavior to suit the particular demands of their habitat.

Harmful Effects

The coyote has a few friends, a lot of acquaintances who admire him for his cunning and adaptibility, and a few enemies. The friends are mostly misguided preservationists who find it popular to defend the coyote from the rest of the

Coyotes will feed on jackrabbits if they are plentiful. If not, he turns readily to juniper berries, cactus fruit, carrion or domestic stock. *Photo Gerry Blair.*

This coyote will be fitted with a radio transmitter and released. Game biologists learn much about coyote behavior through these studies. They learned that this northern Arizona coyote, along with a bunch of his buddies, takes most of the antelope fawn born in certain areas. *Photo Gerry Blair.*

world. Most of this crowd advocates complete protection for the coyote and all other critters except for those they personally like to eat.

Most hunters and trappers, and I am one of them, are neither friend nor foe of the coyote. I certainly admire the canny critter for his ability to survive in an unfriendly world, and I consider him a worthy adversary afield. However, I do not let this respect cloud my good judgment when it comes time to control the coyote.

The strong enemies of the coyote usually are sheep or goat ranchers who have trouble in raising enough stock to feed the coyote and also make a profit. Many of these folks take the hard position that the coyote should be exterminated. Although I sympathize with the ranchers' losses, I cannot agree with his response. The critter, in my opinion, has as much right to be on this earth as I do. I do not feel that his right to survive takes precedence over other species. If too many coyotes are wiping out deer, or antelope, or sheep, I believe that their numbers should be reduced. I also look upon the coyote as a resource of the land, just as the trees are a resource. With enlightened management, man can harvest this resource for his needs for years to come.

The coyote probably kills more big and small game than the rest of the predators combined. This is mainly due to his nature and the number of coyotes. The Anderson Mesa studies on antelope fawn survival has been previously mentioned. That study indicated that the antelope on the mesa had a reproductive rate of 1 to 1.8. Translated, that means that each adult doe would give birth to 1.8 fawns each spring. As antelope normally throw twins, this is an excellent reproductive rate that indicates very few of the adult female are barren. The survival rate of the antelope fawn is, however, dismal. The study indicates that nine of ten fawns born on the mesa fail to survive the first few days of life. The coyote, biologists say, is mainly responsible.

In another area of Arizona, Game Department studies have also shown the coyote is a major cause of deer fawn mortality. Sheepmen and cattlemen in the West know that the coyote is the main cause of calf and lamb mortality. The coyote also takes a heavy toll on small game and non-game animals as well. Biologists estimate that more than fifty percent of young pheasants, quail and grouse fall to predation.

Value as a Fur Bearer

Coyote fur will show wide fluctuations in price. The price the buyer pays will be governed by fashion industry demands, the number of pelts available and the size and condition of the hide. At the present time (1980), coyote pelts sell from a high of more than a hundred dollars to a low of twenty-five dollars. Callers will receive the best price for pelts that have been properly skinned, stretched, cleaned and stored.

Calling Coyotes

The coyote is always hungry. Surplus food goes to fat as insurance against leaner times. He is likely to come to the call at any hour of the day or night, but certain conditions will give the caller better odds.

Coyotes are primarily night hunters, but can also be found shortly after first light and at dusk. They are hunting and hungry at these times and are most likely to answer an invitation to eat. I have had good luck at the crack of dawn. Here in the West the early part of the day often has the least wind. A lack of wind makes it easier for the critter to hear the call, while windy days tend to keep both the predator and his prey bushed up. Often the last clear day before a storm or the first clear day after a storm will be productive. A coyote must be a realist to stay in business. He knows from experience that storms of short duration cause prey animals to hole up. Hunting forays during the storm will likely end with an empty belly. If he can, the coyote will wait out these short storms in the comfort of a brush patch. When the storm passes he will take to the field and will enjoy a better food return for the energy he spends hunting.

Moon Phases

There is little research available to document predator and prey movement during the phases of the moon. Tom Britt, a wildlife biologist for the Arizona Game Department, once participated in a nighttime study of whitetail deer populations in a southern state. The aim of the project was to determine the rough numbers of deer in certain areas. The researchers used spotlights to make an eye count. They made few sightings during the dark phases of the moon. They saw few deer, few rabbits and few predators, and most of those were logged during the increasing or full phases of the moon.

This information can be helpful to a coyote caller. If the coyote is not hunting during the dark phases of the moon he is more likely to be out and hunting the next day. Coyotes must eat on a more or less regular basis. If they do not visit the grocery at night they will likely make the trip the following day. A daytime caller who calls during the dark phases of the moon should be playing to a hungrier audience.

Prime Fur

The coyote caller who hopes to sell the fur must schedule his hunts when the fur is prime. When cold winter weather hits, the hide of all furbearers undergoes a physical change. It thins and turns a creamy color. At the same time, the fur thickens and grows longer and guard hair forms to give the hair a lush appearence. Unprime fur will show a grey or black hide and the fur will be thin with no guard hair.

Coyote fur will begin priming at the start of the winter. The exact time will vary depending on the area. In colder regions the fur may be nearly prime in early October; in warmer areas, a month or two later. The fur will remain prime until the sun of late spring and summer causes other physical changes in the hide and fur. The first change noticed will be a condition called rubbing. This will be apparent on the hips and will show up in the coyote sometime in March. All coyotes will not exhibit rubbing at precisely the same time; two coyotes from the same territory may be a month apart in the degrading of their fur. As warm weather continues the fur will begin to thin. The hair of the back will show sun curling. The fur will be patchy and uneven. Soon shedding has removed most of the winter fur. When any of these conditions appear the hunter should put away the calls. The fur buyer will have little interest in the fur and it would be a waste of a valuable resource to pursue the hunt.

High country coyotes prime about mid-November in Arizona. This is part of the collection called and trapped by Bill Musgrove and myself in 1977–1978 season. *Photo Gerry Blair.*

Perry Shirley of Flagstaff, Arizona, combs the fur on a large prime coyote. This hide brought sixty dollars at the start of the 1979–80 season. *Photo Gerry Blair.*

Virgin Ears

The coyote is the Einstein of the dog family and is quick to learn from his mistakes. If he is called and escapes he will be reluctant to answer the call in the future. When he has made the long run a couple of times to find nothing but hot lead waiting, he will ignore the call completely. I suckered a coyote into three appearances one winter and believe this to be about the maximum number of times one can be fooled. On the first call, I called and killed a big silver and caught a fleeting glimpse of the second as he left. Two hours later I made a call in the same area and coaxed in a sneaker that spooked two hundred yards out. It appeared to be the same critter — smallish and with a definite red cast to the fur. On the second call the coyote came in slow and carefully and spooked for no apparent reason. Two weeks later I called the same territory using a different tape. The persistent coyote came in from downwind. Tracks in the snow showed she came within eight feet of my hiding bush before she spooked. I heard snow crunching and turned in time to get a snap shot at her butt as she rounded a pile of pushdowns. The shot connected and I felt a little better about some of the easy shots I have blown.

Fortunately for the hunter, a new crop of virgin ears appears yearly. Young coyotes—like teenagers—are always willing to eat. Their lack of sophistication makes them particularly vulnerable to the call. Hunters who call during the fall and early winter usually see more coyotes.

Reading the Country

The best way to learn unfamiliar country is to seek expert advice. The Animal Control Division of the U.S. Fish and Wildlife Service responds to complaints of animal predation. Much of their work, particularly in the West and Southwest, deals with the coyote. Usually they will gladly steer the caller to areas with problem populations of the coyote.

State game departments are another source of information. Their fieldmen know the type of habitat attractive to predators. From personal observation, they often know of areas containing high coyote populations. The coyote has a taste for the young of most game animals, and most of the time the wardens will be happy to assist in a bit of predator control.

Ranchers also know about coyotes. In sheep country, the coyote has mutton on his breath most of the time and the growers are glad to make him pay for the meal. Mention the word coyote to most ranchers and they get squinty eyed and their trigger fingers begin to twitch. Introduce yourself, state your purpose, behave like a guest and you likely will have no problem finding calling areas.

In sheep country the coyote has mutton on his breath much of the time. A researcher for the U.S. Fish & Wildlife Service took this picture during a controlled study of sheep and coyote interaction. *Photo Guy Connolly, U.S. Fish & Wildlife Service.*

The Carrion Eaters

The coyote hunter also should watch for scavenger activity. Find the remains of a large animal and you can bet that coyotes are not far away. Usually the vultures, crows, ravens and eagles get there first; this can be the tip-off. Once a gang of coyotes begins work on a carcass, it will disappear fast. I located the carcass of a Black Angus cow once by investigating raven activity. The lady had died while calving. The flying scavengers had barely started work and I knew that the coyotes would soon appear. My first stand in the area produced three coyotes. They were all singles and came to the call from different directions. I checked the carcass six days later and found it was gone. Only the skull and a few ribs remained and even the hide and hair had been consumed. The technique in these instances is for the resident coyote to advertise. They realize that they have more food than they can handle, and they let their neighbors share in the good luck. Soon a dozen hungry coyotes will appear to divide the booty. When it is gone, everyone goes home with a full belly.

Tracks

The coyote has a track like that of a medium-sized dog. Most tracks are about the size of a fifty-cent piece. A pad and four toes will be apparent, and the front foot will be noticeably larger than the rear. The coyote has non-retractible claws which show in deep dust, mud or snow. Look for tracks along little-used roads, in sand washes, along game and stock trails and in the mud of creek and lake banks.

A good time to scout for calling locations is after a light snow. Every critter that walks will leave some evidence. You should make note of movement patterns and concentrations and if your memory is like mine, you will soon forget most of the data unless you commit it to paper.

The Anvil Chorus

Most hunters have heard the haunting cry of the coyote, most often at dawn and dusk. I have heard it at all hours of the day and night. The song consists of a series of yip-like howls. One coyote can sound like a dozen. The main purpose of the howl, I think, is coyote-to-coyote communication. Research on coyote communication is spotty, but it is certain that this highly intelligent animal has a good vocabulary. He is telling all other coyotes within howling distance that he is alive and well and will defend his little piece of turf against the world. The howl may have other meanings. A breeder may have lost a mate and the howl is his want ad for a replacement. Telemetry studies in northern Arizona have proven that coyotes communicate, and that coyotes from neighboring territories obey their territorial boundaries rigidly.

Hunters who use electronic calls may want to try a cassette which contains the taped howl of the coyote. Play the tape in coyote country at dawn and dusk and make a notation of the approximate location of the answering howls. This will give you a good idea of coyote numbers in the area. It will also tell you where to go to make your stands.

Most hunters agree that the coyote is the smartest of the predators. He has been able to extend his range by adapting to new habitat and feeding patterns. *Photo Gerry Blair.*

Coyote IQ

If all predators were rated on intelligence on a scale of one to ten, the coyote would be a ten. This intelligence coupled with his omniverous nature has allowed him to extend his range at a time when every hand was turned against him. The coyote will eat about anything he can wrap a lip around. Fresh meat is always welcome, so are insects, carrion, vegetables and fruit. I once saw a coyote following a whiteface cow with twin calves. I thought at first the critter was after a veal lunch and set up the spotting scope to watch the action. The critter would have likely taken one of the calves if he had been able, but on this day he was after something a bit lower to the ground. The calves' droppings, rich in undigested mother's milk, were being gulped down with gusto. The coyote, frugal critter that he is, could not bear to let all of that good nourishment go to waste.

Characteristics When Called

How a coyote comes to the call will be determined by his age and previous experience with the dying rabbit calls. A young coyote hearing the song for the first time will come at full speed. I have had these virgins come to within five feet before they decide that two hundred pounds is a bit large for a rabbit. I called a double at one stand that stuck their nose into the speaker of the electronic call. These youngsters, while they are eager, do not have the fur that an older coyote has. The younger coyotes seem to put all their chow into growth and none into making good fur. If you call too early in the year you will likely be disappointed when the fur buyer writes the check.

Many times young coyotes who have no home territory will roam the country in two's and three's. When they respond to the call for the first time they are likely to make a foot race of it. Each extends himself to take the first bite from the rabbit. Multiples can be a frustrating challenge to the rifle shooter. The first one is easy as the critters are close and co-operative, but the second shot can be tough. I usually expect to get one, consider myself fortunate if I double, and plan on writing home to mother if I get all three.

I have read articles on shooting where the reader is advised to take the toughest shot first and then swing on the easy one. That is poor advice. In the first place, there is no such thing as an easy shot at a coyote. Second, I know I am not the world's greatest off-hand rifle shot. If I shot at the tough one I would probably miss. I would then have two tough shots instead of one easy shot. If you are like me and are not able to hit dead center on every shot as some outdoorsmen do, take the best shot offered. You will have more fur on the stretcher at season's end.

The Sneaker

When a coyote has been fooled a time or two he loses much of his gusto for rabbit. He may come to the call, but he will come slowly and will make frequent stops to size up the land. A hunter who makes any minor mistake will lose this coyote. Take your shot the first decent chance you get. He will usually stop a hundred yards out to give you the bad eye — that is as far as he intends to come. If one of the bushes ahead looks a little fat he will turn tail and leave in a rush.

I called a big male from a brushy canyon last year and watched him come for a quarter mile. The country had been called hard by other hunters and I knew this coyote had heard the song several times. The critter used every bush and rock in that quarter mile to make his sneak. I was well hidden on a high rim and had a good seat for the show. The coyote used fifteen minutes to make it to shooting range. He stopped every hundred feet to smell the wind and survey the country. He finally stopped two hundred yards out. All I could see was the top half of his head. I put the cross hairs on the grass and shot about where I thought the critter's chest should be. I missed, of course, and the coyote took thirty seconds to retrace his route of travel. That coyote, I am certain, will never trust a dying rabbit again.

Coyote come close on the first call but they learn fast and will answer each succeeding call with less enthusiasm. This handsome fellow is about ready to leave. Two hundred pounds, he figures, is a bit large for a jackrabbit. *Photo Gerry Blair.*

The Circler

Educated coyotes sometimes will make wide circles around the call hoping for a smell of rabbit. If the rabbit smells like aftershave lotion the critter will slip away and not be seen again. Masking scents will sometimes fool these nose hunters. If none is used the critters are not likely to be taken; in most instances, you may never sight them. You may find it interesting to make a two-hundred-yard circle in the snow when you have completed an unsuccessful call. You may be surprised at the number of fresh tracks in the snow.

Take your chance at one of these circlers at the first opportunity. They won't offer you much, but a poor chance is better than no chance at all.

The Howler

Some educated coyotes come to the call and stop about three hundred yards out, usually out of sight. They won't budge an inch closer even if you beg, but they will announce their presence by howling pitifully. Some callers believe that the coyote is trying to warn other coyotes that the squalling rabbit is really a man. When the howls start, they pack up their junk and leave.

I don't think this is so. A coyote is too smart an animal to come even that close if he thinks someone might be pulling his leg. I think the critter howls for a couple of reasons. He has probably been called before and knows there may be skullduggery afoot. He also knows that the call may indicate a bonafide rabbit lunch. It is, therefore, the frustration of making this decision which causes him to howl. He may also howl hoping that another coyote is torturing the rabbit. If he howls and gets an answer he knows it is safe to move in.

A hunter can do a number of things in response to a howler. The best course of action is to ignore the howler and continue with the call. You will be surprised at the number of critters that will respond in spite of the loudmouth in the brush. I was calling with a partner one winter when we were plagued with a howler. The critter set up shop about two hundred yards into the trees and really sounded off. We had the electronic call going and I turned up the volume a bit to drown out the coyote's solo. Five minutes later a worried-looking bitch coyote trotted in begging for the rabbit. A minute after I gave it to her, the howling started again. I motioned for my partner to stay with the call and worked my way crosswind of the coyote. The .22-250 ended his musical career.

I did the same thing on another hunt when I was using a tube. The howling started two minutes into the call and never let up. I finished the call with no action. I motioned for my hunting partner to keep blowing and worked cross-wind. I got to within fifty feet of the critter before I saw him. He never saw me at all—he was too busy enjoying the sound of his own voice. The Ruger ended that coyote's career also. Do not attempt to walk directly from the call to the coyote as he will be sure to spot you and slip away.

Another technique I have used on howlers is to finish the call and have my partner pick up the junk and head back for the truck. I stay hidden in the stand. Several times, about five minutes after the rabbit stops squealing, the coyote will pussy-foot in to see if we forgot anything.

Squeezing the Rabbit

Squeezing the rabbit is the easiest part of the hunt. Most calls are factory tuned to produce the correct sound. A rabbit that is staring at a set of coyote tonsils is probably not the best singer in the world. I am sure that the dying rabbit screams, even when they come from a dying rabbit, are not all the same. There are a few refinements, however, that will increase the critter response to your call.

Contrary to much of the published advice on calling, I like to start the stand with low volume. There will be times when a coyote is bedded within a few hundred feet of your stand. Full-volume calls may bring him in but they may also send him hot-footing into the next county with a pair of aching ears.

I was calling a grassy flat a few years ago. It was a perfect place for a coyote to hunt for an early morning snack. I had made a silent approach and knew there might be a hungry predator close by. I found my stand, hid myself, and waited about five minutes to give the nearby birds a chance to forget about me. When they resumed their noisy chatter I blew a few soft notes on Burnham Mini-Squeal. At the first chirp, a bobcat jumped straight into the air. He was trying to see over the grass to learn what kind of critter was volunteering to be his breakfast. I got that cat, but I probably would have missed him if I had blown into one of the Circes with my usual gusto.

Next time you're out, try low-volume calls for a couple of minutes. If nothing shows, go to long-range blasts to spread the word far and wide that a rabbit is about to be eaten. I blow these high-volume blasts for about thirty seconds and then pause a minute or two to watch the country. Some callers do not pause. They call constantly from the time they start the stand until they finish. This is the wrong approach for two reasons; it is a lot harder on the caller to be blowing constantly for ten or fifteen minutes, and it is not necessary. I think the critters come just as well to the interval calls. After five minutes of the call-and-pause sequence, go back to the low-volume calls again. There may be a suspicious coyote out of sight in the brush who has come as far as he intends to. The low volume call might be the urging he needs to finish the trip.

If I sight a critter coming toward me, I stop calling. The object of the hunt is to get a critter coming your way, and when you have accomplished this, further calling cannot improve the situation. If the varmint stops, though, or shows other signs of losing interest, you will need to resume the song. If he is close and seems unsure of your location, give a couple of chirps on the close-range call or let loose with a pair of lip squeaks.

Most of the predator hunters afield, I am convinced, are folks who never really made a study of the sport. Most will read the instruction sheet packed with the call and will never progress much beyond that level of skill. They will call critters but will not call the numbers I would need to keep me going through the winter. If you join the majority, your calling will sound just about the same as every other hunter who uses that brand of call. The critters soon develop a critical ear and will be bashful about giving you a shot. I try to put individuality into my screams to make them unique and different from every other caller. This draws coyotes that won't come to some of the standard sounds.

One technique I use is to flutter my hands over the end of the tube as I blow. This produces a pitiful, moaning whimper that is hard for a coyote to ignore. At times I also vary the wind I am putting into the call, to accentuate the whimper. It is a sound most coyotes find hard to ignore.

Another technique is to vary the tone of the individual screams. Blow hard into the tube at the start of the scream, then ease off a bit to get a mid-range moan, and finish the call by letting your breath ease away to nothing. The call will do the same and the sound produced will be the frantic scream of a rabbit that is being eaten alive trailing off to a hopeless moan of despair. I try to put a few drops of blood on every scream.

If you are hunting with a partner and are in heavily called country, another technique may produce results. Blow two calls at the same time. This will work best if the calls are of different tones, maybe a coarse mid-tone call and a high-pitched call. This duet will sometimes bring coyote when nothing else will.

One more piece of advice on blowing for coyote: Lower your volume. At times you will hunt good coyote country and have trouble in calling them to the stand. If the country has not been heavily hunted you can sometimes get results by lowering the volume of your calling. Forget about range and concentrate on variety of sound. You will need to make your calling stands closer together as the subdued calls will not carry as far.

Blow softly on the first series of calls. There may be a coyote bedded nearby and loud sounds may send him across the mountain. *Photo Harley Shaw, Arizona Game Department.*

Playing the Tape

If you are using an electronic call, you do not have to concern yourself with pauses. You should make it a point, however, to vary the volume of the speaker. I start each stand with the tape on low volume to attract those critters that may be underfoot. If nothing shows after two minutes, I turn up the volume. Let the tape play at full volume for five minutes. If nothing shows, either turn down the volume or play one of the close-range tapes. The baby cottontail and the baby cardinal tape made by Burnham Brothers are both good.

Speaker Placement

The placement of the speaker can make the difference between a good shot and a tough one. Coyotes usually do not come right up to a speaker. They will stop fifty or a hundred feet out to look things over. Keep this in mind when you set up the speaker. Make sure there are no trees or large bushes on the far side of the speaker. If there are, you can bet that brother coyote will use them to his best advantage.

I try to evaluate the potential of a stand before I set up. I decide the route that a sneaking coyote is likely to take and then place the speaker so that his course of travel will bring him through an open area on his way to the speaker. Do not always place the speaker directly in front of you. The coyote will come in looking at the source of the sound and will look over the speaker directly at your hidey hole. He may see a flaw in your camouflage and spook. Another reason you won't want the speaker directly in front is the natural caution of the critter. If you have a fifty-foot wire on the speaker and the coyote keeps a safe distance between him and the speaker, this will put the critter about fifty yards away—a little farther than I like to shoot with a shotgun, even a three-incher.

I run the speaker off to the side, at about a forty-five degree angle. The distance I place it away from me depends on the country. Most of the time I don't use all of the fifty feet of wire—maybe thirty feet. I have taken more coyote than I can remember who didn't even know they were in danger until the bullet hit them.

Locating the Customer

A coyote coming to the call can be tough or easy to spot depending on the cover and his style. Chargers are usually easy. Their pell-mell movement makes them visible against a still landscape. A sneaker can be tougher. He comes slowly and uses every scrap of cover to hide his approach. I had a big coyote sneak almost into my lap on one hunt and I never saw his approach. I had made a mid-day stand in an area that was mostly open with a few scattered junipers. The area immediately in front was open and over-grazed meadow. There was a stingy clump or two of rabbit brush. I kept my head swinging slowly, scanning as much of the landscape as possible. I swung by the area directly in front of the stand. There was nothing there. On the return swing, maybe ten seconds later, there was a big silver coyote giving me the bad eye. To this day I don't know where he came from. I know where he went though. I put a 52-grain piece of lead through his motor and he will sneak no more.

Ghosts

Some hunters call them boogers, some call them spooks and others call them by a wide variety of unprintable names. I call them ghosts. They are the bushes and rocks that take on a coyote's configuration a few minutes into the call. Many callers miss a bet by not studying all of these features before they start the call. Search out all of these coyote look-alikes before you start squeezing the rabbit. If you don't, you may be tempted to raise your scope during the call. This movement may scare off a customer that was getting ready to surrender.

Most of the time a caller has no problem in recognizing a critter when he comes. I can only remember being fooled one time. I was calling the rim of a brushy canyon where I had found fresh coyote droppings. Five minutes into the call I located a ghost in the shade of a tree a hundred yards out. I was almost certain it wasn't a coyote and resisted the temptation to take a closer look. Finally I could stand it no longer. I put the scope on the suspicious object. I was right: It wasn't a coyote. It was a huge tom bobcat. The cat's camouflage was good but not good enough to keep the hollowpoint from tickling his ribs.

Stool Pigeons

Always stay alert to the actions of the animals around you. They will often sic you onto a critter you might not have seen. I was calling the push-downs one winter when a staring cow put me onto a pair of coyotes that had come in through the back door. On another hunt, a timid coyote snitched on his big brother. I was calling the pushdowns and had interested a sneaker that stopped about two hundred yards out. He was partially hidden in a pile of pushdowns and it would have been a tough shot. I considered my past batting average on shots of this type and decided I would be wasting a shell. I begged and pleaded for three or four minutes and never budged that critter an inch. Through the scope I could see him pacing nervously and swinging his gaze from me to a point about fifty yards to my rear. I was backed up to a big alligator juniper and turned as slowly as possible to check out my rear flank. I discovered a big roan coyote standing fifty feet away. The smaller coyote would have been a tough shot but he tipped me off to an easy one.

Let me give one more example on this and I will shut up about it. I was calling the lip of a rocky canyon one evening just before dark. The country looked super catty and I was almost sure I could pull in a bobcat. Ten minutes into the call I heard a worried momma quail sound off a hundred yards down the hill. I called with enthusiasm, putting blood in every note. The quail began flushing, one by one. I was sure the biggest bobcat in the world was on his way. It was somewhat anti-climatic when a big gray fox poked his pointed nose through the brush. If the quail had not encouraged me, I might have abandoned the stand before the fox arrived.

The Length of a Stand

The proper length of a coyote stand is a question that is sure to start an argument among callers. One may suggest staying five minutes, while another maintains that ten minutes is the absolute minimum, and the third will hold out for fifteen. They may all be right. The time I spend at a stand for coyote will depend on a number of factors. It is never less than seven minutes and may stretch out to a half an hour in a few instances. The length of the stand will be determined by the amount of wind noise, the terrain, and my evaluation of how heavily the country has been called. Let's take them one at a time.

Wind noise will cut down on the carrying power of your call. Instead of carrying for a mile or more, the call may reach out for a half or a quarter of a mile. Critters that close can make it to the rabbit in a few minutes if they are interested. I usually end such a call after the seven minute minimum.

Predator calls will carry a great distance under ideal conditions. If there is an absence of wind the call will carry farther. Open country with a minimum of brush and trees also allows the call to extend to a greater range. Timber particularly has a dampening effect on sound. If you are calling from a high point, the call is likely to reach more distant ears. Under these conditions I will likely put in the full thirty minutes at a stand.

Calling pressure will slow down the critter response. Late in the calling season, when I am sure that most coyotes know the dying rabbit blues by heart, I spend more time on each stand. Most of the time I will stay at a coyote stand for about fifteen minutes. Under average conditions, I figure, a coyote can cover a mile of decent country in two or three minutes. If he doesn't show up in fifteen, he has missed his chance at the rabbit.

There are exceptions of course. I called last winter with a friend from the Arizona Game Department. Actually we had been scouting for the spring turkey hunt and had decided to do a bit of predator control before we called it a day. I was calling high timber—Ponderosa pine with a lot of open area on the forest floor. We got howls back from two different coyotes shortly after we started the stand. I played around with those howlers for fifteen minutes. I didn't expect them to come but we were in a comfortable shady swale listening to the coyote music. After twenty minutes, I figured we were whipping a dead horse and got to my feet. I was amazed to see a hard-charging coyote coming from three hundred yards out. She hadn't spotted me and I fell back down. She kept coming and almost ran up the barrel of my friend's rifle. I have no idea why it took her so long to come to the call, but I am almost sure she was not one of the singers. They were still at it when we carried her back to the truck.

Calling After Shooting

Many callers leave a stand as soon as they have taken a shot or made a kill. They are making a big mistake. Most of the critters I have killed do not seem unduly alarmed at a rifle shot. Perhaps the frequency of sonic booms in this area has made them tolerant of explosions. I have called a number of coyotes into stands where I had one of their brothers kicking on the ground.

The most recent that comes to mind is the trip George Oakey and I made a week after Christmas 1979. It was one of those miserably cold winter dawns after a storm. The clouds were still hanging around the San Francisco Peaks and the slope we called had a thick fog bank that cut visibility to about a hundred feet. I wriggled myself into a snowbank and thought how great a day it was for calling coyote.

I cranked up the electronic call and George and I waited for action. It wasn't long in coming. Two shadowy figures half-materialized from the fog. I turned the volume of the call down so the critters had to strain to hear it. It was apparent that they were having trouble, homing in on the call. The fog diffused the sound and made it seem to come from everywhere and nowhere. Soon one of the shadows began moving our way—the second disappeared back into the fog. One coyote came plodding deliberately through the snow and stopped thirty feet out. I nodded and George put a .243 through his ribs. We let the tape continue and watched. Two minutes later, a second coyote appeared from my right, running hard. I dumped him at thirty yards and he rolled dead three feet from the first customer. We sat still and let the tape play. When nothing showed for ten minutes we gathered up our junk and the two coyotes and left.

I could tell you stories of second kills until you would cry for mercy but I won't. Be convinced, however, that all critters will come to a call even after a shot. You know you must be in good country or you would not have called the first animal. When you get a called critter down keep calling. Start your timer from the shot and call just as long as you would on a new stand.

Leaving the Stand

A good hunter maintains his alertness when leaving the stand. I have sighted coyote several times as I walked back to the truck. One time I had made it back to the truck and was driving off when I spotted a big silver standing two hundred yards out. He spooked when I left the truck. Running shots at two hundred yards are not my specialty and I fully expected to miss. I swung a couple of coyote lengths ahead of the critter's nose and stroked. He went down with one in his ear. If I had led him another few inches I would have missed. My hunting companion was immensely impressed with my fine shooting and proceeded to commend me. Honesty made me admit that the shot was pure luck and that I miss nine out of ten shots at that range. I did tell him, however, that this shot might help compensate somewhat for all of the easy ones I have missed.

Shooting at the Customers

I am not the best qualified person to give instruction on rifle shooting. On second thought, perhaps I am. I have made every one of the possible mistakes at least once. I suffered through a shooting slump once that had me ready to sell the guns. I missed eight coyotes in a row. Some were tough chances that I would have missed on my best day; others were medium hard, the ones that I get about half the time. One was downright embarrassing: I missed a running coyote at fifteen feet. I was lucky enough to have a friend along on that trip to spread the word to all of our other friends. "Yes," he would say, "it is possible to miss a coyote with a scope-sighted rifle at fifteen feet. I saw Blair do it."

I checked the scope alignment. Unfortunately it was dead on. I even checked the cartridges to see if I had inadvertently loaded a box of blanks. No such luck. I finally decided the shooting slump started about the time I bought a new pair of camo gloves. The trigger on the Ruger was crisp and the gloves destroyed my squeeze. I cut a slit down the trigger finger and my rifle shooting returned to normal—not good but not humiliating.

When to Shoot

Most of the time I don't shoot at a coyote as long as he is coming my way. The critter will usually stop before he gets in my lap to size things up. I love those standing shots at thirty feet. They do wonders for my coyote shooting percentages. If a coyote stops a hundred yards out and gives you the bad eye, shoot. At that distance he can count the hair in your eyebrows and will likely come no closer.

I don't want the critter closer than about fifty feet if he is running and I am holding a rifle. My Ruger has a 6X scope and a close coyote fills the scope, making it tough to swing with him. I am always convinced I can't miss those shots and I always do.

Running coyotes are almost always missed because of not enough lead. A scared coyote covers ground at about thirty miles per hour. That's forty-three feet per second. My bullet has a muzzle velocity of 3,500 fps and will slow to 2,340 fps at two hundred yards. That's an average of 2,920 fps. At that speed it will take the slug one-fifth of a second to get to that coyote two hundred yards away. The coyote will have covered about eight feet in that time. That means I have to lead him by about two coyote lengths if I want to stretch his hide. I lead a hard-running coyote about one body length for each hundred yards of distance between us.

Where to Shoot

Where you put the bullet will be determined by the type of gun and the bullet being used. With the .22-250, or with any of the other flat-shooting centerfires, I go for the chest cavity. Stay away from the shoulder; the fast-moving hollowpoint will blow up on the surface when it hits meat backed by the shoulder bone. Your coyote will go down but you will hate yourself when you spend a couple of hours with a needle and thread. A hit in the chest cavity causes the bullet to explode among the critter's necessaries. There is a small entry hole and no exit. Many times I don't even have to wash the hide.

On tough shots I aim at the easiest part of the critter to hit. A mangled coyote, I figure, is better than no coyote. If he is going straight away I go for the butt. If the distance is extreme—say a couple of hundred yards—I shoot for the coyote. I know I am not skillful enough to call my shots at that range and try to put a bullet in the coyote's vicinity and hope he runs into it. I have made hits on

Coyotes on the run can make for tough shooting. Try to aim for the part that is easiest to hit. I would aim for mid-body on this shot. *Photo Gerry Blair.*

most parts of a coyote's body with the .22-250 and have never lost a cripple. That is one advantage of the rifle: If they bleed they usually die.

Shotgun Shooting

Some hunters use a shotgun exclusively for coyote and have good luck, while some states prohibit the use of centerfires and the hunter has no choice. A shotgun does a good job on a coyote if the cover is heavy enough to hide the hunter. I like the shotgun particularly early in the year, when the young are still running together. The multiples that come to the call are easier to take with a shotgun.

Killing Cripples

There will be a few times when the hunter needs to administer the *coup de grace* to a wounded coyote. It is well to remember that such coyotes have long, sharp teeth. You could shoot him again but that would increase the bleeding and the sewing problems—more work when you handle the fur. He can be put away cleanly and humanely by using the trapper's method. Find a stout section of limb and stroke the critter forward of the eyes with moderate enthusiasm. The blow should knock him out but if it doesn't, whack him again. When he goes limp raise one of your feet and bring it down hard on his chest, just behind the front shoulder.

Calling the Roads

Calling the roads can be a good technique to use in good country. Some coyotes are road scavengers who travel a certain piece of blacktop picking up road kills. Make a notation of the locations where you have sighted coyote crossing the road. Get the same information from friends who travel the highway. Calling stands in those areas will be productive.

If you travel much through good coyote habitat you will spot travelling coyotes on a more or less regular basis. Don't try to take these critters from the road. It is unlawful in most states and is always dangerous. Besides, you have little chance of success; the coyote will sell out the moment you touch the brakes. You will have better luck if you drive until you are out of sight, upwind if possible.

Park your vehicle and walk a few hundred feet from the road, then set up a quick stand and blow the whistle. I took two huge coyotes in this manner last January. A friend and I were driving to an early morning pig hunt when we spotted the critters trotting through the timber. We drove a quarter-mile south on the busy interstate and parked in a pullout. My friend took the Ruger and I packed the 1100. A toot or two on the tube brought quick action. Seconds later we had the two big dogs stretched out in the snow.

Second Opinion

Ed Sceery is a predator control specialist who works with ranchers near his home in Santa Fe, New Mexico. He has a Ph.D. in the field of livestock management and is also a talented predator caller. He has been calling for fifteen years and has called more than two thousand critters, mostly coyotes. Ed is the author of *Professional Predator Calling* published by Spearman Publishing Company in 1979. He designed and now markets his own line of predator calls under the name *Varmint Getter*. Here are his views on coyote calling and some of the techniques which have made him successful.

Ed Sceery
I guess I am a skeptic on most things. When two friends told me they could bring wild predators to gun or camera range by blowing a whistle I did not believe them. That was sixteen years ago and I have been calling ever since.

Most of the critters I have called have been coyote. I do most of my calling in coyote country and have had days when I brought sixteen of the big hides home to be stretched. I call every day I can during the fur season. When I am not calling I write about calling or work at perfecting my new line of calls. It has taken me five years to come up with the design for the *Varmint Getter* but it has been worth it. I really believe this is the best predator call on the market for the serious caller.

I do very well calling fur bearers and selling the pelts. One reason I am successful is the knowledge I have of the country and the critter. Most callers, I think, don't take the critters they should because they underestimate them. The coyote is the smartest of the bunch; he has the best sight, the best hearing and the best nose. I think he also has the best brain. You may find a few dumb ones around early in the calling year but they lose their hides fast.

I skin most of the critters I call. This is where most fur hunters fail. They do everything right until it is time to shoot, and then they miss the critter. I kept track of all the shots I missed one year and it almost threw my wallet into deep shock. Now I spend a lot of time before calling season practicing my shooting. I cut coyote- and fox-shaped targets out of plywood and punch holes in them at about a hundred yards until it becomes second nature. I miss very few now. It is not uncommon for me to run a string of twelve hits on coyote without a miss, and once I ran a string of sixteen.

Another reason I call a lot of fur is the pre-season scouting. I check for good critter habitat more than anything else. If you are after cats you will look for a different kind of country than you would for coyotes. You won't pick many peaches in an apple orchard and you won't find too many cats in good coyote country. Their needs and hunting style are different and so is their habitat. A gray fox's habitat requirements are more like the cat's than the coyote's.

When you find a good calling area, mark it down and go back there forever. Don't tell even your best friend where it is. I have one spot I discovered last season that is a hotspot for coyote. I went there about twenty-five different times during the calling year and called critters eighty percent of the time. One morning I called there and had coyotes coming in on schedule like Greyhound buses. The first one showed up thirty seconds into the call and I dumped him. Thirty seconds later, here came another. Another shot and another dead coyote. Thirty seconds later, and here came a third. In less than three minutes of calling, I had three prime pelts on the ground.

When I am hunting fur, I plan my day so I can be at my first stand a few minutes before shooting light. I drive in slow and quiet and drink a cup of coffee from the thermos while I wait for shooting light. This lets the critters in the area forget about my presence. When I can see to walk, I go to the first stand. I don't walk any farther from the truck than I have to. I am after fur, not exercise, and I usually set up about a hundred yards from the truck. The minute it is light enough to shoot I start the music.

I blow at medium volume for about fifteen seconds and then pause for thirty seconds. I repeat this sequence for a couple of minutes and then pause for a minute or two. I would rather not be blowing when the coyote appears. He is liable to see the fluttering of my hands on the tube and decide he has no taste for rabbit. Most of my coyotes show up about four minutes into the call and I usually have my gun up and ready to shoot when he arrives.

Here is a tip that will improve your shooting percentages. I am not the best shot in the world, even with practice, and have found my hits on running coyotes are few and far between. When the critter gets about thirty or forty yards out I let out a high-pitched *whooooop*. This always stops the coyote and gives me the three or four seconds I need to tickle his ribs with my .22-250.

I hunt in full camo including facepaint. My gun and the bipod are hidden. I don't want anything to scare the critter away before I take my shot. I pick my stands with great care. If I am in good coyote country I am pretty sure I will call critters but this is not the main purpose of my hunt. I want to call *and kill* critters and to do that I have to pick a stand that offers concealment, vision and shooting opportunity. If you are making a call before sunup, be sure you sit on the shady side of a tree or bush. If you don't, the sun will be full on you when it rises and any coyote coming will see you easily. The shady side will make you harder to see and will put the sun in the coyote's eyes instead of your own.

When the stand is done I pick up my critters and drive to the next good stand. I know where it is from pre-season scouting. It may be a mile away or a few hundred yards.

I have heard a lot about resting stands between calls, but I don't think this is necessary. I believe that the coyote population is moving most of the time and they are attracted to the best areas. I have called the same stand five days in a row and called critters every time. I really believe I could call that stand in the morning, kill a coyote, and go back a couple of hours later and call another.

If I am calling for coyote, as I do most of the time, I use a call that sounds like a jackrabbit in trouble. I have tried most of the sounds on the market and am convinced that the jackrabbit squall is the best sound for coyotes. I take a lot of lessons on coyote calling from jackrabbits. They have called a hell of a lot of coyotes and have to be considered the real experts. Listen to a jackrabbit squall sometime and tune your call to that sound.

Most of the time I hunt alone. A partner is all right if you just want companionship and a good time in the field, but I get more fur if I am by myself. I don't have to worry about a partner who might cough, sneeze or scratch at the wrong time. If you do hunt with a buddy try and pick someone as good as you are. Set up signals before the hunt so you can communicate.

I hear a lot of talk about the volume of predator calls. I try to blow at the same volume a rabbit does—no more and no less. I have found that super-loud screams will scare off about as many critters as it brings, and I think that the low-volume calls are unnecessary.

I use a Model 77 Ruger in .22-250 for all of my calling and a 6x18 Redfield scope. A coyote or a fox at 200 yards is a small target. All of my fur hunting is done with a 55-grain full-metal-jacket bullet. Load the bullet down to around 3,000 fps muzzle and you won't get much pelt damage. My load is 30 grains of 4064 behind a Hornaday 55-grainer. I weigh every single load; I don't want to take a chance on a bad load costing me a critter. I have chronographed my loads and find less than 25 fps variance.

One last tip: Pairs or groups of coyotes are harder to fool than singles. Two coyotes have twice the nose, eyes and ears to discover the fraud and any small mistake will lose both of them. Stay well-hidden and don't make your move until you are ready to do the dirty deed. Then shoot fast and sure.

9

The Bobcat

The bobcat is a secretive animal who hunts mostly at night. To take cats consistently the caller must know the animal and its habits. The successful hunter must also learn to recognize bobcat sign and bobcat habitat.

The bobcat is found from southern Canada to Central America and from coast-to-coast in the United States. Bobcat will vary greatly in size. A cat taken in Colorado in 1951 weighed sixty-nine pounds, and cats weighing more than fifty pounds have been taken from Nevada, New Mexico and Ohio. It should be noted that these are exceptional weights; the average adult male bobcat will weigh about twenty pounds. The color of the bobcat also varies. Cats of the Northwest often show a chocolate color; Southwestern cats vary from light gray to silver. The color of all cats is a mixture of brown, buff and white, with black and brown being the prominent head colors. Body fur is usually spotted. The legs are long and strong. The tail is insignificant and the ears are often tufted.

The bobcat is a night skulker for the most part. In areas frequented by man, he may turn totally to a nocturnal existence but usually the cat will move about during the day in wilderness areas. They will also live close to humans at times. They may never be discovered, however, as their secretive habits and nocturnal nature allow them to remain unobserved.

Bobcats make their living by being sneaky. A study of 176 bobcat scats in Arizona revealed that they live mostly on rabbits and other rodents. He will supplement this diet with birds, snakes, lizards, insects, fox and fish. Although mostly carnivorous, the cat will take grass occasionally, perhaps as a source of bulk, and has been known to eat prickly pear. If times are really tough the cat may turn to carrion. The cat is also likely to take young antelope and deer if the opportunity is presented and he will also take an occasional adult deer. This usually occurs

Bobcat show a wide color range. This West Virginia cat is a deep chocolate, darker and less valuable than the western cats. *Photo U.S. Forest Service.*

when the deer is winter-weak or snowbound. The cat will stalk an adult deer when they are bedded. When he is close enough he will charge in a blur of speed and leap to the deer's neck. The startled animal will bound off carrying the cat on a wild ride. If the deer is lucky, he will scrape off the passenger on a low limb. If not the cat stays and bites increasingly deeper into the deer's neck until he rides it to the ground. On a large carcass, such as a deer, the cat may eat his fill and cover the remains with debris in the manner of a mountain lion. He will not return, however, if he has the opportunity for a fresh kill.

Bobcats make their living being sneaky. The brushy habitat selected by this cottontail rabbit is also good cat country. The cat uses the cover to sneak close and makes the kill with a lightning pounce. *Photo Gerry Blair.*

The hunting technique of a bobcat is essentially that of all other cats, including the domestic housecat. The bobcat will locate his prey by sight or sound and will stalk as quietly as incoming fog. He pauses whenever the prey raises its head. When the cat is close he makes a fast bound or two and takes his prey. Cats have been known to travel five to eight miles in a night's hunting. He follows the same hunting route on most of his trips through his territory. At selected points along the route he will pause to deposit scat, urine and a thick yellow paste from his anal gland. These are his territorial markings and give notice to other cats that the territory is occupied and will be defended.

The territory of a bobcat will vary with the geographic features of the land and the amount of prey. The territory may be as small as a few square miles. The males have larger territories and these may overlap the territory of the female. The male and female do not hunt together and actually avoid each other except for one brief meeting in the winter when they mate.

Bobcat territory will vary in relation to the prey animals available. If groceries are plentiful this Florida swamp cat may range less than a square mile. *Photo U.S. Forest Service.*

Mating

A bobcat love affair is a mixture of aggression and submission. It is always noisy, and the discordant caterwauling can be heard for a great distance. The males, prompted by the mating urge, will leave their territories to seek out females. When one is found he announces his intention in a series of growls, snarls and howls. The female will crouch and allow the male to walk around her singing his song for as long as an hour. Finally the female will signify her passion by joining the song. Both cats howl and growl and mate. When the copulation is done the two go off on their separate ways without a backward look. The female returns to the business of hunting and the male looks for other willing maidens.

Denning

A bobcat den may be in a jumble of boulders, in a natural cave, or in a dugout under tree roots. The young are delivered about two months after breeding. They will be blind and helpless. There may be as many as seven kittens although the average is much less. The female must leave the kittens alone frequently to hunt, and if a male bobcat happens across the den he is likely to kill and eat the young. This dries up the milk of the female and forces her back into estrus. The male then has another opportunity to breed her.

The young are nursed for the first few weeks of life. Their diet is then supplemented with fresh meat. Often the female will bring live mice and rabbits to the den, and the young then are allowed to practice their killing technique.

Bobcat may den in natural caves or under rock overhangs. They also use these areas during the day to escape the sun. *Photo Gerry Blair.*

Summer Fun

The summer is a carefree time for young bobcats. They travel with the female on her nightly hunts and learn the skills they will need to survive on their own. Game is usually plentiful. Young rabbits and rodents are about and the cats will have little problem in filling their bellies. Hunting instruction continues through the summer. The kits may stay with the female until cold weather hits, but when the food supply begins to dry up the young are encouraged to leave. They will likely stay together for awhile. If they have learned their hunting skills well, and if there is a plentiful supply of cottontail rabbits, a good percentage will survive. If not, most or all will perish. They are young and inexperienced and must hunt in strange territory. Usually they are confined to marginal habitat as the older and larger cats claim and defend the best hunting grounds.

Hybridization

As the coyote is a dog the bobcat is a cat. It is not common but bobcats have been known to mate with domestic cats. Two successful matings I know of took place between a bobcat and a black domestic cat. Four of the kittens produced were black and resembled the domestic parent. The other three kittens had bobtails, tufted ears and were light grey. All of the kits had feet that were noticeably larger than those of domestic cats.

Longevity

Fifteen years appears to be about the tops for bobcat in the wild. Considering the high infant mortality rate and the toll taken by trappers and hunters, the average lifespan is much lower. One bobcat in captivity lived thirty-two years. The main enemies of the cat, aside from man, are the flying predators, other land predators such as the coyote and the mountain lion, and domestic dogs.

Bobcat Numbers

Many states are presently concerned that bobcat numbers may be diminishing. This does not seem to be the case in the West and Southwest. States such as Colorado, Nevada, Utah, Arizona and New Mexico have healthy populations.

Spotted fur is currently in demand and fur industry competition has raised bobcat prices to record highs. This full-furred fellow brought more than three hundred dollars in 1978. *Photo Gerry Blair.*

New Mexico may have the most with an estimated population of almost fifty thousand.

Value as a Furbearer

Historically, bobcat has not been an attractive fur to the industry. Prices were never very high. The fur was considered sparse and the hide thin. In the 1970's however, a series of events caused a dramatic increase in demand. The export of leopard and cheetah was banned in many of the countries which produced them and bobcat became the only spotted fur available to the industry. Prices skyrocketed and by the late seventies large, well-handled pelts fetched more than five hundred dollars. But prices became depressed in 1979. A federal suit filed by one of the self-proclaimed conservation agencies threatened the ability of the industry to continue to export the bobcat. Prices dropped by half almost overnight. As this is written (spring 1980), they have not recovered. Based on prices paid at the end of the 1979-80 season, bobcat fur should be worth from $125 to $225.

As with all fur, individual pelts will vary greatly in worth. Price determinants are size, color, primeness and handling. The highest prices are currently paid for the lighter colored furs with dramatic markings.

Calling Cats

Bobcats are much easier to call than either fox or coyote. The fact that they're not often called is due to a combination of factors. The cat by his nature is a solitary animal. There is usually one resident cat in any given territory which may encompass several square miles. It is unlikely that a caller will set up in the exact area where the cat happens to be at the time. Another factor is the manner in which the cat responds to the call. He does not come charging as the coyote or fox often does. Instead the cat comes as he hunts, deliberately and utilizing every scrap of available cover. Many hunters, I am convinced, never see most of the cats they call. As an illustration, I was making a dawn call from the lip of a rough canyon with an out-of-state friend. I had previously scouted the area and had discovered scat and scratches from a mountain lion. Five minutes into the call my friend signaled that he had sighted game. It took him almost three minutes to point the big bobcat out. The critter was sitting in a fairly open area and was less than sixty yards distant. His natural camouflage protected him well. If there had

Stubby Fleming of Las Vegas, Nevada, calls the brushy border of a shallow lake, perfect habitat for the spotted cat. *Photo Gerry Blair.*

been two eyes instead of four on that trip the cat likely would have gone un-discovered. I hurried my first shot and missed. The cat exhibited another characteristic of feline behavior—he never budged. The second shot from the .22-250 took him under the throat and did a neat job.

Most hunters fail to call cats because they are not hunting cat territory. The cat is not a lover of the open spaces. He must have fairly thick cover to survive. The cover hides the rodents on which he lives and provides the cat enough cover to make a successful stalk. Cover also provides the cat with a means of protection from the larger predators who might be intent on a bobcat brunch. The cat needs brush, trees or rimrock country to survive.

A lack of hunter patience will also keep bobcat hides off the stretcher. Hunters who may have experience calling coyote will become impatient when fifteen minutes of calling does not pay off. This is not nearly enough time for the cat unless he happens to be at your elbow when the call begins. The cat comes to the call slowly and deliberately; he is really moving along if he breaks into a trot. He will make frequent stops to size up the land ahead and deliberate on the cause of the ruckus. Many hunters, I suspect, get up and leave the stand in disgust while there is an interested pair of feline eyes watching every move from forty yards out.

The Repeat Customer

Now for some good news. The cat is not as smart as a coyote or even a fox. They cannot, it seems, associate the sound of the distress call with the human who plods through the woods. If a cat is called and escapes he will come to the call just about as readily the next day. The fact that he may be shot and wounded at the termination of the call does not seem to make a difference. If he lives, and if he is able, he will explore the call with the same interest. I was calling to the camera in one rocky canyon in the Mazatal Wilderness Area late one spring. The trapping season and calling season had passed, and as I often do, I returned to the field for some calling and photography. In a week's time I called a cat from the brushy canyon five times. I have no way of knowing if it was the same cat but I suspect that it was. The cat came as readily to the call the last time as he did the first. On almost every call he appeared about twenty-five minutes after the call had started.

The most important aspect in a successful bobcat hunt is choosing country which is likely to house a cat. Look for country with brushy canyons and rimrock. Bobcat tracks may be found along dusty, little-used roads, around water or in fresh snow. The track will be almost round. An average track might measure 1¾" wide by 2¼" long. Adult tracks resemble those of domestic cats in configuration but larger. The heel pad differs noticeably. The track will show four toes and a heel pad. Usually the claws are retracted and do not show in the track. Like most cats the bobcat will place the rear foot in the same spot as the front. This will often result in a double print or a blurred print. In poor ground a partial track may be visible. With practice the hunter will learn to recognize the track. The gait of the walking cat will be about fifteen inches.

Scat

Bobcat scat is usually larger than fox droppings and smaller than coyote droppings. The offal is also more segmented. When first evacuated the scat will be a wet black. It soon crusts and if left undisturbed will turn a grayish color, then, eventually, it will turn white and disintegrate. The bobcat has an efficient stomach and little except hair, bone fragments and lubricant will be evacuated. The scat seldom contains vegetable matter but occasionally grass will be present. The grass is probably ingested as bulk and not for any nutrient value. If times are tough, the scat may contain some fruit. Southwestern cats will eat the purple pears from the prickly pear cactus if their belly is growling. This will turn the scat a reddish purple and seeds and peel will be visible. The bobcat's scat is more con-

Bobcat stay close to water most of the time. Check muddy banks of waterways for cat tracks. *Photo Gerry Blair.*

A bobcat comes better if there is brush to hide his advance. His mottled coat makes him tough to spot in brush. *Photo Harley Shaw, Arizona Game Department.*

sistent than either the coyote or the fox. Often these piles will contain scat from a number of visits. At times a fox who feels daring or a coyote who feels aggressive will evacuate atop the cat scat. When these multiple deposits are found, the hunter can be sure that there is a territorial cat in the neighborhood. A single pile of dung may be from a transient who is just passing through.

A bobcat will sometimes cover his urine and offal by scratching dirt and debris over it. This scratch is also a good indicator of a territorial cat. Coyotes and fox will also scratch but a close examination of the area should determine which critter clawed the ground.

Stand Selection

Stand selection is crucial in bobcat hunting. When correct habitat has been located, the caller should attempt to determine where the cat might be at that particular time of day. If it is early in the morning or late in the evening, the nocturnal tabby wil likely be out and hunting. Look for him in heavy brush which may border fields. If the call is made at midday it is almost certain that the cat will be bedded. If it is hot he will choose the shady side of a hill where it is cooler. Look for him fairly high on the rims of the canyon where he can take advantage of any wind movement that might be available. He will bed under brush, in natural caves or in the gaps of a rock jumble.

The stand selected must offer a number of advantages. There must be sufficient cover to hide the hunter and enough cover to let the approaching cat feel comfortable. Cats do not enjoy walking across broad open areas in daylight. He will come more readily if there is scattered brush to hide his advance. The cover must not be too thick, however. It must be open enough so that the hunter has a fair chance to spot the cat as he approaches.

The strength of a bobcat is in his exceptional eyesight. He can see the flutter of a bird wing at half a mile. The caller must be well concealed or the cat will discover the hoax and will likely never be seen. The cat also has excellent hearing and he appears to be much more curious than members of the canine family. The only sound I have found that is sure to spook a bobcat is the human voice. The bobcat has a poor nose when compared to the coyote. His sense of smell, I suspect, is mainly for close work. I have had cats come from downwind on a number of occasions but it is still a good idea to use a masking scent when cat calling. The cat may not mind your odor but the volunteer fox or coyote you might occasionally harvest will certainly object.

Cats are not predictable in their reaction to the call. I have had a number of cats stop a hundred yards out and absolutely refuse to budge an inch. Others come until the hunter becomes alarmed. I called a cat to thirty feet one summer and was busy photographing with a telephoto lens. Something about the click of the shutter and the rasp of the rewind turned the cat on and he went into a classic stalk position and started to come my way. I chickened out when he was ten feet away. "Get the hell out of here," I yelled. The cat lost no time in following the suggestion.

A neighbor who was calling south of Flagstaff a few years ago brought a cat even closer. He was hidden in a clump of brush making a twilight call for coyote. Ten minutes into the call he sensed a presence behind him. Before he could turn he had a very surprised bobcat on his back. Both the hunter and the cat decided that they had made a mistake; the hunter left in one direction and the cat went the other. Such confrontations are rare but I know of a few instances where a rabid cat attacked a human. A cat in his right mind, however, knows his own capabilities. He is not about to get into a scrap where he may be outweighed by two hundred pounds.

Brushy canyons with rimrock are attractive to bobcat. Pick a spot with good visibility and call for thirty minutes, more if there is lion sign about. *Photo Gerry Blair.*

Cat Calls

A cat will respond to a surprising variety of sounds. All of the rabbit squeals will attract them as will squeaks and whimpers. They will come to bleating goats and screaming birds and the distress cry of a fox. I have called them using most of the hand calls and with electronic tapes. I seldom use the tape on cats, I might point out, as much of my cat hunting involves long walks into the wilderness areas. The electronic calls are just too bulky and heavy to pack. A skilled caller, I feel, can do as well or better with a tube, and it weighs a hell of a lot less. I have had my best luck calling cats using the calls with the high-pitched reeds. I like the Burnham WF-4 for the prime call and usually back it up with their S-2 close-range call.

Calling Technique

I have found that a lot of volume is not critical in cat calling. I start the call with a few low moans on the WF-4. I keep the groans short, seldom calling more than ten or fifteen seconds before I pause to let it take effect. In a minute or two, I will repeat the low moan for another few seconds. Another pause. Sometimes this is all that is needed. If the bobcat is close he likely will respond in short order. If I don't get action in four or five minutes I will lay into the call with gusto, producing a 20-second series of heartrending screams. I pause for about a minute and blow another 20-second series, then pause for a minute and change to the close-range call. Blow low moans for about twenty seconds and start the pause-blow sequence, and stay on the stand at least thirty minutes, or longer if the country looks promising. Many times a hunter can sense the approach of a cat by watching the birds. A daytime cat seems to drive birds nuts. They will squawk and raise hell. Often they will fly above him hurling the vilest of profanities in his direction. If any such activity is observed the hunter is well advised to stay put and keep squeezing the rabbit.

If your trigger finger is apt to twitch under stress, as mine does, you will find that you frequently miss a standing or sitting cat at absurdly close ranges, but don't worry. Most cats seem unafraid of a rifle shot. If they are not hit it is likely they will not blink an eye as you reload and make a more careful shot. An acquaintance once missed a sitting cat six times running with a scope-sighted revolver. I will not use his name for humanitarian reasons. He reloaded the six-shooter and took the tabby dead between the headlights with the first shot. See what practice does for you?

Hunter's Luck

Not every stand produces action and not every hunt puts fur on the stretcher. Varmint callers are like other hunters. They like to talk about the trips where they connected, but you don't hear much about the times they have been skunked. I have come home empty-handed many times and so have most of the other good callers I hunt with. Like other hunts, varmint calling has its good and bad days. Even on the good days if I sight critters at half the stands, I think my luck is exceptional. Don't expect to hit the jackpot every time out. You are sure to be disappointed.

Cats are not hard to call. They are curious and are not as smart as a coyote. A lot of hunters walk away from a stand leaving a bobcat watching in the brush. *Photo Harley Shaw, Arizona Game Department.*

A Second Opinion

Tom Morton is a former World Champion Predator Caller who may be the best cat caller around today. According to Tom, a cat is a cat. He will come to the call about the same whether he is a bobcat, a mountain lion or a jaguar. The techniques offered in this interview helped make Tom take more than sixty cats during the 1979-80 season.

Tom Morton

I don't have any idea how many bobcat I have called. When I first started calling twenty-five years ago, the fur was not worth skinning and we never kept count. I do know I called and killed eighty-five bobcats in one fifteen-week period. I was working a full time job and was only able to call weekends. I have called hundreds of cats, maybe more than a thousand. Cats are not hard to call if you go about it right. They are a curious critter and are not as smart as a coyote. They don't get call smart. I know I have called the same cat two and three times. Sometimes I'm not able to get him the first or second try but I just keep going back and the cat keeps coming in until I get lucky. You could smarten a cat up if you fooled him two or three times in a short period, but even then you could probably call him back if you changed the tone of your reed slightly.

Like other cats the bobcat is primarily a night hunter but he can be called in the daytime consistently if you set up right and call right. They are easy to call at night and that is the best way to hunt cats if it is legal. They are out and hunting and are not light-shy like a coyote. They come in good and usually stick around until they take a bullet.

I blow for cats the same way I do for lion. Maybe the reed in the tube should be a little higher pitched than for lion. I like the jackrabbit reeds straight out of the box for bobs. Blow a loud series for fifteen seconds and pause for a full minute, then count to a hundred and fifty and blow another fifteen-second series and pause another minute. Keep this up till you quit the stand. I usually call thirty minutes for bobcats and will stick it out for forty-five minutes if I have any encouragement at all. A bobcat comes in slow and sneaking like a lion and is hard to see. They have a natural camouflage that helps them out. If I know I will be calling cat country I carry a set of binoculars to help locate cats.

Night calls for bobcats can be made anytime except when there is strong wind. Wind kills the call and the cats can't hear you. I don't believe the moon phases affect a bobcat's feeding habits like it does a coyote. Night calling for coyote is best during the dark phases. Moonlit nights are a poor choice. I really think that a caller can have better luck on coyotes during the day. They are so light-shy that you have a tough time getting the gun on them at night.

Day calls for cats are usually best right at daybreak because the cat has not bedded down from his night hunting yet. If hunting is poor he may

Good bobcat country is rocky, bluffy canyons with a lot of quail. A bobcat would pass up ten rabbits to get one quail. *Photo Gerry Blair.*

be going to bed with an empty belly and a rabbit might sound good to him. Late calls might be all right too. You have the same danger here you do with lions. The cat comes slow and it might be too dark to see him when he shows up. I like early calls the best.

Good bobcat habitat is a rocky bluff canyon with a lot of quail. I have read a lot of books that state the cottontail rabbit is the cat's favorite food but I think a bobcat would turn his nose up at a dozen rabbits to get to one quail. Twice I have watched cats take quail. Both times the cat cornered a covey of quail under a bush. The cat trotted around the bush continually. The quail couldn't stand much of that and they flushed out. The cat leaped in the air and batted them down with a forepaw. One of the cats took five quail out of one covey that way.

I took five bobcats on one hunt. I think that is the best bobcat day I ever had. Most of the time the bobcat comes in singles. They are a solitary animal and usually hunt alone. A few times I have called doubles. On one hunt, in December of 1978, I called four bobcat to one stand. I was deer hunting with a friend in the Superstitions when we found fresh bobcat tracks around a waterhole. I knew we had to make a call. We set up and the four cats came running, all grouped together. We shot one apiece with our deer rifles but the other two ran off. The two we killed were toms and I suspect the others were to. I don't know why they were running together. I have not seen that happen before or since.

I did a lot of cat calling with my boy last season (1979-80). One day we made our first stand at daylight and the last one at dark. We went home with three bobcat, a coyote and two fox. We were using shotguns and got top dollar for all of the fur.

I usually carry a shotgun when I am calling for fur except when I'm calling for mountain lion. A mountain lion is too big to depend on a shotgun. I use a 10-gauge single shot with a thirty-six inch barrel and I use No. 2 birdshot. I once did a test for the Winchester people. They gave me a case of about every kind of shotgun shell they make. I found that the No. 2 did the best job on fox, coyote and bobcat. Anything closer than forty yards is almost a sure kill and the small size of the shot doesn't hurt the fur.

I have also shot a lot of predators with a .222. I load 21 grains of 4198 behind a 55-grain Speer hollowpoint. I figure I am getting about 3,000 fps muzzle. I think the deuce is the best gun going for predators. It is accurate and won't tear up a coyote or bobcat, but it messes up a fox sometimes if you hit him wrong. I like it for bobcat because sometimes they show up too close for the shotgun, which would blow them to pieces.

I usually travel a mile or maybe two miles between bobcat stands if I am calling open country. If you are in the cluttered-up canyon country that cats like best you only need to move from one canyon to the next. Your call doesn't carry as far here and you don't need to move as far.

The best thing to remember on cats is they come slow. Give them plenty of time. If you will spend at least thirty minutes on each cat stand and watch carefully, you will increase your kill on bobcat. With bobbies selling for two or three hundred dollars a piece you sure don't want to throw any back.

10

The Gray Fox

I made the stand as the morning sun cast its first red rays over hardscrabble Mesa. I had made the ten-mile drive over the miserable dirt road to spend a day calling fox and cats in the brushy canyons that lay between Hardscrabble and the Verde River. The country was a series of rolling ridges and canyons with thick brush on the sidehills. The tops and north sides of the ridges had scrawny stringbark juniper. Caprock formed slight rims on most of the ridges. Perfect country, in my opinion, for gray fox and bobcat.

I located a juniper big enough to hide my bulk and put the sun at my back. The fox could fight the sun. I was shooting a scope-sighted .22 rimfire magnum and I sure didn't want sun flare in the scope about the time I got ready to lay down on a three-hundred-dollar cat.

I spent thirty minutes on that first stand and didn't even call a crow. I was using the high-pitched Burnham long-range predator call and I blew it with feeling. I was about ready to give up and made a slow look to my rear before crawling out of the juniper. The cat was on the rimrock exactly between me and the sun. I have no idea how long he had been there listening to the music. I eased the magnum around and fought the sun flare in the scope until I had a hazy outline of the bobcat centered in the dual X. I was shooting at an awkward angle. If these sound like excuses, they are; I missed that cat but hit close enough to scare the hell out of him. He took one step backward off that rock and disappeared.

I went back to the truck and drove a mile down the road. If I hadn't shot at the bobcat I would have driven only a half a mile. A fox in broken country like this probably can't hear a call more than half a mile away, particularly if he is down in one of the canyons.

I made about a dozen stands that day and sighted ten fox. Two of the

Gray fox prefer brushy country that has a good rodent population. This Arizona gray came to 20 feet and spooked at the camera shutter. *Photo Gerry Blair.*

stands produced doubles. I took two fox from one stand and four from the others. Six fox out of ten sighted is not a bad average for me.

The last call of the day was the most exciting. I was calling from a ridge top and watching the sidehill of the next ridge across a shallow canyon. A fox appeared in the brush across the way about three minutes into the call. That fox did his level best to ignore me and the call; he seemed to be hunting the hillside and had no interest in the best sounds I could blow. He was smart enough to keep moving when he was in the open and do his standing in the thick brush. I finally laid the call down and picked a piece of flat-bladed grass about four inches long. I stretched the grass between my thumbs and formed a reed. Blowing through this makeshift call provides a very high-pitched scream, a sound that most fox find irresistible.

This fox was no exception. He came out of the brush at a run and didn't stop until he was thirty feet out begging for the bird. The angle was bad for a good lung shot and I hit a little far back. The fox flipped into the brush and began a piteous screaming. I sat tight. If the fox came out of the clump of brush he was in he would have to cross an open space and I would have another chance. Forty seconds later another fox appeared running hard. He ran right up to the crybaby and stood looking at him in disgust. I made a better shot on the second fox. At the shot the screaming stopped and I made a slow stalk. Both foxes were dead when I found them. The hollowpoint from the good old boys at Speers had done its work well. A small entrance hole, massive blowup in the chest cavity, and no exit.

Gray Fox Distribution

The gray fox is a common critter in the Southwest as well as most of the United States. He is also found in good numbers in most of Mexico. He is found nowhere else in the world. The gray is absent from the high plains states, the northern Rockies, the northern parts of the Great Basin Desert and the coastal rain forests of Washington and Oregon. Much of the gray fox range overlaps that of the red fox. The shared range causes few problems. The gray is an animal of the brush and forests and the red seems to prefer the more open country.

It is in the Southwest where the gray is found in the greatest numbers. He thrives in the diverse chaparral midlands and is equally at home in the low desert and the high mountains. In Arizona, the gray is found in every part of the state except the high grasslands of the Four Corners area. The red has moved into this foxless void and is found there in moderate numbers. The Arizona red is different than his eastern relatives. The coat is a tannish-blond and seldom has any hint of red.

Look for the gray fox in rough country interrupted with many small canyons. The gray needs the cover to make his stalk. Unlike other members of the dog family, the fox makes his living by stalking his prey and ending the stalk with a lightning pounce. The presence of trees makes the habitat even more attractive to the gray. He is the only fox that is a tree climber and will often use this skill to escape unfriendly neighbors such as the coyote and the bobcat. In the absence of forest, the fox needs heavy brush or rimrock where he can outmaneuver the coyote and outrun the bobcat. Don't look for many fox in well developed conifer and spruce-fir forests. The absence of undergrowth and the small population of year-round rodents makes it tough for him to make a living in a forest.

Fur Value

Fur prices are determined by fashion trends and by the availability of the fur. Gray fox fur is not as fine or full as the red and will usually bring less money.

In 1979 I averaged forty-eight dollars for my Arizona grays. That price has remained stable for the past three years. Southwestern grays will prime about mid-November in the higher elevations and perhaps a month later in the desert.

Description

The gray fox is about three feet long from nose-tip to tail-tip. A third of that length is devoted to the gray's grizzled bushy tail. Large adult fox may weigh ten pounds or more, but most average less, around eight pounds.

Gray fox fur is salt-and-pepper gray on top of the back and tail. The under fur is buff. The fur turns a reddish brown on the stomach and chest. This will sometimes confuse beginning hunters and they will swear they have bagged a red fox. It is a fact that the gray fox in Arizona have more red on their bodies than the red fox. The center of the gray fox belly will often be a spotless white. The tail is black-tipped and will have an apparent black stripe running its entire upper length.

Gray fox do not show the color variation found in the reds. They are usually almost identical except for size. The white throat patch and salt and pepper body hair is typical. *Photo Gerry Blair.*

Habits

The gray fox is a night feeder for the most part. He is also secretive in his habits. He will avoid close contact with man if he has any choice. It is not surprising that few non-hunters encounter a gray fox in their travels. Campers may hear the high-pitched yap-yap-yap barking of a gray and not recognize it for what it is. The bark somewhat resembles the barking of an immature coyote.

Gray fox are territorial. Their home range will be determined by the variety and amount of food available. It may extend to three or four square miles in stingy country. The gray is omniverous. He will eat about anything he can get in his mouth. Prey animals are anything the gray can catch and kill. Gray fox have killed jackrabbits that were almost as big as they were. They also take cottontail rabbits, ground squirrels and mice. Small birds, particularly those that are ground roosters or who roost on low brush, also see the inside of a gray fox stomach. The gray will take insects such as grasshoppers, crickets and beetles. Along waterways, the gray will hunt the shoreline for crawfish, frogs and water snakes. Preferred fruits for the gray are juniper and manzanita berries and the fruit of most cactus.

The main predator of the gray fox is the coyote, but bobcat and mountain lion will also take a few. The fox will avoid, therefore, country that houses an abundant population of large predators, particularly the coyote. If the fox's range overlaps with that of the coyote, the fox stays in the brush and rough country where his speed and maneuverability lets him escape most of the time.

The black tail jackrabbit is often as large as a gray fox and doesn't often see the inside of a gray's stomach. One is taken occasionally but the grays usually pick smaller prey. *Photo Gerry Blair.*

Quail and other ground nesting birds feed a lot of fox. *Photo Gerry Blair.*

Mating

The vixen is monestrous, coming into heat in January or February. The pups are born two months later in litters that average four or five pups. The pups are born fully furred and blind. The den will be located in an abandoned badger hole, a dugout area under a brush pile or in a natural cavity in a rock slide area. The pups stay in the den for about five weeks and then make short trips outside to see the world. These forays will be confined to the area immediately outside the den at first, but the pups will be hunting with the adults by midsummer and will be taught the hunting skills they will need to survive on their own. If it is a poor year for groceries the young will be forced to leave the territory at the onset of cold weather. If they are reluctant to leave they may be nipped severely around the hips. But if food is plentiful in the parent's territory, the young are permitted to stay and will share the territory with the old folks.

Fox are mostly monogamous; the males stay with the females and help raise the kids. I have seen fox pairs travelling together in late winter, before the breeding season, and am of the opinion that they pair permanently until one dies.

This pocket mouse is a night feeder and never travels far from his den because of fox and other predators. Areas with an abundant rodent population usually host fox. *Photo Gerry Blair.*

Calling Fox

Fox are night hunters for the most part, but if they are hungry they will hunt both night and day. If your state allows night calling, you will find that they respond to a call much better at night. You will sight more fox and will find they will approach closer to the stand.

If you are not permitted night calling you will find that the hours after dawn and before dusk will be the most productive. The critter seems to be up on his feet and thinking about groceries then and will answer the call with more enthusiasm.

Look for the fox in brushy basins or canyons. Stay away from mature forests where the undergrowth has been starved out because of a lack of sun—you will not find many fox there. The open country under these mature forests also make the fox vulnerable to his cousin the coyote. Areas with alternating brushy canyons and juniper ridges also house fox. The brush provides cover and chow and the junipers provide a handy climbing tree if a hungry neighbor drops by. The juniper also offers a succulent berry to satisfy the fox's sweet tooth and provide variety to his diet. Fox country is easy to find if you remember the fox's needs, the first of which is food. Look for manzanita thickets, prickly pear patches, or areas with a high rodent population. Any such area will satisfy the food requirement.

The gray fox must also have cover. The best food supply in the world will not sustain him if he does not have the proper terrain to elude his enemies. He does not have the endurance to run long distances as the red does and must therefore rely on his ability to hide and maneuver. Heavy brush offers the type of country the fox needs to display these talents. He can hide, he can maneuver and he can sneak up on the rabbit or mouse he chooses for supper.

Fox will be found in country that appears to be surprisingly open. If you look close you will find that some open country has frequent patches of brush, clusters of trees, or rocky outcrops which meets the fox's requirements.

Gray fox will also be found in the desert. This may be the habitat, as a matter of fact, that suits him best. The cactus offers an abundance of sweet fruits as well as maneuvering room if he encounters a hungry coyote. The desert also contains a high rodent population. Mice and rats, as well as rabbits, snakes and birds are plentiful. The desert also offers brush which may not be obvious at first glance, but it is there. This brush will form stringers along the low sides of sand washes and will also cover drainage hillsides particularly on the north sides. There also will be brush along the infrequent waterways.

The last requirement of the fox is a habitat free of a great number of fox predators. If the area is lousy with coyotes you are not apt to see many fox. Man, it must be remembered, is also a fox predator. Considering the high price paid for fox fur he also may be the most dangerous. Therefore, areas that are easily trapped or called will also have few fox, so it takes a bit of scouting to find fox hot spots. Look for wilderness areas with no roads where it is unlikely the trapper has traveled. Look for small areas near cities or urban developments which trappers usually avoid because of dogs. Look for small brushy basins isolated in open country. If you do find a fox hot spot, don't do a lot of bragging about it down at Joe's Place. You may have a lot of company the next time you go calling.

At the present time, the fox population is controlled by hunters and trappers. If that control was not present the numbers would be regulated in other ways. Wildlife personnel have recorded falling fox populations at various times for a number of reasons. An investigation into several cases revealed that all of the animals found dead were rabid. Biologists suspect that in times of population explosions, this dreaded disease will return fox numbers to manageable levels. Rabid fox attacks on humans and domestic animals were not uncommon in the days of low fur prices and high fox populations, but since the population has been reduced by hunting and trapping, such attacks are seldom reported.

Rock squirrel are also a favorite fox food. At times the fox will dig the critters from their den and wipe out an entire family. *Photo Gerry Blair.*

Fox Guns

Gray fox can be shot and killed with all centerfire rifles, most shotguns and a few rimfires. The field of available firearms is reduced considerably if the hunter wants to sell or mount the fur. The fox is a small-bodied critter, not much bigger than some of our big western jackrabbits in some instances, and his fragile frame will not withstand much lead. Too much gun and your trophy will look like a jigsaw puzzle with a few of the pieces missing. The three guns listed below have done the job for me.

Rimfires

I have shot fox with the .22 long rifle hollowpoint and have had inconsistent results. Some fox drop dead in their tracks, while others only howl and run off. They probably die later but they die alone and usually die slowly. I think we owe them a quicker, more humane death and, therefore, I do not recommend the .22 rimfire as a fox gun.

Most gray fox come close. The .22 rimfire magnum does a good job if the range is under 70 yards. *Photo Gerry Blair.*

The .22 rimfire magnum is a different matter. It is a faster-shooting gun than the standard rimfire and delivers more energy. The 40-grain pill should leave a rifle barrel at a bit over 2,000 fps. Use the hollowpoints; the solid slugs often go all the way through the critter without expansion. I have had good results with the .22 mag at ranges of up to seventy-five yards, but past that the slug loses energy and kills were not consistent. The occasional coyote or bobcat that comes to the call in fox country can be handled with the mag if the animal is within the seventy-five-yard kill range. I shot seven coyote and four cats with the magnum this year. All of the cats were close and went down enthusiastically, and five of the coyotes were closer than thirty-five yards and went down without a fuss. The other two coyotes were about sixty yards out and neither went down on the first shot. Both were killed but it took more than one shot to do the job.

My .22 magnum is a Model 700 H&R. I like the autoloading feature as it provides five fast shots with the standard clip, and an auxiliary ten-shot clip is also available. The ten shots can be sprayed at a disappearing coyote in about as many seconds. Try that with a bolt-action sometime.

The gun is equipped with a Weaver 4X scope with the dual-X cross hairs. Get the one-inch tube, the same one you would mount on your centerfires. The optics will be better, you will have a wider field of view, and you will get on target faster. My gun is also equipped with a sling. I usually carry a lot of junk when I am hunting and like the rifle out of my way over the shoulder.

Now for the bad news. The ammo for the .22 mag is expensive. Mag rounds cost a bit more than nine dollars a hundred according to a 1979 price list from CCI. That's about a dime apiece. A handloader who buys at sales or patronizes the discount stores can reload centerfire for less.

The mag has one other disadvantage. You may get a surprise bear or mountain lion when calling for fox. The little rimfire is not enough gun for either. In some states it would also be unlawful to use on bear or lion.

Centerfires

Most of the flat-shooting varmint guns will not mess up the outside of a fox if the correct bullet and powder combination is used. I have already mentioned Murry Burnham's load for fox. He uses a .222 and loads it so slow that it has been passed by VW Bugs on upgrades. The slow muzzle velocity has a tendency to do all of the dirty work inside. Murry tells me the load is good to about seventy-five or one hundred yards. That is no disadvantage to Murry as most of his hunts are night hunts but a day hunter may have some problems. The West and Southwest have a lot of wide open space and it is not unusual to take a fox at a hundred plus yards.

This fine Arizona gray was lip-squeaked on a hunt for Gambel Quail. He was shot with No. 3 buckshot from a 20 gauge. Note absence of blood. *Photo Gerry Blair.*

FMJ for Fox I have had fair luck shooting full-metal-jacket bullets through my .22-250 for fox. The FMJ's do less damage if they are loaded between 2,000 and 3,000 fps muzzle velocity. My Speer book (*Reloading Manual No. 9*) gives a page of loads for .22 centerfires shooting the FMJ. The speed varies from about 1,600 fps to about 2,700 fps. As with other loads the slower the bullet, the less the tissue damage. The FMJ does not expand as spitzers and hollowpoints do, but the pure velocity of a hot-loaded .22 may cause more pelt damage than the fur buyer likes. I mentioned in an earlier chapter that I did not like the FMJ for coyote, but they do a good job on the smaller-bodied fox. I have never lost a fox that was well-hit with the FMJ out of my .22-250. But the slower-loaded FMJ's may cause a loss of accuracy so you will need to experiment to get the load that does the best job in your gun.

Shotgunning Fox

The scattergun is usually my first choice if I am hunting fox in heavy brush. A daytime fox can move like quicksilver if he suspects that the rabbit is actually a hunter. The shotgun gets on the critter fast and throws out a whole bunch of lead for him to run into. The famed Morton Burnham used the shotgun almost exclusively. His choice of birdshot instead of buckshot was probably a good choice for the country he was hunting but I like a little heavier shot. My 1100 Remington is loaded with a three-inch magnum holding No. 4 buckshot. The .224 diameter buck has a muzzle velocity of a bit more than 1,200 fps—plenty of punch to put down a fox without a lot of exterior damage. I have made clean kills on fox out to sixty yards with the magnum. I like the autoloading feature as it gives a fast second and third shot in case of multiples.

Don't give up fox hunting with a shotgun if your bird gun happens to be lighter than a 12 magnum. I have killed fox cleanly with a standard 12 pump, a Sweet Sixteen Browning Autoloader and a 20-gauge, three-inch Silver Snipe over-and-under. The lighter guns will kill fox about as well, but the effective range is reduced. Most of the fox taken with the lightweights were taken as a bonus while I was afield for quail or cottontail. I make it a practice to carry a couple of buckshot loads on my small game hunts. If I see promising fox country or fresh fox sign, I invest a few minutes in a stand. It is usually productive. Good country for quail and rabbits means good fox country.

There is no such thing as "the best" fox gun. Every choice has advantages and disadvantages. All a caller can do is evaluate the type of country he will be calling and make a guess at which gun will do the best job. Sometimes I guess wrong. You will too unless you are a better guesser than I.

Second Opinion

Mike Mell is one of the best callers in Arizona. You don't hear much about him because he spends most of his time hunting and not much talking about it. Mike has called seven bear, two mountain lion and more coyote, bobcat and fox than he can remember. He has been calling for 20 years.

Mike Mell

I called my first gray fox when I was sixteen—twenty years ago. My first predator call was an Olts, which had a sort of a ducky tone. I had trouble convincing the desert critters around Phoenix, Arizona, that ducks were nesting in the cactus patches. The Olt calls have been improved since those early days.

Few gray fox escape after being called. They come close and stubbornly stick around until they get the rabbit. *Photo Harley Shaw, Arizona Game Department.*

I have had my best luck calling fox sucking on the back of my hand or blowing through a blade of grass. I hold a three-inch piece of grass, or a section of leaf, between my thumbs and leave a little air space between. When I blow through the air space, the grass acts as a reed and causes a high-pitched scream. The sound is a killer for fox if they are close enough to hear.

I like the Circe calls and use them most of the time when I hand call. I use the cottontail reed when calling brush and the jackrabbit in open country. The coarser tones of the jackrabbit seem to work better on lion and bear.

I have my best luck fox hunting in canyon country with a lot of scrub oak and chaparral. Fox need cover and brush gives them cover and also a food supply. The fox eats rodents and any fruit and berries he can find.

It is not legal in Arizona to shoot wildlife after dark (except raccoon) and I do all of my hunting during the day. I usually shoot a three-inch 12 loaded with BB's. It is good out to sixty yards. I also use a .22 rimfire magnum shooting hollowpoints.

I always keep calling at a stand after I shoot a fox. Ten times last year I called fox after I had one on the ground. Once I called four fox to one stand —I took three.

Fox are not as spooky as coyote when they come to a call. They don't have the intelligence and they don't get call-smart as quick. Before fur prices went up we called a lot more fox than we do now. A lot of the areas are trapped and there are more callers in the field, but you can still call a lot of fox if you get into virgin areas.

I use a hand call most of the time and occasionally a tape player. I think a hand call is better in the hands of an experienced caller who can do more with it but tapes might be better for a caller who is just learning. I use the tape occasionally to keep from blowing my lip and when a day of heavy calling will make me tone deaf and I have a hard time keeping the notes pure.

I also use masking scent when calling fox. It is not critical, as it is with coyotes, but it helps me take a few extra fox every year. I sometimes call coyote at fox stands too, and if I didn't use the masking scent I would probably lose some of them.

A fox comes to the call differently than a cat or coyote. A coyote comes in charging most of the time. A cat comes sneaking. A fox comes trotting, looking over the country ahead to see if there are other predators about. If he is convinced it is safe, he won't leave until he gets the rabbit.

11

The Red Fox

The red fox ranges most of the United States, but there are a few gaps that should be noted. The coastal areas of some of the Southeastern states have no reds, nor do the desert portions of the Southwest. A large multi-state gap also appears in the Great Plains. The fox is found in good numbers in that part of North America that lies north of the Mexican border and his range is steadily increasing.

The red fox found in the United States today is probably a mutant. Our native red fox, formerly known as *Vulpes fulva* (tawny fox) was not widely distributed in many of the Eastern seaboard states. Our English forebears missed the foxhunts on the rolling hills of home and sicced the hounds on the local gray fox, but the gray wasn't much fun. He had a tendency to hole up soon after the chase started, and sometimes he would show very unfoxlike behavior and climb a tree. It didn't take long for the settlers to import a boatload or two of reds. The refugees thrived in the new habitat and mixed with the few local reds. The red fox found through most of the country is the product of that friendship.

Just as all black bear are not black, all red fox are not red. The few reds found in Arizona, for example, have a coat that is typical in every respect except color. Most are a creamy tan which is about the shade of a blond cocker spaniel. He is actually much less red than the gray fox found a bit farther south. Red fox may also be crossed, silver, and black. The crossed fox is a red with a dark cross over his shoulders and down his back. Silvers and blacks are melanistic phases of the red. All of the colors may be found in a single litter of pups.

One other strain of red fox should be mentioned. The Samson fox has been found in northwestern Europe and in certain parts of the United States. This critter lacks guard hair and its underfur is matted and curled. The wooly appearance of the fur does not generally excite the fur buyer who seldom reaches deeply into his wallet for a Samson pelt.

The typical red will range from ten to fifteen pounds when fully grown. The coat is full and fine—rich, reddish underfur protected by long guard hair. The body is a bit over two feet long with another foot or so of bushy tail, the tip of which is characteristically white. The throat, neck and chest are also white or cream and the feet are black. His lush fur gives the red fox a larger appearance than he deserves. One look at a skinned fox carcass will convince you that he is a small target indeed.

The red's handsome coat is always in demand and fur prices for reds stay consistently high. In 1979-80 some large prime reds brought a hundred-dollar bill. The fur has marvellous insulating qualities. A red can bed down when the temperature is 50° below zero and stay warm enough to keep alive. He will curl into a ball and cover his nose and the pads of his feet with his lush tail. He breathes into the tail, and the warmth from his breath is retained in the hair. During blizzards the red is likely to hole up in an underground den or burrow. He will come out as soon as the storm ends and will spend non-stormy periods sleeping above ground.

Food

Like most other predators, the red is an opportunist in his feeding habits; he eats both meat and vegetables. Most of his fresh meat intake is from mice and voles. On a still night the red can hear a mouse whisper from fifty yards away. He will stand motionless with a front paw raised and when he has zeroed in on

Red fox like all rodents including prairie dogs. If the dog town is located in high weeds the red has an easier stalk. *Photo Gerry Blair.*

the mouse's location and direction of travel, he will pounce and imprison his victim in a mat of grass and leaves. He seldom misses. The fox also takes other fresh meat, usually rats, rabbits, birds, eggs and poultry.

Carrion tastes pretty good to a fox. I have often seen hide and bones from young antelope and deer decorating the front of a fox den. The red kills these young critters occasionally, but cannot be considered a serious predator of so large an animal. It is likely that the scraps were stolen from a buzzard and packed home for the kids to play with.

Reds eat most fruits, vegetables, insects and snakes. It would be easier, perhaps, to list those things a fox doesn't eat.

Mating

The vixen red comes into heat in late January and there usually is a lot of competition for her favors. The male reds often fight over the vixens and a red fox fight is truly something to see. They stand nose to nose with front feet interlocked straining for dominance, leaping and cavorting with their full tails flowing. When it is over the winner leaves with the girl and the loser skulks off to lick his wounds.

Red fox usually mate for life although the pair does not stay together continuously. They are together during courtship, mating, and while the kids are being raised. When the youngsters are big enough and smart enough to make it on their own, the two adults go their separate ways and lead their own lives until the mating urge returns. Most biologists feel that the same two fox get together year after year.

The Den

Fox mate in late January, after which they are together constantly. They hunt and sleep together, and when the female senses motherhood approaching they go househunting. The den will be established in an old badger or woodchuck hole, or if no tailormade home can be found, the fox will dig a den under the roots of a tree or under a rock. The den will be a four- or five-foot tunnel. Several entrances will be dug, including a main entry hole and several escape tunnels in case something unfriendly comes calling. A side tunnel will be dug off the main hall to serve as a nursery. The main tunnel entrance will likely face the rising sun to keep the den warmer on cold mornings.

Most reds have more than one den. They will live in one and use the others as alternates in threatening situations. The pair can vacate a discovered den rapidly, carrying the young pups in their mouths to one of the back-up dens.

When the den is finished, the female gets serious about having kids. She runs the male out of the den and settles down to being a mother. The pups are born about the first week of April and the male will not be allowed inside the den until the kids are grown. He stays nearby, however, and brings food which is placed at the den entrance for the vixen if she is hungry. Is she is not, she takes it into the nursery and stores it in a handy spot.

The Young

The red fox litter will have from one to ten pups with six being average. The pups are blind and deaf at birth. The vixen does not leave the den for at least ten days, tending constantly to the pups. The pups nurse frequently. Red fox milk is much richer than cow's milk and the youngsters grow fast. Their eyes open at nine days after which the vixen leaves the den to hunt and replenish her emaciated frame. She returns to the pups frequently to let them nurse. The rich milk is supplemented by a soft and rich mixture of regurgitated flesh. Momma also brings bits of feathers and fur for the pup's enjoyment. After a time the playthings are replaced by the dead carcasses of mice and voles. When the pups are able to handle these with no trouble the female will capture a mouse alive and bring it home to the pups. They do their own killing.

The pups leave the den for the first time when they are about a month old but they will not venture far from the entrance at this stage. The slightest shadow will send them scurrying back to the safety of the den. They gain self confidence rapidly, however, and will likely sunbathe in the soft dirt at the den entrance within a week or two. When they are two months old, their eyes turn from baby blue to a foxy yellow. At about this time, they begin to accompany the adults on the hunt. They have about three months to learn about life. The parents break the pups in easy, usually on grasshoppers. They are taken to a meadow to learn the stalking technique they will need to keep alive, and when they have mastered grasshoppers they will graduate to mice and other fox delicacies. The young fox will be about five months old when the first frost hits, at which time the parents immediately suggest they leave the den. If the youngsters are reluctant, they will be encouraged with sharp bites on the butt and other hostile behavior.

The young fox always leave but they may not go far. If the area around the den has a good food supply, the youngsters will likely set up a territory close to the old folks. If times are hard, they may travel a great distance looking for a piece of ground that will support them through the winter. Ernest Ables, a member of the Wildlife Management Institute at the University of Wisconsin, has documented a truly remarkable migration. A young red fox was caught and tagged near Madison, Wisconsin. Nine months later the fox was shot by a woodchuck hunter in Montgomery County, Indiana, a straight line distance of almost 250 miles. A littermate of the traveller was tagged at the same time, and he was recaptured a year later a few hundred yards from the original capture site. Another red fox study by Charles M. Pils showed that red fox pups disperse readily from the home territory. He has had recoveries more than twenty miles away from the home area.

Territories

Most animals are territorial and fox are no exception. The size of the territory will vary greatly and may be determined by how good the hunting is. A pair

Young reds are taught to hunt at two months. This youngster works a grassy meadow for mice and grasshoppers. *Photo U.S. Forest Service.*

of fox could make a go of it on a few hundred acres if there are plenty of groceries and a lot of cover. Less generous areas may see a red fox territory of more than five miles. Al Sargent, a biologist for the U.S. Fish and Wildlife Service, did a study of reds in Minnesota who averaged about two square miles in their territories. The study also showed that a territorial fox seldom visited their neighbors. When a territory is established the fox, or the pair, will likely spend their life within the territory. If one or both dies a new pair will set up housekeeping shortly thereafter.

Fox are like other dogs; they mark their territory with urine posts, scat and audible signals. If the fox from the next territory comes to visit, or if a nonterritorial fox happens to wander through, the landowners will attack him and drive him off.

Fox Sign

Fox droppings are often seen along paths, fence borders and primitive roads. The scat will vary in size and appearance. It is doglike and is generally smaller than a coyote scat. It is usually somewhat larger than gray fox scat. All of these critters, however, will eat essentially the same groceries when their ranges overlap. The scat of all three will also show a radical size range. It is difficult to make a positive identification unless a track is found.

The red fox track is distinctive. It is doglike and is almost always smaller than the coyote and larger than the gray fox. If a trail is found, the paw prints will appear in almost a straight line. The front feet are larger than the rear and all four are well-furred and the fur often shows in a distinct print. Prints left on firm ground will show only a partial cast of the toes and pad. This will create an appearance of a great distance between the two, more so than others of the dog family. The pad print will sometimes appear as a Y-shaped bar only.

A good technique for locating fox territories is to drive the section roads on the morning after a light snow and look for fox tracks crossing the road. Most smart fox avoid these roads during daylight but cross them readily at night. When you have located a fox territory, the fox can be yours if you play your cards right.

Fox dens will usually be found near elevated land features. Steve Allen, a biologist in North Dakota, found that his foxes denned on mounds and hillocks scattered over grazed, hayed or idle land. Most of these dens had more than one entrance. Allen also established that the Dakota reds did not hibernate.

Habits

Red fox are primarily night hunters. They are sometimes seen hunting during daylight hours, however, particularly in the dead of winter when food intake does not meet energy demands. The fox will curl up on a high point to spend the day and will go underground only in the most severe weather. Look for them with binoculars on these high points. Favorite bedding spots are bulldozer piles, hay mounds, hillocks on open ground and rockpiles. These viewpoints give them a view in all directions and a chance to escape from approaching danger. Some hunters drive the roads on winter days and glass every high point. If a fox is located they try a stalk or hide downwind and call the fox to rifle range. Be sure to get permission from the landowner before trying for his fox.

Calling Fox

A red can be tricky to call, particularly if he has heard the song a time or two before. He is easier to call at night. Most fox callers see more fox on night calls but don't skin as many. Night calls and day calls will likely produce about the same number of hides on the stretcher.

If you are night calling, it is critical to scout the area of the hunt during daylight hours. Get the lay of the land and try to decide where the fox is likely to be when you make the call. This will give you some idea of his route of approach. If you have a constant wind, plan your stand so you will be downwind or crosswind of his approach and use skunk musk as a masker. Read the chapter on night calling for more information.

Day calls for red fox can be productive if you go about it correctly. You likely will have your best luck calling reds in the hungry months of January and February. The fox has used up most of his summer fat by this time and has to keep busy to stay alive. Hunger will probably make him investigate all food sources even if he suspects his leg is being pulled. Fox taken at this time of year will be at the peak of their prime and should bring the best price from the fur buyer.

Any time you call fox you will get a few customers. Certain types of weather will increase your business. As with other predators the red seems to be out and hunting just before a major storm hits. He will usually hole up to wait out the storm and return to the hunt when the storm clears. The last day before

Although the red and the fisher sometimes share the same range, face-to-face confrontations are rare. Neither is large enough to eat the other without a tough fight. *Photo U.S. Forest Service.*

a storm and the first day after a storm are always good and they will be even better if there is an absence of strong winds. I have also had good luck calling on very cloudy days. Periods of unsettled weather seem to make the critters restless and they will interrupt their regular routine and can be seen hunting and travelling during daylight. Foggy conditions are particularly good for day calls because the fog helps to hide the hunter, but it also hides the fox and seems to increase his confidence. If you are calling on foggy days you should decrease the distance between your stands. The moisture in the air seems to break up the sound waves from the call and your advertisement will not carry as far. Calling on foggy nights can be frustrating. The fog disperses the beam of the light and you will find it difficult to locate the critters.

Watching the Wind

Red fox do not usually come to the call with the same eagerness seen in a gray fox or a naive coyote. The red is wary by nature and his suspicions increase each time he is fooled by a predator call. A downwind red fox will probably never be seen. His keen nose will soon uncover the fraud and he will slink away into the weeds. Some upwind fox will make a slow circle to get downwind. I have seen call-wise coyotes do the same thing. They are hungry and want the rabbit but experience has taught them this survival technique. The use of skunk musk usually will solve a good part of the problem. You may also have good luck calling crosswind. Position yourself so that the prevailing wind comes either from your right or your left. Many times the call-wise fox will move into shooting range as he tries to move downwind to get your scent.

Windy days create other problems. All of the critters I have hunted are edgy on windy days. I suspect that they are kept nervous by all of the moving leaves and tree limbs. The critters sight-hunt at times and often use movement to lock in on their prey, but when everything is moving they are not able to do this. They also use movement to warn them of critters that may be intent on having them for supper. A lot of the time the critter will hole up on really windy days and save his energy for a time when it will provide a better return. Wind also affects call volume; it creates a lot of ground noise and the critter may have a hard time hearing the call if he is any great distance away.

Time of Day

I have already pointed out that a fox is primarily a night hunter. He will come to a day call but will not come as far or as fast as he will at night. You will have your best luck calling in the hour or two after daylight and the hour or two before dark. The fox is about ready to go to work anyway and will answer the call with more enthusiasm. Most nocturnal critters are also crepuscular.

Day hunters will also have to set up closer to the fox, a fact which makes stand selection critical. Where you look for reds will depend largely on where you live. If you are hunting cultivated land or prairie country you likely will find your fox bedded on high points, taking the sun and watching for fox hunters. Use a good pair of binoculars to locate these snoozers and try to stalk to rifle range. If that is impossible, get close enough to make a call. Remember to tailor the volume of the call to fit the distance between you and the fox. Don't overblow. Blow only loud enough to reach the fox. The lower the volume, the better in this instance.

If there are fingers of trees or brush bordering the fields, the fox may choose this cover as his bedroom. Field borders are always productive, and areas of high grass which border cultivated fields are also good bets. Sunny hillsides will host fox in cold weather, and you may also find them around haystacks, baled hay, snowdrifts and weedy areas along fencelines.

Squeezing the Rabbit

The method you use in blowing the call is more critical when calling reds. I have met a lot of coyotes that had no taste for music at all; they came as quickly to a sour note as a sweet one. Every gray fox I have encountered has had a tin ear and most cats are not much better. The red fox, though, will be turned off by a clinker. Make sure your call stays in tune. If it begins to blow sour, change the reed immediately.

Unlike the coyote and the cat, the fox makes his living hunting mice. The rabbit call works great on the larger predators but you likely will have better luck on fox using something that resembles the distress cry of a mouse or a bird. I like the Olt close-in caller, Burnham's S-2 and S-4, and Major Boddicker's Crit'r Call for the first series. If you use the Crit'r Call put your teeth about a quarter of an inch onto the exposed reed and blow softly with no hand muffling. Use one of these calls for a thirty-second series and end with a forlorn moan. Put a little blood into it. Wait and watch for about a minute to see if you have customers coming. If not, repeat for another thirty seconds and watch for another minute. If nothing shows go to a longer range call and try again.

I have had my best luck calling fox using a call that is reeded a bit on the high side. The Burnham C-3 is a good one, so is the WF-4. The Crit'r Call is also effective as you can vary the tone by moving your lips up or down the exposed reed. Blow a thirty-second series at medium volume, pause for a minute, and repeat the thirty-second series. Blow a fairly short blast, starting low and going high. Repeat this two or three times fast and then blow a long call starting high and fading off to a low moan. Continue these series for two or three minutes and then reduce the volume again and repeat the low series. You may have a fox on the way that you can't see. Blowing softly may make him think the injured critter is about to disappear down a competitor's gullet and if that's what he thinks, he will come in faster.

Red fox seem to get call-smart pretty fast. They have to or they won't last long. If your area is heavily called, you may find it necessary to give the fox a new sound. If most of the hunters in your area are using a particular type of call, you should use something different. Even a call-wise red will come if the sound is new to him. I often go into heavily called areas and come out with fur, using an electronic call and experimenting with tapes until I find a winner. I have found the baby cottontail squeaks to be effective as are the baby redbirds. The distress cry of the yellowhammer woodpecker seems very effective on fox.

I do not usually try to tune the reeds of calls I buy. They are factory tuned and are about as good as they can be. However, if I am working a heavily called area and having no luck I will sometimes make an exception. I will manipulate the reed in an attempt to produce a sound that is slightly different than the one my neighbor makes with the same call. This small difference will sometimes fool the fox. The Crit'r Call, I feel, is a good choice of a call to use in late season when the critters have a discriminating ear. The exposed-reed type of call never seems to sound exactly the same when blown by different callers. The sound is influenced by the position of the lips or teeth on the reed, the amount of hand muffle, the volume and even the thickness of the lips. I have taken the Crit'r Call into "called out" areas and have brought home respectable amounts of fur.

Second Opinion

Major Boddicker makes a good part of his living calling and selling fur, which he has been doing for almost thirty years. He bought a Herters call in 1952 with money earned trapping pocket gophers from a neighbor's alfalfa field. Major was ten years old at the time. Since that time he has called thousands of critters, almost a thousand of which were wily red fox. Five years ago he designed a new type of varmint call which is marketed under the name Crit'r Call. He took the prototype call out for a field test just north of Fort Collins, Colorado (an area that had been called heavily with conventional calls), and called three coyotes to the first stand. The Crit'r Call has been a favorite with serious callers ever since. Major Boddicker has generously offered to share his thirty years of calling experience with the readers of this book.

Major Boddicker
The red fox can be called from several different habitats. In the western states, they can be called from an irrigated agricultural area. I usually call the field borders, the creeks and standing crops that leave material after the crop is harvested. Irrigation ditches and irrigation ponds are also good bets, and old farmsteads are really good. I also call the borders that surround that kind of habitat.

The red fox is also a critter of the high mountain parks in many of the western states, but in those areas he will stay close to cover. I hunt the willow bottoms and the hedges. I call one area in Colorado called Middle Park and South Park. It is at 8,000 feet elevation. These parks are filled with lush grass and there is quite a bit of water.

In my opinion the red fox is smarter than any other predator except the coyote. If a coyote was a ten on the intelligence scale I would rate the red at about eight. Actually, I have called just about as many coyote as I have reds and they act quite a lot alike in their response to the call. The red comes at you in much the same way a coyote does—hard and fast. I have killed reds when they were ten yards out and have had them roll dead at my feet. At other times, reds will come slow and stop a hundred yards out with just their ears and eyes visible above the weeds.

I don't think that reds get call smart as quick as a coyote does. I have called the same fox several times on many hunts. In South Dakota we hunted the marsh country and would often get a quick snap shot at a red as he ran through the weeds. If we missed, we could come back a week later and call from the exact same place. The red would come back in and poke his head through the weeds at the exact spot he had appeared the week before. I don't think a coyote would do that. If you call a coyote and miss, your chance of calling that same critter back using the same call is slim. If you change calls or change delivery though, the coyote can be called back.

I vary my calling technique as the season progresses to take advantage of this feature. I start the season making a sound like a grown cottontail rabbit. As the season progresses, I will blow more like a jackrabbit, lower-toned and gravelly. If you really listen to a jackrabbit squall you will notice that it is not really a scream. It is more of a guttural squall. To me, the rabbit seems to be saying, "You are killing me, you SOB, but I am cussing you all the way." It is not so much a pleading wail as it is an aggressive squall. That is the sound I try to get from my call. Really late in the season, say March or April, I switch to an even lower-pitched call, something like a deer fawn or an antelope fawn might make. If I summer call, doing damage control work, I use what I call my *kee-kee* pup whine. This sound is really dynamite on males. Put the Crit'r Call about the same place in your mouth you would for a cottontail rabbit sound but don't close your hand around the end of the tube. Vary your breath as you blow, making a short sound then a long sound. It is really a killer call for late spring or summer calling.

I think red fox are easier to call at night. Most predators are. Late in the winter when the critters are call-shy you can go out at night and have good luck. The trouble with night calling though, is that you may call more critters, but you don't kill as many. I get about the same number of reds on day calls as I do on night calls. I prefer the dark of the moon or a cloudy night, and the same kind of weather I would pick for my day calls—cloudy with a weather front moving in. Anything but fog. Your light won't work well in the fog and the call sound won't travel as far. Just before a snow or right at the start of a snow is always good. Just after a storm is usually good.

I blow for reds about the same way I blow for all critters. I assume there might be a critter bedded down fifty yards away and I don't want to bust his eardrums. I start out low and tender. When I start calling I stick to it; I really call a lot. I will pause but the pauses are only 20 seconds or so. I have watched a lot of critters coming to the call and usually when the screaming stops, they stop. I start calling quietly for about the first two minutes, trying to get the critters that may be fairly close. If I don't get results, I will increase the volume—really lay in to it. I give them a sound that I know carries for two miles. I have heard howl backs from that far. The distance the call carries will depend on the terrain, of course. Brush, hills and canyons will break up the noise and muffle it. Open areas, particularly bowl-shaped basins, contain the noise and allow good penetration.

Many times a fox will be sighted about a hundred yards out and will refuse to come closer or come into the open for a shot. Some fox are sneakers, like a cat. They will use every available blade of grass to hide their approach. I have had them sneak to within twenty yards across open areas you swear couldn't hide a gnat. They seem just to loom up out of nowhere. When I see one of these fox that won't come into the open, I make the most authentic rabbit sound I am capable of. When you are blowing hard, trying for distance, the sound you make sounds like no rabbit ever did. If you sight a bashful fox, put just that volume into the call that a rabbit would. You don't really need a lot of volume on fox because their hearing is exceptional. I will also use lip squeaks. I can take my call and put my teeth on the first quarter-inch of reed and make low-volume toots. I bring the air in my nose and out my mouth in little *hoo hoo hoo*'s. It makes a great close-in call.

I shoot most of my fox with a .222. I use 20 grains of 4198 behind a 50-grain SX Hornaday. That gives me about 2,900 to 3,000 fps muzzle. I know that some hunters in brushy country use a .222 loaded down to less than 2,000 fps muzzle. I would probably do that too if I was hunting their type of country. Up here we may get one shot at ten yards and the next one at three hundred. I have to have a load that will work both times. If I am shooting open prairie with wind I switch to a .25-06. I use 57 grains of 4831 behind a 100-grain Sierra. It messes up the hide but I figure a holey hide is better than none at all. I just figure on sewing them. The .222 does a pretty good job on fox. I usually try for the chest if I have a choice. My load will exit on the far side and leave a fifty-cent-sized hole which takes me about eight stitches to sew up. I get top price for the hide. If I am shooting the .25-06 and need to take a fox, I aim for the head. I just scratch the head as I know there won't be anything left. I have a 4-12 Weaver variable on the .25-06 with a Lee dot. The .222 carries a 4X Weaver with a duplex.

I don't do a lot of pre-season scouting because gas is too high. If I am going into new country I don't go until I can take some fur to pay for expenses. I know I will call fewer animals than usual as I will spend a lot of time talking to farmers getting permission and locating stands. But I am able to scout while I hunt. The animals picked up will at least buy a tank of gas. If I find a spot that produces, I mark it on my map and go there every time I am in the area. A stand has to be rested between calls, though. Good stands, I feel, are somewhat like good fishing holes. If a big one is caught, another one will move in. I once called five critters on five consecutive tries at the same stand.

If you call and shoot a fox at a stand, don't give up. You may get another at the same stand. The sound of the shot doesn't seem to bother any of the predators. Use common sense. If you have been calling ten or fifteen minutes and a fox shows up that is probably the only one you will get at that stand. If you are only a couple of minutes into the call and you get a fox, you have a good chance of getting another if you keep calling.

Red fox prime at different times here in Colorado. We have an elevation range of ten thousand feet. Fox will prime in the high country about the first of November. The low elevations will prime two or three weeks later. The low fox will probably be fair the first of November, but will not bring top price—maybe three-fourths of the price for high country reds. When I talk high country I am talking eight or nine thousand feet elevation.

If I am night calling for fox, particularly in heavy brush, I may use a shotgun. I don't use it if I am hunting alone, but if I have a partner one of us carries a rifle and the other a shotgun. I use a 10-gauge double barrel. I load up 3½-inch magnums up to 2¼ ounces. I will use Lubaloy BB's in one barrel and No. 4 buck in the other. If a fox comes in, he gets the BB's. A coyote or a cat takes the buck. I have double triggers so I can select the barrel I want.

Shoot at reds when they have been set up. If I have a critter coming I will stop him about sixty yards out if I am rifle hunting. Change the tone of the call or make a mouse squeak and they will stop to evaluate this new noise. Take them while they are standing. With a shotgun I pull them in to about thirty yards and will probably take them on the run.

I don't like full-jacketed bullets for predators. Barnes Bullet Company sells a bullet that is not quite fully jacketed and it does a good job. I went back to the softnose bullets because a full-jacketed bullet doesn't expand, and if you don't hit a critter in exactly the right place there is not enough damage to put him down. There are lots of hunters who are better shots than I and maybe they do all right with the FMJ's. Distance or wind drift may cause me to make a poor hit sometimes and I want a bullet that will put them down anywhere they are hit. I have hit a couple of critters in the hind legs and the softnose has opened up the big arteries so I have been able to skin them. With an FMJ the critter would have run off. I started shooting Hornaday SX bullets in 1968 and have used them ever since. I like that thin jacket. It really lets the bullet blow up.

I don't usually use camo either. I hunt in a pair of jeans and a dark-colored shirt. I have called coyotes and fox wearing bright orange. They are colorblind and don't seem to notice. Stay away from rayons and nylons though. The coyote or the fox will see the shine and spook. I don't use a face mask or facepaint either. I have muttonchop whiskers which hide part of my face. The rest of my face looks like sand with chicken tracks. I don't use masking scent as I feel that a coyote can smell a human through any masker. I hunt birds a lot and have seen my bird dogs get a dose of skunk square in the face and smell up a quail a half-hour later. If a dog can smell a quail through skunk musk, a coyote can smell a human through it. If it is really cold I wear a pullover face mask to keep my face warm. I wear white in snow country and a camo khaki other times. Sometimes I will use a decoy—a piece of rabbit fur on a stick out front. It gives the critter something to look at while I do the dirty deed.

The more people you take on a hunt the less chance for success you have. I like to hunt with a partner if he is a good hunter and if we work as a team. Two good hunters can probably take more fur than one. If I have more than two along it seems I always get a cougher or a sneezer or a guy who slams the door. I have called coyotes with sixty people watching on demonstrations. It's tough to do and I may have to make ten or twelve stands before I can get one in. I called a coyote at a demonstration near Pueblo, Colorado, once when I had sixty people scattered through the brush. The coyote came in to about two hundred yards, took a look at that crowded hillside, and almost broke his back changing directions.

I have had some strange things happen calling predators. I was laying on a cutbank calling once and had a buddy laying on another bank about thirty yards off. I called for twenty minutes and got no response. I heard a noise behind me and thought it was my buddy ready to leave. I looked back and saw a coyote smelling the soles of my boots.

Another time I was calling right at dark. I had called for twenty minutes and gave it up. I saw a coyote track in the last footprint I had made before I sat down. He must have been within feet of me and I never knew it.

The hardest fox I ever chased ended up getting a free pass. A friend and I made a daylight stand just after a snow. A big red came in fast and we missed the shot. We went after the fox tracking him in the soft snow. One of us would track and the other would drive the section roads to intercept, and then we would trade off. We followed that track until almost dark—almost ten hours of tracking. My buddy was a crack shot and he was tracking when he came to within sixty yards of that tired fox. The red was bedded in a snow bank ready to give up. My buddy took one look at him through the 6X scope and put the gun back on safe. The fox, he figured, had earned another chance.

12

The Mountain Lion

It was late in the year to be calling fur. Ordinarily I would not be perched atop the rubble of an ancient Indian village playing the dying-rabbit blues to a pair of state biologists and a pregnant coyote. The reason I found myself trying to do just that on that early June morning had to do with coyotes, antelope and a strong desire to get the stink of asphalt out of my nose for a few days. I was on Anderson Mesa, southeast of Flagstaff, Arizona, a place where gangs of hungry coyotes gobble the yearly crop of new antelope in a few short weeks beginning about the last week of May. The Arizona Game and Fish Department and the U.S. Fish and Wildlife Service move into the area about the same time as the coyotes and set steel traps across the mesa in an attempt to thin out the killers so that a few of the antelope fawn will have a decent chance at adulthood. They asked me to help sing in a few critters for the federal trappers. With proper instruction they hoped the trappers might use the varmint call as a supplement to their trapline. I was glad to oblige. I hooked up the trailer one night and made the forty-mile drive to the mesa camp at daylight the next morning.

The Indian ruin call was the third call we had made that morning. The first two had taken place looking out over the grassy meadows which interrupted the junipers on this part of the mesa. Both calls had been duds. We were after coyote and I terminated both calls after fifteen minutes of fruitless calling. The Indian ruin stand was in different country: To the east of us the hundred-foot depth of Kinnikinick Canyon. A mile down the canyon, Kinnikinick intersected another major canyon. The point of land bordered by Kinnikinick and Grapevine Canyons was a brushy juniper-forested plot of land that housed important summer populations of both deer and elk. The country where I made my call was more cat country than it was coyote country.

I leaned into the high-pitched Burnham tube, standing for the first series of squalls so that the invitation would reach out through the ground cover a bit better. When the first thirty-second series ended I settled into the brush and readied the .22-250. Behind me I heard either Don Neff or Norm Woolsey do the same. Both of the wardens carried rifles. If we saw any action we were sure to have enough firepower.

When I first saw a movement sixty yards out, I thought it might be a tawny coyote answering my invitation to share a rabbit breakfast. I changed my mind fast when a handsome mountain lion stepped into full view. He stood on the west side of the tree and the morning sun cast a long shadow that made the cat nearly invisible. The cat looked straight at my bush and I eased the barrel of the Ruger through the brush and centered the small middle X of the 6X Weaver just under the lion's throat. As I began to stroke at the Ruger's sensitive trigger I was struck by a horrible thought. Lion are classified as big game animals in Arizona and hunters must have a license and a lion tag. I had a license alright but was not completely sure about the tag; some years I buy them and some years I don't. With two game wardens watching, I figured, was no time to gamble. I eased off the trigger, laid the rifle down, and searched through my wallet three times for a lion tag. The bottom line was always the same; no tag. The lion hadn't moved. I belly-crawled to Norm and whispered the question, "Do you have a lion tag?" He did not. Neither did Don. The lion soon tired of waiting and slipped his long hundred-pound body back into the secrecy of the forest.

As we discussed the sighting and checked the fresh lion tracks around the junipers Don remembered he had heard a rock roll in the rubble behind him about two minutes into the call. We checked the area and discovered a second lion had crept to within twenty feet of Don. It was a larger lion from the look of the track. Two days later Herb Metzger, the owner of the Flying M Ranch, found a cow elk and her calf killed and partially eaten by a pair of lions. The kill was less than a mile from the ruins.

The mountain lion is considered uncommon throughout most of the United States. The large predator is fairly common in Arizona and several of the other western and southwestern states. Harley Shaw, a game biologist for the Arizona Game and Fish Department, estimates there are more than 2,000 adult breeders in the state. Harley has spent the past six years working exclusively with the Arizona lions. He has treed, tranquilized and radio collared a number of lions in habitat ranging from scrub to tall timber. Harley is one of the few researchers who is qualified to make educated guesses of lion numbers and habits. I talked to him at length to obtain information for this chapter. The information presented, it should be remembered, came from studies of lions in Arizona. Lions in other locations likely will modify their behavior to some degree.

Description

Felis concolor is Latin for cat of the same color. It likely refers to the fact that the coloration of the mountain lion is a smooth blending of a tawny brown. An adult lion will be about five feet from nose to the rear of the hips and the long slender tail will extend for another three feet. An adult will weigh from eighty to two hundred pounds, with the male being larger than the female. Bill Powers, a northern Arizona hunter, took a male lion during the winter of 1979-80 that weighed 175 pounds. Harley Shaw treed and tranquilized another tom the same winter that scaled 160 pounds. Both cats came off the North Kaibab. Those are the two largest lions Shaw has encountered in his six-year study.

Lion kittens are spotted and might be confused with young bobcats if it were not for the long tail. The head and ears of the lion appear small when compared to the lithe and muscular body. The lion has large feet with razor-sharp, retractable claws. The paw print is similar to bobcat except it is much larger. A big dog track can be mistaken for a lion track if it is indistinct, but clear tracks will show claw marks for the dog and none for the lion. A clear lion track will show a large pad with four toes.

Habitat

Most of the current lion population is confined to the western United States, all of Mexico, and parts of Canada. Other states have minor populations with many eastern and some southern states reporting increased lion sightings in recent years. It is not known if the populations are actually increasing or if more sophisticated techniques are presenting a more efficient census.

Western lions seem to prefer rimrock country in the Transition Life Zone (6,500-8,000 feet), but they are commonly found from sea level to above the timberline. The Transition Life Zone the lion favors is characterized by the ponderosa pine tree. Ponderosa forests interrupted by steep canyons and rocky rims would be the habitat most likely to house lion.

Food

The main business of the lion is hunting deer, and he will go wherever they are. If, for instance, the deer retreat to lower elevations ahead of the winter snows, the lion will follow. Shaw estimates that lion make a major kill every eight days

This night feeding deer would be easy prey for a hungry lion. The big cat would use the cover of the night to stalk as close as possible. The last few feet would be covered in a blurring burst of speed. *Photo Gerry Blair.*

and that kill is usually a deer. If deer is not available the kill might be an elk, a burro, or a young domestic beef. Cattle depredation seems to be greatest in the states of Arizona, New Mexico and Texas, and in areas where calves are born in lion habitat. The problem is compounded if deer densities are low. In Arizona, ninety-three percent of cattle kills found were animals under a year old.

The lion is also an eater of mutton. Sheep kills occur mostly in the summer as sheep are usually wintered away from lion habitat. The lion seems to prefer lamb if it is available but will take adult sheep readily. One lion may kill more than a dozen sheep from a single bedground, but only one or two normally are eaten. The lion may return on subsequent nights to feed on the dead sheep. If live sheep are available he will make a fresh kill and ignore the day-old carcasses.

One of the fifteen recognized subspecies of lion is called *hippolestes*, which is Greek for "horse thief." Modern lions are not important predators of the horse, but they did kill many colts in the early days when the mares were allowed to foal in lion country. Most ranches now move their brood mares away from lion habitat as foaling season approaches.

The lion is an important predator of many big game animals. All ages of deer are taken although fawns seem to be preferred during the season. Bucks seem to be selected during the rut and immediately after fall hunts. Kills at other times of the year seem to reflect the percentage of animals in the herd makeup.

Elk are common prey of the mountain lion, but they try to avoid mature bulls and concentrate on fawns when possible. Lion-killed big-horn sheep and antelope are comparatively rare but have been documented. Recent data from the Three Bar Study indicate that the lion is a frequent predator of the peccary or javelina. Smaller prey, such as rabbits and rodents, are sometimes taken by the lion, but no evidence has been found to indicate the lion depends on these species to any great degree.

The Kill

Recent advances in radio telemetry have provided the game biologist with new insight into lion behavior. Radio transmitting collars have led researchers to fresh lion kills and they have been able to document much new information. It is a fallacy, Shaw believes, that the lion will take only the old and the sick in his search for food. Lions in the Shaw study take whatever critter they have the best shots at. On many occasions his supper may be the herd buck. The next critter may be a pregnant doe; next week it will be newborn twin fawns. The argument advanced by self-styled preservationists that the lion maintains a healthy herd by weeding out the sick and the weak is like most of their other "facts"—so much hogwash.

Young burros are a lion delicacy. I once snuck up on a lion that was sneaking up on a herd of burros. I did the donkeys a favor and took the cat home with me. *Photo Gerry Blair.*

The lion makes his kill in about the same way a bobcat makes his: He sights his quarry and immediately begins a slow and stealthy stalk. If the intended victim is a feeding mule deer, the lion will advance only when the deer's head is down. When the head comes up the lion turns to stone; the head goes down and the lion takes a few more stealthy steps. When he is a bound or two away, the lion makes his move. He turns into a blurred streak of tawny lightning as he leaps atop the frightened deer's back. Razor sharp talons dig into the shoulders. The huge canines bite into the deer's neck muscles searching for the backbone. If the deer is not large it goes to the ground, but a larger animal might run a short way, frantically trying to remove the rider by scraping against low limbs. But this does not often work and the lion usually wins.

On large kills the lion will eat his fill and cover the remaining carcass with dirt and debris. He will then return to the kill nightly to eat his fill, and he will keep coming back until the meat is completely consumed or it taints. On each visit he uncovers the groceries and drags the carcass a hundred feet or so before dining. There are usually drag marks which can lead an observant hunter to the buried kill. A series of varmint calls in the surrounding area will almost surely produce action. If the weather is cold, the lion may feed from a large kill for more than two weeks. One lion in an Idaho study fed from an elk carcass for nineteen days. The lion will not go far from the carcass; he will likely be within one mile and probably much closer.

The lion eats fawn in the summer because they are easily killed. They have the strength and skill to take the biggest bucks and often do. *Photo Gerry Blair.*

Lion are most likely to kill elk when they are winter-weak and slowed by heavy snow. Big bulls are taken as readily as other elk. *Photo Montana Department of Highways.*

Biologists have established that lion are most likely to take adult healthy deer. The claim of "preservationists" that the lion take only the weak and sick is hogwash. *Photo Gerry Blair.*

Mating

Adult male lions are loners. They get together with the ladies during mating but are invited to leave when the act is finished. Like bobcats, they caterwaul, but of course they are much louder. The young may be born at any time of the year but it is most likely to be summer, and only one litter is born every two or three years. The average litter numbers three. Females will use a natural cave in a rimrock or other cavities. They probably do not return to the same den the following year, although it is likely they will return to the same general area. The cubs will be almost totally dependent on the mother for the first year, but by the middle of the second year they will show signs of independence and will probably strike out on their own by the end of that year.

The Pecking Order

The lion is territorial. Adult lions which have their own territories are the top of the pecking order. These are usually the largest and most experienced lions and may be of either sex. On the Spider Ranch study area near Prescott, Arizona, lions used their total territory with no seasonal change. Lions on the North Kaibab Study Area, which is at a considerably higher elevation, seem to have winter and summer territories which are some distance apart. Male and female lions seem to associate only at breeding time. They have been known to occasionally share kills but the reason for this association is not known. Male lions will have home areas which vary in size. Spider Ranch lions (chaparral vegetation) averaged about fifty-nine square miles. Female lions on the same study area had home areas which ranged from ten square miles to almost seventy square miles.

Immature lions are offspring of resident adults and remain with the female. They will strike out on their own at about the end of the second year, and it is not uncommon for litter mates to remain together after the separation. Unestablished lions are critters that have left the female and have not found a home territory. They will move into an area, stay a few days, and move on.

A lion travelling after a fresh snow leaves distinctive tracks. Note the drag marks in between paw prints. Many hunters scout for fresh sign after a snow and make their call in that area. *Photo Colorado Game and Fish.*

Lion Sign

Large dogs are usually the only animals that leave tracks as large as a lion's. A dog track will differ from a lion track in a number of ways. First of all, the lion heel pad is divided into three distinct lobes at the rear and it is also much broader and flatter than the heel pad of a dog. The presence of claw marks can also be used to distinguish between the track of a lion and a dog. Lion claws are retractable and do not usually show in the track but lion in a hurry may show indistinct claw marks. Not all dog tracks will show the claw marks; some dogs will travel on hard ground without showing distinct claw marks.

A lion is also a more efficient traveler than either a dog or a coyote. Unless he is pursued or is in close pursuit of groceries, a lion will not move faster than a deliberate walk. They set their feet firmly and leave no disturbance outside the track, but they may leave drag marks between tracks in deep snow. If they are moving on level ground in a straight line, the rear feet of the lion will print partially or totally over the track left by the front foot. Double prints or the print of only the hind foot are often seen. Members of the dog family usually travel at a trot and dirt and gravel around the imprint is usually disturbed. They also frequently move with the body at a slight angle to the line of travel causing an offset in the front and hind feet and preventing overlap.

Scratches

Lion scratches may be found along rims, along major drainages used as travelling routes, and in saddles. The scratches are made by mature males and are used as a territorial marking. They are likely to occur more frequently where the home range of two adult males overlap. The scratch will be a series of long furrows in the ground and may be accompanied by dung or urine.

Dung Heaps

Dung heaps may be made by a male or female lion. Most merely represent a site where fecal material is buried, but some occur near kills and may serve as an aid in relocating the kill site. Droppings may be left in random patterns all through a lion's travels.

Mounds

Lion mounds are probably made by females. They are rare and may have something to do with the presence of a young litter. These mounds will be four or five feet in diameter and will be composed of pine needles or other debris. They somewhat resemble a buried kill but contain no animal remains.

Kill Sites

The cats and the grizzly bear are the only two United States predators that cover their kills but an uncovered kill does not necessarily rule out the lion. Deer and calf kills are sometimes left uncovered. In multiple kills, as in sheep herds, one, two, or none of the kills may be covered. Most of the time though, some attempt at covering is made. If the kill is on bare hard ground there will be obvious scratching and scrapings indicating an attempt to cover. If these efforts are not successful the lion will often drag the carcass to a tree or bush and bury it. If the kill is more than one day old, several burial sites likely will be found with drag marks indicating the location of each site.

As a general rule the paunch and its contents will remain buried at the first site. Lions mostly enter the body just behind the ribs, sometimes breaking them as they enter. The carcass is eviscerated and the heart, liver and lungs are consumed. They almost never eat the paunch. The lion goes from the body cavity to the hams and usually feeds from the inside out.

Shaw's blue tick hounds have discovered a yearling steer killed and covered by a mountain lion. In cold weather the lion will return to these kills until they are consumed. A kill site is an excellent place for a call. *Photo Harley Shaw.*

Many hunters miss seeing nearby lions. The cats come quietly and will use every scrap of cover. *Photo Harley Shaw, Arizona Game Department.*

Calling Lions

The relative scarcity of lions and the wide-ranging nature of the critter make it tough for a caller. Most call-killed lions are taken as a bonus. The caller is usually interested in bobcat, fox or coyote and fools the lion by accident. Ray Parent of Flagstaff shot and killed a mountain lion while on a varmint hunt north of Seligman, Arizona. Dave Niehuis of Phoenix killed a called lion while hunting the Fort Apache Indian Reservation near Whiteriver. Bob Lake of Tempe, Arizona, fooled a hungry lion by clucking for turkey south of Happy Jack. The hungry critter had stalked to within fifty feet of the camouflaged hunter when a hunting buddy gave it a load of chilled fours in the head. The big cat died instantly. I could have killed a called lion if I had had the foresight to spend a buck for a lion tag.

I am convinced that a dedicated caller could call and kill a lion if he was willing to work at it. The first step would be to locate lion country. I would think that Arizona, New Mexico, Utah or Colorado would be good bets. They are all states with healthy mountain lion populations. State Game Departments might provide information on lion concentrations. The U.S. Fish and Wildlife Service might also be helpful and so would associations of sheep and cattle ranchers. I would check prominent saddles and rims for lion sign. If I could find a fresh kill I would consider myself extremely fortunate. Although any call could call lion I believe that I would choose a call that has the deeper, coarser tones, maybe the Circe Jackrabbit Model. A lion might come more eagerly if he thought the walk would produce a meal that would come close to filling him. I would call near the rims and rocky canyons, places that a lion would likely spend the day. I would choose my stand for vision and comfort and I would stay at least an hour on each stand, and if my heart was set on lion I would not shoot the other critters that responded to the call.

Another technique—one frequently used by dog hunters—is to patrol primitive roads after a fresh snow searching for lion tracks. When tracks are found I would follow them, pausing frequently to make a call.

Lion Guns

Any gun that will take a deer should take a lion. The body weight range is similar—about one hundred to two hundred pounds. I normally carry a hot loaded .22-250 on my varmint hunts and would not hesitate to take a lion with it. I would hesitate to move much lower than the .22-250, although the .222 magnum would likely do the job if the range was not extreme. I know that many lions are killed with handguns. These lions, however, are usually treed animals and are headshot at close range. That is a different matter than shooting a called lion that skulks in the brush a hundred yards out.

Second Opinion

Tom Morton has been calling for twenty-five years and has called every state west of the Mississippi. He also has called for wolves in Alaska and for jaguar in Mexico. Tom is one of the best callers in the country. He won a world calling championship in 1967.

Tom Morton
I think lions are like other cats in that you call in two for every one you see. Half the lions I have called came as a surprise. Most callers probably get their lion this way. I have learned certain techniques that work well

on lion, and I am certain that I could leave right now to hunt a lion and could have one out front begging for the rabbit in two days. I would spend the first day scouting for fresh lion sign. I would probably hunt the rugged Superstition Mountain Range in central Arizona. It has that combination of high desert, rough rocky canyons and good deer numbers. I would make a check of all of the water holes looking for fresh lion sign — either tracks or scat. If I found fresh sign I would make a call. If I was really lucky I might find a fresh kill. A lion usually won't eat a major kill such as a deer or a cow in one night. They pull the carcass into a shady area and cover it with sticks and leaves, and then they will hole up in the area and feed on the carcass until it is gone or it taints. I have called over kills twice and have called lions both times. I never got either of them though because it was really brushy country and I just glimpsed them in heavy brush.

I called my first lion not far from the mining town of Ray, Arizona, where I grew up. I was calling Little Willie Wash, a brushy broken-up piece of country. I had been on the stand for twenty minutes and hadn't seen a thing. I had called three gray fox at previous stands and hoped I might call another here. I was about ready to give up on the stand when I caught a flash of movement in the brush — just a hint of movement, really, and I couldn't be sure what it was. I guessed it might be another fox. I quit blowing the tube and started lip squeaking. The animal was only eighty yards out but it was so brushy I couldn't see it. I kept squeaking, sucking on the back of my hand, and I saw a movement again. I still couldn't tell what it was. I convinced myself it was a call-wise fox and kept trying. I was slobbering on the back of my hand when the critter moved through a small opening. It was fast, like the blink of an eye, and I still couldn't be sure what it was. I knew it wasn't a fox because it was too big. Maybe it was a young deer, I thought. I had never called a mountain lion and it didn't even cross my mind it might be a lion. Half an hour later, the cat stepped into the open and I about fell over. It was a mature tom, maybe a hundred pounds, and he was looking right at me forty yards out. I was using a .270 with a Leupold variable and I made short work of the cat. Fur wasn't worth anything in those days and I did a lot of hunting with the .270. I was using a Weems call at the time. Up to 1965 that's all I used. About 1965 I tried a Circe Long Range tube and have used it mostly every since. I used the Circe in 1967 when I won the world's championship. But I still have two Weems walnut tubes that were made for me by Bowen Weems. I still use them once in a while.

If I am calling strictly for cats I begin the stand blowing as hard as I can for fifteen or twenty seconds. I tune a jackrabbit reed so that it produces a guttural sound that approaches the death scream of a deer. Get the reed open as much as you can to get the low sounds but don't open it too wide or you will split the reed on the first series. I think it is important to tune the reed for lion as you want them to think the critter in trouble is big enough to be worth the walk. Tuning the reed gives your call a little different sound than similarly reeded calls and that helps too.

Make your first series of calls as loud as you can and put blood on every note. Some good callers I know blow soft for the first couple of minutes because they are afraid of scaring off close critters. Both Jim Dougherty and Bill Dudley blew that way and they both did great. I blow loud straight through and that works for me. After the first fifteen-second series I pause for a full minute. To me, that's the secret; the pauses between the calls. When the minute is up, blow another fifteen-second series and pause for another minute. Keep up this call-pause ratio until you are ready to quit the stand. Most callers quit too soon on lion. A lot of them probably walk away with a lion watching them a hundred yards out. If I am in good lion country and have seen sign I don't hesitate to call an hour. I spent two hours on one stand because I knew the lion was out there. I was calling a rocky rim in the Superstitions and caught just a glimpse of the cat skylined for a second on a ridge a couple of hundred yards out. I never saw that lion again for almost an hour but I kept calling and lip squeaking. Finally the lion stepped into the open thirty-five feet away. It was a young female and I put her away with the .270.

I like a canyon below me when I make a stand for lion. I back away from the canyon lip about thirty yards. There is no way that cat can stay below the lip and see me. They have to come over the top to see what is making all the racket and it gives me a good chance. Most of the time the cat will jump suddenly into view up out of the canyon. One second there is nothing and the next second you have a lion sizing you up for supper.

I killed a big lion under the Payson Rim (Mogollon Rim) in 1967. A rancher found where a lion had killed one of his whiteface and covered it with debris. A local man set a couple of traps but didn't get the lion. The rancher called me and asked me to try and call the lion. The kill was three or four days old by this time. I walked into the kill in the dark. I guess I got set up about an hour before daylight. It is against the law to shoot at night in Arizona so I sat and waited for dawn. That made it about right because it gave the forest a chance to forget I was there. As soon as it got light enough to see, I started the call. I was using a Circe Long Range with one of the modified jackrabbit reeds. I used the sequence calls I always use on cats. Thirty-five minutes into the call I saw him coming. He came different than most cats, moving at a fast trot and coming straight at me. I guess because he had food there he behaved differently. He trotted up to the carcass and I was hidden about thirty-five yards away. I shot him through the shoulder with a .222. He was a big lion; weighed a hundred and fifty pounds and measured nine feet from tip of nose to tip of tail. That was the only lion I ever had mounted.

Don't expect to call more than one lion to a stand. They run alone most of the time. I did call a female and a cub to one stand but that was the only lion double I ever called. It was in the Superstitions again and I was calling over a fresh track at a waterhole. They came in fast for lion – about ten minutes – and I shot them both.

The easiest time to call lion is in the spring when the cubs are born. The females are gaunt and hungry and they come to every call they hear.

I don't call then myself, as you only get small lion, females and cubs. Most of the lion I have shot have been toms – about ninety percent. Lions will come in any weather condition except bad wind. Wind can be bad two ways: If there is too much wind you can't get your sound out at all; if it is dead calm it is almost as bad because the sound seems to float and not carry. A four- or five-mile-an-hour wind is just right. Like other critters, a lion will get serious about feeding just before a major storm hits. They seem to know that bad weather is on the way and want to hole up with a full belly. They also feed hard after a storm ends, particularly if it is a major storm. They may hole up for several days waiting for the storm to end and they are super hungry when it ends.

I don't use a masking scent such as skunk musk. I will give you a trade secret on calling cats. Put a little squirt of Ben-Gay on the toe of each boot. It has an oil of wintergreen in it that is attractive to cats. I guess that pure oil of wintergreen would do just as good.

I do all of my cat calling from a blind. I took a twelve foot piece of thirty-six-inch chicken wire and covered it with camo netting. It folds up and only weighs about 1½ pounds and is just big enough for two men. I also carry a little stool to sit on. You have to be comfortable if you are going to be at a stand for an hour without squirming. Your face is the only thing visible above the blind. I use camo face net with places cut out for the eyes and the ends hanging clear down around my shoulders.

The best time to call any kind of cat is at night. I don't think it makes much difference on cats if there is a full moon or if it's pitch black. If I am night calling, I usually set up just after dark. The cat has been holed up all day and is just starting to hunt. If you wait too late he may have already made a kill and be reluctant to come to a call. The best time to make day calls is right at sunup. I don't like late afternoon calls for cats. It takes them so long to come in that it may be after dark before they show. In states where night hunting is unlawful you are out of luck.

Most callers lose their lion because they don't have the patience to play the lion's game. I have watched several lion come from a good distance off, one of which was the ridge lion I have already mentioned. Another time I was calling the high desert when I saw a flash of movement two hundred yards out. It was a lion. He came about ten yards to the call and laid down under a bush. I kept blowing and finally got him on his feet again. He came another ten yards and sat down. I started lip squeaking and got him up. It was one step at a time from then on. The lion came in like he was on a stalk; I almost sucked a hole in the back of my hand from lip squeaking. The lion finally stopped forty yards out and I could tell he was getting edgy and starting to circle. Whenever a cat, or any critter, does this, it is time to take him because he won't be around long. I shot him with the .270. He was a tom, about seventy pounds, just an average lion. It had taken him forty minutes to cover two hundred yards.

Almost everybody knows that lion are territorial and they run patterns. I ran into a prospector in the Superstitions once who told me lions in that country run seven-day patterns. According to the Lost Dutch-man Mine hunter if you saw a lion at a certain place and came back seven days later you would see him in the same place. I jumped a lion deer hunting once and couldn't call him back. I went back the next couple days and tried again at different parts of that area. No luck. Then I remembered what the miner had said about seven-day patterns and tried to go back a week after I had seen the lion but I couldn't make it. I waited another seven days and went back and made a call. This was fourteen days after I had seen the cat originally. I called the critter in and shot it. I also did the same thing on another lion. I know that two times does not make it definite, but I think that old prospector may have known what he was talking about.

There are a lot more lion in the West than most people know about. If you want to kill a lion you have to hunt in the places where the deer winter. Check for lion tracks when you deer hunt or when you are varmint calling. If you find fresh sign you should make your stand a little higher than most of the country around you. This will let you see better. Blow fifteen seconds and wait for a full minute. Most of all, don't get in a hurry. Call for at least an hour. You will be surprised at the number of lions you will attract.

13

The Bear

We hadn't seen the bear in ten hours and it didn't seem likely he would make it to us before dark. The sun slid behind the jagged peaks of the Mazatzal Mountains west of us and I knew we had one or maybe two hours before it got dead dark. We were three miles from the truck and ten miles from camp. Time was running out and that damn lazy bear was bedded down somewhere on the ridge above us snoring his hairy head off. Mike Mell took the varmint call from his shirt pocket and knocked the reed free of lint. "This might send him running the other way," he whispered, "but we're running out of time. Let's gamble." I scrunched deeper into the limbs of the juniper and listened to the familiar notes of the dying rabbit blues. It wouldn't take us long to find out if this bear was one of the fifty percent that would come to a predator call. He might come scooting down the mountain intent on a rabbit supper or he might move out for the next county. We would soon know.

Mike had glassed up the bear at daylight that morning. The critter was three miles off munching on a mess of prickly pear. He showed up as a fuzzy black speck in the 20x eyepiece of Mike's spotting scope. Even at that early hour in October the heat waves caused distortion. We couldn't be sure it was a bear at that distance. The new sun cast long black shadows on the west side of the cactus clumps. Was it really a bear or just another shadow? The spot detached itself from the cactus clump and walked to another twenty feet away. Hell, it *was* a bear. We watched the dancing speck for almost an hour. Finally the bear left the cactus patch and ambled out of sight over a low ridge. "He is going off to bed," Mike predicted. "Let's surprise him when he comes back for supper." I didn't argue. Mike, I knew, had guided friends to almost two dozen bear in the past five years.

We took our gear back to camp and ate a hurried breakfast. When it was

Mike Mell with the cactus-eating bear we called from the brush. The critter was a sow that weighed 175 pounds. *Photo Gerry Blair.*

down we drove the truck back to the scanning point and saddled up. I took my Ruger .25-06, a flashlight and a canteen of water. Mike took water and a half dozen sandwiches. We cut across the high desert, setting a straight course for the distant saddle where we had last seen the bear.

We reached the saddle early in the afternoon and found a point above it where we could hide and not be seen. Like most other critters bear are more or less predictable in their habits. The bear had left a good supply of sweet and juicy prickly pear when he went off to bed. The first thing he would do when he woke up would be to return to this generous feast. The pears were a dark purple and were as large as avocados. We were both sure he would be back. The wind was in our face and we knew we hadn't been winded. If the wind changed slightly we hoped the can of skunk musk Mike carried around his waist would overpower the odor of two sweaty hunters.

Five minutes after Mike started blowing, a pair of javelina showed up on a ridge a hundred feet away. Mike stopped blowing. The pigs got bored and left. We didn't need two scared javelina running through the bear's bedroom. More

Mike Mell and a hunter check out a brushy canyon. Mike called a big red out of the canyon that may have weighed 400 pounds. *Photo Gerry Blair.*

blowing brought in a scrawny-looking coyote. He was obviously the young of the year as his pelt was dull and thin. His tail looked like a piece of one-inch rope. He sure didn't know anything about predator calls. He played around for several minutes coming closer every time Mike blew a series. When he stopped thirty feet out, I lobbed a fist-sized chunk of rock his way. The casual shot almost connected, hitting the ground a few feet away from the startled teenager. The coyote tucked his scrawny rope between his legs and ran off like a whipped hound. Mike and I were giggling so hard we almost didn't see the bear.

He was on ridgetop five hundred yards above. He was backed up to a big round rock when we first saw him. He was looking our way. Mike blew again, lower this time. The bear moved away from the rock and headed our way. He was in no hurry but he was coming in the right direction. Mike kept blowing, coaxing him in. When he stopped a hundred feet out Mike nodded for me to shoot. The 100-grainer took him in the ribs just behind the shoulder. I heard the diaphragm break with an encouraging thump. The bear went down bawling, got up, and ran about eighty yards. I was fighting my way out of the brush cranking another chance into the chamber of the Model 77. Before I could shoot the bear went down and stayed down. He was dead when we walked to him.

The he, it turned out, was a she; a young sow maybe five years old. We guessed her to be about 225 pounds on the hoof. We then subtracted fifty pounds to compensate for hunter excitement. Looking back, a hundred and seventy five pounds was about right. We did the dirty work and packed out by flashlight. Mike carried the bear on a packframe while I walked ahead on snake patrol. It was near midnight when we made the truck.

Range

Black bear are found in good numbers through most of Alaska and Canada. They inhabit mountainous areas in most of the continental United States as well as the swamps of many of the Gulf States. North central Mexico has a fair number. Most states, in my opinion, have no idea of the number of bear they host. Arizona didn't until the game department assigned wildlife biologist Al LeCount to a bear project.

Al LeCount and his aides caught bear using foot snares. When the bears were tranquilized, Al fitted compact radio transmitter collars around their necks. Only adults were collared because if the collar was placed on a sub-adult he would likely choke as his neck grew. The transmitter told Al the movements of the individual and the size of his home territory.

Arizona biologists had a number of surprises as a result of Al's seven-year study. They were initially surprised at the number of bear ranging in the study area. The country was mostly chaparral—heavy brush more than stirrup-high to a man on horseback. Most of the study took place on the north side of the Mazatzal Mountains. Al established that the brushy country contained a bear per square mile. Only in one other part of the United States has such a high bear density been established and that is in the rain forests along the coast in Washington State.

Studies have shown that certain areas of Arizona contain a bear a square mile. This high country bear will need to travel farther to eat and will have a larger range. *Photo U.S. Fish & Wildlife Service.*

The chaparral offers everything the bear needs to exist: Thick high brush to hide his movements; a primitive area with few roads that keep out most humans; plenty of fruits to keep his big belly full; and an almost complete lack of hunting pressure from houndsmen. The high brush is hard on dogs and horses. The bear knows his territory and can easily confuse even the most experienced hound. If the bear is bayed the men are usually too far behind to take advantage. Before they arrive at the "tree," the bear has broken through the dogs and the chase is renewed.

A few bear are taken from the chaparral every year. Patient hunters find a high point and glass the prickly pear slopes to catch a late feeder. The glassing is done early in the morning before the bear beds for the day. Early morning glassing also minimizes the heat distortion caused by the sun. The bear leave the chaparral in late September and early October to harvest the prickly pear crop. When the pears drop—usually in mid-October—the bears leave the cactus and return to the brush.

Al LeCount believes that varmint calling is the most productive way to hunt the bear when they are in the chaparral. I agree with him. Later in this chapter is an interview with Mike Mell who shares his technique for bear hunting.

Black bears, it should be noted, do not live only in the Arizona chaparral. They are found at almost every elevation in the states and in similar areas in other states. The highest bear concentration may be the chaparral but that is only conjecture at this point. Al LeCount is just starting a bear study in the high country, and when that study is finished, we all might be surprised at the number of bear there.

Territories

The Mazatzal bears have territories of approximately one square mile. Between June of 1973 and September of 1976, Al LeCount snared forty-four bears. About half were males and half were females. The territorial boundaries were so precise that Al was able to predict the presence of an untrapped bear by finding the territorial gaps on his project map. He once trapped for forty-four days to catch a bear he had never seen. He knew the bear existed because there was an empty territory on his map, and the size of the territory told him it was a female. He approached his snare on the forty-fourth day. The loud growling and breaking of limbs told him he had won. She was a fine big sow with a glossy black coat.

Territorial bear are the biggest bear and are the toughest to hunt. Young bear are not allowed to hang around when they get to be about two years old.

Both the San Carlos and Fort Apache Indian Reservations have good bear populations. Black River, a wilderness stream that divides the reservations, has high numbers. *Photo Arizona Game and Fish Department.*

Momma is tired of fooling with them and is ready to mate again. If they are hard-headed about taking a trip they will likely be killed. So much for the old wives' tale that man is the only critter that kills his own kind. These young bear – the wanderers – are most likely to blunder into a deer hunter and be bagged. They are also the bear that cause trouble at campgrounds. These bear without a country are doomed to wander the wastelands until they find an empty territory or grow big enough to boot another bear off his piece of real estate.

Prickly pears are a favorite bear food in the Southwest. Some years the cactus has bumper crops and the bears come into the low country to build fat. *Photo Gerry Blair.*

Bear Numbers

Most states have no good idea of their bear population. Even Arizona, with LeCount's fine study, can only guess at the state population. A recent Game and Fish Department estimate puts the state total at 2,000 to 3,000 bear on non-Indian lands. Much of the state, it should be noted, is Indian reservation. Much of the reservation land is prime bear country. The San Carlos Apache Indian Reservation has a lot of bear. So does the neighboring Fort Apache Reservation. The Navajo and the Hualapai reservations have smaller numbers. It would not surprise me if the Indian reservation population equaled the game department estimate for non-Indian lands. That would produce an estimate of 4,000 to 7,000 bear in the state.

Game department figures for the number of bear killed in the state during 1979 are more precise. Department figures show 256 bear were killed in Arizona during the calendar year. Most of these were taken by hunters who were afield after other game. Hunters with hounds took a significant amount of the total also. It is encouraging to note that the number of varmint-called bear is increasing. The game department figures that predator calls accounted for thirty bear.

Bear Diet

Like most other predators the bear is not fussy about what he eats. He will kill and eat livestock under certain conditions. The kills are mostly young calves who have been freshly branded. The sight of a frisky calf and the smell of burned hair is a combination few bear can resist.

The bear also eats carrion. Livestock that die of natural causes, or those killed by predators such as the mountain lion, often end up in a bear's belly. Bear are sometimes killed as stock killers because a rancher has found a bear's tracks around a half-eaten whiteface. Most of the time it is a bum rap. The bear probably are guilty of nothing more serious than stealing a buzzard's lunch.

The main meal of the bear is berries, fruits and nuts. The prickly pear and other cactus fruit provide a sweet and nourishing staple in the fall of the year. A bear will also eat acorns. They have been known to tear a stout limb from an oak tree to get at a new crop of acorns. The bear also eats berries. Manzanita and juniper berries are a staple in the Southwest. He supplements this vegetarian diet with insects. He will travel down a ridge overturning every large rock he can handle. Ants, grubs and beetles make a run for it as soon as the rock starts moving but the bear's sticky tongue laps them up. Bear will also tear into a rotten log with a gusto that is a marvel to behold. Again, they are hunting ants and other insects. Bears eat garbage and fish where it is available. They are opportunists and will take what the country has to offer.

Bear are not fussy eaters. This Alaskan Black tears into a rotten log to get at the insects inside. *Photo U.S. Forest Service.*

All black bear are not black. This brown or "cinnamon bear" is a color phase of the black and may have a littermate that was totally black. *Photo U.S. Fish & Wildlife Service.*

Description

Black bear are not always black. Like some other animals the critter has color phases that may range from light blonde to jet black and some have been sighted that were piebald. Cubs from the same litter may show the entire spectrum of color. Mike Mell once called a sow bear that was trailed by a pair of two-year-old cubs. One was jet black and the other was a handsome roan.

Black bear will vary greatly in size. An adult female will average about 150 pounds here in Arizona; males will be larger. Ed Scarla of Phoenix killed a huge boar near Young in 1959 that weighed 520 pounds with the intestines removed. Bear usually lose about fifteen percent of their body weight when they are field dressed. Scarla's bear probably weighed close to 600 pounds live weight. Big males in other parts of the country have been known to reach 700 pounds, but any black bear over 350 pounds has to be considered large.

A bear on four feet is not tall, maybe three feet at the shoulder. If he stands on his hind legs, as they sometimes do, he may be well over six feet tall. Most hunters, according to LeCount, tend to overestimate the size and weight of the bear they see or kill. (So, what else is new?) LeCount has designed a measurement system that allows a hunter in the field to closely estimate the weight of his bear. There is a close correlation between the circumference of a bear's chest and his body weight. Carry a small tape measure on your next bear hunt and use it to measure the chest circumference immediately behind the front legs. If the circumference is thirty inches the bear will weigh about a hundred pounds. Sorry, that is all. Forty inches will equal two hundred pounds. Fifty inches will indicate you have bagged a whopper, maybe close to four hundred pounds. If the tape reads sixty inches, check to see if the critter has horns. You may have shot a Black Angus bull by mistake.

Recognizing a Trophy

Most hunters have never seen a bear in the wild and may have trouble in determining if the first one they see is a good trophy. Boone and Crockett and most state lists rate bear by the way they score on two measurements of the skull. The length of the skull is added to the width of the skull to get the total score. The current world's record measures $13^{11}/_{16}$ inches long and $8^{11}/_{16}$ inches wide for a score of $22^{3}/_{8}$ inches. A bear skull must measure more than 21 points to be listed in Boone and Crockett.

Here is a simple way to estimate bear size. A bear's ears are five inches long. This is true if he is a year old or ten years old. If the ears are quite noticeable on the bear you see, they are large in relation to his head and you are likely looking at a young bear. If the nose is also pointed, like a coyote, you can be sure of it. A young bear's ears will also be set close together. As he gets older his skull widens and the ears are separated. They will also be less conspicuous. The heads on bigger bear will take on a triangular shape. A bear with the triangle-shaped head, wide-spread ears, and small ears in relation to the head is an adult bear that will likely weigh more than three hundred pounds.

Some idea of bear size can be determined from an examination of the track. A front foot track that measures more than $4^{1}/_{4}$ inches from heel to toe and more than $4^{1}/_{4}$ inches wide probably belongs to an adult male. A front foot track less than $4^{1}/_{4}$ inches long or wide is probably made by an adult female or a young male. A hind foot track that measures more than $7^{1}/_{2}$ inches long and more than four inches wide is likely the track of an adult male. Smaller hindfoot tracks would probably be either an adult female or a sub-adult. A front foot track which measures more than 5½ inches long or wide, or a hind foot track that is more than nine inches long or five inches wide was likely made by a big bear, probably over 350 pounds.

Bear Sign

The most unusual bear sign I ever saw was in the Coconino National Forest on the east side of Leonard Canyon. The forest service had erected a stained redwood sign which indicated the number of the primitive road I was on. This sign had been in one hell of a fight with a bear and had gotten the worst of the fracas. The critter had chewed away most of the top part of the sign and had clawed and mauled the four-inch-square post.

But other bear sign may be less obvious. The evidence most hunters see and recognize is droppings. The scat is usually loose with no discernable form—a dishpan-sized pile of pulverized animal and vegetable material. The droppings will give a clue on what the bear had for supper. A smart hunter can figure out where the bear goes for lunch if the droppings are fresh. Juniper berry seeds in the scat indicate the bear spends his nights in the junipers chowing down on the nut-flavored berries. If the droppings are found away from the junipers you may assume the critter was on his way from his feeding grounds to his bed grounds when he answered Nature's call. Other material noticed in the scat might be manzanita berries, acorn hulls, prickly pear seeds and peelings, and animal hair. The hair likely will indicate the bear is feeding on a piece of carrion. Droppings from a carrion-eating bear are darker than other droppings and will have the consistency of a thin pudding. Hair, and sometimes bone, will be visible.

If you discover droppings which indicate the bear is feeding on prickly pear fruit and the pears are still on the cactus you can bet the critter is still close. He is not apt to leave the area until cold weather in late October causes the fruit to fall to the ground. Even then he may stick around for a week or so feeding on the fruit until it has rotted away. The same thing goes for acorns and berries.

Freshness of bear scat can be estimated with a fair degree of accuracy. If the scat has been rained on and you know the last time it rained you can make a good guess. If there has been no rain, examine the offal for moisture. Bear scat holds a lot of water when it is fresh. If there is surface moisture you can be sure the sign is fresh and it might be a good idea to look over your shoulder to see if anything is creeping up on you. If the droppings are crusted on the surface but moist just below the crust the deposit was probably made within the past 24 hours. If it is completely dry with no moisture in evidence, it is likely days or weeks old.

Rear bear tracks are shaped a bit like the human foot. The hind feet are considerably larger than the front. The heel and ball of the foot will be fronted by five toes. If the track is in deep dust, mud or snow the claws will show and sometimes the hair.

Look for bear tracks along the muddy banks of waterways, along the dust of little-used roads and along well-defined game trails leading in and out of canyons. A fresh track will show sharp edges and a clear imprint. Bear are plantigrade and put their entire weight on all of the foot. This well-defined track will lose sharpness as the wind blows dust into the depression.

Check around rotten logs that have been torn apart. Many of these logs contain interior water. If the exposed surfaces have moisture, and it has not rained recently, you can assume the bear is close by. Overturned rocks are another indication of bear activity. This type of bear foraging will most likely be found near the top of rocky ridges. If the depression left by the rock is wetter than the surrounding ground, the bear passed by recently. If the depression looks dry check beneath the crust to see if moisture is present at a shallow depth.

Bear eat carrion. They seldom make the kill themselves, particularly if it is a large animal such as domestic livestock. The period just after a hunting season is sometimes a good time to hunt for bear. Let your nose guide you through good bear habitat. If you smell carrion, investigate. You may find a bear is doing a buzzard's job for him. He will be cleaning up the critters that were wounded and later died.

When a carcass is located that shows sign of bear activity it may be productive to visit the area at dawn and dusk. Use the varmint call then, as it is likely the bear will continue to visit the sight until nothing remains but stink and hide. At times the bear will visit the carcass to harvest the crop of maggots that have developed since his last visit. I found an elk carcass once that was intact except for the contents of the abdominal cavity. The bear was making daily visits to harvest the crop of his maggot farm.

Habits

Bear mate in early summer. The mating period usually will last about a month. During this time the bear will caress each other and engage in much grunting and bawling. When the love affair is over each bear goes a separate way. They don't even remain good friends. The male returns to his territory and the female to hers. The cubs are born the following winter when the sow is denned in that fitful sleep sometimes called bear hibernation. The cubs are incredibly tiny at birth. The sow may have only one or as many as four. The little critters grow fast on a nourishing diet of momma's milk and are about a foot and a half long when they follow the sow out of the den at the start of the summer. The cubs stay with the sow for almost two years. When she gets ready to look up her boyfriend again, the cubs are booted.

Bear spend most of the summer and fall building enough fat to last the winter. Yearling cubs are taken back into the den with her at summer's end. The den may be a hollow log, the base of a fire-gutted tree, cavities in a jumble of boulders or a natural cave. The hibernation is a troubled sleep interrupted by frequent periods of sluggish wakefulness. This lack of activity lets the bear exist on stored fat until summer brings a new food supply.

In addition to vegetable matter and carrion, a bear will hunt and eat a variety of small critters; ground squirrels, mice and other rodents dug from their dens. He also takes young deer and elk if he gets a chance. His hunting technique is to stalk as closely as possible and then make a charge that is surprisingly fast for so large a critter. Bears, as everyone knows, love honey. They will spend hours digging into a bee cave or a bee tree. When the honey is exposed the critter is in bear heaven. The honey, comb and angry bees will be eaten with gusto .

Bear also eat grass and a wide variety of roots and tubers. I have seen bear droppings that contain pine needles. I doubt that the bear ate them knowingly. He probably gobbled them up while he was after something tasty, perhaps a maggoty hunk of meat. Pinion nuts, choke cherries and other stone fruits are gathered in season, as are wild grapes. The bear, in short, will eat anything he can wrap a lip around.

Bear Getters

The size and weight of bear vary. Almost any centerfire rifle or handgun will take a small bear. As the critter increases in size more firepower is needed. I would not feel completely comfortable shooting a 400-pound bear with any gun lighter than a .270. I know that bear have been killed with a lot less. My last bear was shot with a .25-06 and it did a good job. A bear hunter has no way of knowing the size of the critter he will encounter. It is better to be prepared than surprised. The gun used should carry a load that will penetrate past the thick hide and the surface fat before it explodes. Extremely fast powder-bullet combos are a poor choice. A fall bear is a very fat bear and the bullet may explode on or near the surface doing little real damage. The shooter will be treated to the dismal sight of the bobbing butt of a departing bruin.

I don't want to nag on this, but feel I should make a comment on bullet placement. I do not agree with some writers who suggest shooting all critters through the front shoulder. These writers reason that such a hit will break down one shoulder and maybe two. The bullet also has a fair chance of taking off part of the heart. I have had poor luck with shoulder shots and so have other hunters I know. The best shot, in my opinion, is a lung shot. Aim about midway between the back and the brisket just back of one front shoulder. The bear has a big set of lungs. They extend from the backbone almost to the brisket and from the front legbone back to mid-paunch. A shot here will cause lung hemmorhage and put the critter away humanely. Unlike the shoulder shot little meat is ruined.

If the bear is a big bear that you may want to mount or have measured, do not shoot it in the head. A local hunter took a huge bear using hounds last year. Chest measurements indicated the critter probably weighed somewhere between five and six hundred pounds. The dogs had put the big bruin up a tall pine. A chest shot brought the bear out of the tree. The big bear landed on his head and several bones in the skull were damaged. The bear, which might have been a new Arizona record for black bear, has not been accepted by the scorers because of skull damage.

Pistols and Primitives

I don't shoot muzzle loaders or bows and will make no comment on their effectiveness. I do know handguns, however, and have formed some hard opinions on their use on bear and other large game. I spent 25 years of my life as a law enforcement officer. I packed a Colt Python so long that my right hip still feels a little off balance without it. Part of my police career was spent as a revolver instructor. Another part was spent as a member of the department's traveling pistol team. I have a cigar box full of medals that say I am one hell of a handgunner. I tell you this not to convince you that I am a deadeye with the handgun (although you may draw that conclusion if you desire) but to point out that I know whereof I speak. I am dead set against the use of handguns on big game. I know that many an animal has found his way to critter heaven at the business end of a handgun and I have sent a few there by that method myself. I have also crippled a few and watched them run off to die a slow and lonely death. The critters, I feel, deserve better. I want to give them the quickest and most humane death possible. A handgun is not the best choice to accomplish that goal. The awkward partridge sights are inferior to scope-sighted rifles. They are even inferior to iron-sighted rifles. Ballistically, they cannot compare with the so-called lightweights such as the .234 and the .244. If I was to change my mind and set out after a big bear with a handgun I think I would either borrow Dirty Harry's .44 magnum or go for something bigger.

Calling Bear

Remember Mike Mell, the hunter who has scored on a couple of dozen bear? Here is the interview I promised at the start of the chapter.

Mike Mell

I have probably been on a hundred bear hunts, most of which were not successful. Looking back I can see a number of things I did wrong when I first started hunting bear. When I learned to hunt where the bear are, and in country where I have at least an even chance, my success percentage with bear increased. I have shot four bear myself and could have shot more. I didn't because I look upon the bear as a special creature and feel I have had my share. I have served as a non-paid guide for a number of bear hunting friends. I am a licensed guide in the State of Arizona and could legally charge if I so desired, but I have not because of the special feeling I have for the critter.

Most of the twenty-one bear I have helped bag were not varmint-called bear – most were glassed up from fairly open country and were stalked. Seven of them were called. I located two of the seven by glassing and went into the area and called them to the gun. The others were called cold. The largest called bear we have taken was an estimated 430 pounds. I was sitting with the hunter on a rocky rim that overlooked a brushy canyon. The rimrock dropped sharply for ten feet and the brush sloped gently for another two or three hundred yards to the canyon bottom. We could see water in the stream from where we sat. I was blowing a Circe tube containing a jackrabbit reed. I like the jackrabbit for bear as it is coarser-toned and seems to work better. Both the hunter and I were in full camo and I carried a can of skunk musk as a masking scent. I blew several loud squalls on the tube and paused for thirty seconds. When nothing appeared I blew another series. When I finished I saw the head of a big bear pop out of the brush across the canyon. I kept calling and the bear headed our way. If I stopped calling, he stopped coming. When I called again he would move again. One of the places he stopped had head-high brush. The bear couldn't see over the brush standing four-footed and he raised up on his haunches to peer at us. He kept coming until he was stopped by the rimrock. He stayed there, about twenty feet away, and stared at us, and he

Mike Mell uses shade from his truck to glass the prickly pear ridges in the background. Mike often spots bear feeding 2 miles away and hikes into the area to call. *Photo Gerry Blair.*

gave us several sharp woofs. The hunter was so amazed he forgot to shoot. I asked him if he was all right and he shot the bear in the shoulder with a .25-06. The bullet was a varmint-loaded bullet and it exploded on the surface of the bear's shoulder without doing any real damage. The bear went down, got up, and headed for the brush fast. The hunter put the second shot through the ribs and into the lungs. The bear went down hard and rolled to a stop against a clump of brush. He was dead when we got to him. He had a red silky coat that was the most attractive I have seen. We had the skull scored and found it measured $20^{15}/_{16}$ inches. Another $^{1}/_{16}$ inch and it would have made the Boone and Crockett book. It did score high in the Arizona book.

Most of the bear I have called were in canyons with a lot of brush. Much of the time there was scrub oak on the rims. Scrub oak and manzanita seem to be a good combination for Arizona bear. I have had my best luck calling in September and October. Bear season starts here the first of September but the hides are better in October. Find a place where bear are feeding. Either manzanita, acorns or prickly pear. Use a spotting scope early and late to locate feeding bear. If you spot a bear early, watch him until he heads for the bedground. If you will be there that evening the bear will probably return to the same area. Do not try to flush him out of his bed. Most of the time he will smell or hear you and will slip away into the brush. An evening bear is harder to stalk. You have to leave before daylight the next morning and set up in his feeding area right at dawn. If you are too late it is best to wait until evening when he likely will show up again.

Calling a bear you have already sighted is a chancy business. He may come to you, he may ignore you or he may leave for the next county. I watched a bear go into a brushy canyon on one hunt and figured he had bedded. We made the stalk and sat on the canyon rim for almost an hour hoping to locate him in his bed. When we couldn't, I blew the call. Nothing happened. Finally I heaved a hunk of log off into the brush and the bear walked out. He headed toward me, changed his mind when he saw me standing on the rim, and moved out in the opposite direction. The hunter was about a hundred feet away down the rim. I went to get him and when we got back the bear was gone. Later that afternoon we got tired of calling for bear and moved out into the flats to try for a coyote. On the second stand we called in a bear. He was about a four-year-old bear with a silky black coat.

Most Arizona bear den up in the winter. I don't think it is a true hibernation. I know they come out before spring as I have seen their tracks in the snow, usually in March.

A lot of hunters won't eat the bear they kill. I like bear if it is barbecued. I think the flavor of bear meat changes with what they eat. Prickly pear bear have a good flavor. So do acorn and manzanita bear. Garbage and carrion eaters are not so good.

If you intend to have the hide mounted, you must take certain precautions. Skin the bear by making a cut from the inside of one rear ankle to the inside of the ankle on the opposite leg. Slip the point of the knife under the skin and cut from the inside out. Never cut from the outside in as you will cut away some of the leg hair. Skin the hide away from the bone and cut the ankle bone so that the foot stays inside the hide. Make a cut from the middle of the inside of the rear legs up to the brisket. Again, slip your knife point under the hide and cut from the inside out. Now make a cut from the inside of the front legs to intersect the brisket cut. Make this cut in a gradual curve, not straight, so that it meets the center cut on the point of the brisket. Use your knife to peel away the hide. Cut the front legs off at the ankles leaving the front feet inside the hide. Tube-skin the bear from the brisket forward. Leave the ears, lips and nose on the hide but be very careful when you are cutting around the head. A bad mistake here could ruin your trophy.

When the hide is off the bear, take a knife and cut as much fat as possible away from the hide. Most fall bear are fat. When you have removed all you can with the knife use a scraper to take off the rest. If you will be in the field a day or two the inside of the hide should be salted. Fold the hide meat side to meat side and keep it in a cool place away from the flies. Take the hide and spread it out at night so it will cool. Fold it again the next morning and keep it out of the sun.

Bear meat is very fat and will turn rancid quickly. If the weather is warm it will not keep long without ice. Good luck.

A Second Opinion

Riney Maxwell is a former employee of the Arizona Game Department who now makes his living as a professional guide. His Big Ten Guide Service, Rt 2, Box 2825, Lakeside, Arizona, is one of the best in the West. Riney is one of the best bear callers I know. He hunts mostly south of Springerville, Arizona, in the rugged Blue Country, a miniature Grand Canyon with brush and trees. The following are excerpts from a recent interview with Riney Maxwell.

Riney Maxwell
I called up my first bear in 1967. I wasn't calling strictly for bear then so I was really surprised when he showed up. Since then I have called twenty-five bear, most of them in the last six years. My hunters have taken sixteen of those called bear. Some of them were real whoppers. I remember one that was 400 or 450 pounds. We didn't have any way to weigh him as we were in rough country.

Most of the bear I have called have been in rough country. That's where they stay. If you want to call bear you need to get into the roughest canyons you can find. Some of the places I hunt are even too rough for the horses. I took a bear out of some rough country once and he rolled off into the bottom of the canyon. I tried to lead the horse in as close as I could. We were following a sorry game trail that sidehilled into the canyon. I was leading because it was too rough to ride. The horse stepped on a loose rock and fell off into that canyon. He was dead on the first bounce. I never even went after the saddle.

You have to call bear early in the morning or early in the afternoon. I have had good luck calling up to ten o'clock. I quit then and start again about three in the afternoon. I use the Circe with the walnut tube. I have used both cottontail and jackrabbit reeds but I think the jackrabbit does a better job on bear. I blow hard on the first series. That is the one that will get them coming or send them running. I really lay into it for about thirty seconds and then stop to glass. A minute or two later I blow another series. I keep this up for about half an hour. It takes a bear a long time to come to you in this rough country and you have to give him time.

I try to locate a feeding canyon. In the Blue, the bear territory is in the canyons. They will work up and down about a mile of canyon feeding on new acorns·and on berries. There is some manzanita here and they eat that. They also like the prickly pear where they are available. There is no mistaking the evidence when you find a bear canyon. There will be fifty or sixty big piles in a mile and a half of canyon. Call here and if the bear is not call smart he will come.

In good years you will see a lot of bear just riding the country. I have seen three bear in one day from horseback. I usually see them on the side of a mountain. You need a horse to get into most of the Blue. A good backpacker who is well-equipped might do all right too. Day hunting from a road camp won't produce too many bear; you need to get back away

Arizona guide Riney Maxwell (right) poses with two of his hunters and a called bear. The big black weighed more than 300 pounds. *Photo courtesy Riney Maxwell.*

from the roads. Climb two or three miles up one of the mountains, make camp, and day hunt out of that camp. Look for transition zones where the oak and chaparral meet the pines. They stay close to the oak in the fall if there is an acorn crop. If not they will work the junipers and manzanita for berries and the prickly pear for fruit. I have seen them on bald hills working the prickly pear.

You see some funny things calling bear. I saw a sow whip three cubs once because they wanted to come to my call. One of the cubs started to me at a dead run, the other two were trailing. The sow caught up with them, slapped the snot out of the first one, and got them all turned. The four of them got the hell out of there. She was a smart bear. She had been fooled by the call before and wasn't about to let the cubs make the same mistake.

In 1978 I took a hunter out after bear. We were on the third day of the hunt and I had called a bear every day. The hunter missed each one. One of the bear was big, maybe 400 pounds plus. I called him out of a brushy canyon and gave the hunter a 200-yard shot. The bear rolled off into the brush at the shot and the hunter began jumping up and down wanting to shake my hand. I told him to wait on the congratulations until we found the bear. The big boar got off into the brush and we never saw him again. But the next year a Mexican fellow killed a huge bear about a mile from there that had been shot through the nose. I know it was the same bear. It made the book.

I called seven head of bear on my 1979 hunt and never killed a one. I was working a camp with six hunters. We called early and late. The bears either come in wrong or they were not the right bear. We ended up with three bear on that hunt but never took a one over the call. We either hunted them up, baited them up or ran them with the dogs. One of the three was a boar bear that must have been close to 400 pounds. He had the biggest head I ever saw on a bear. I told the guy who shot the bear that he had one for the book. It turned out the bear only had a 20-inch skull—missed the book by an inch. I would have bet a hundred dollars that the bear would make the book. The trouble was, the bear had so much meat on his head that it made him look bigger than he was.

I have had my best luck with bear making evening calls, usually from about three o'clock on. The big ones come from country that looks like the Grand Canyon—rough country with chaparral, pine, rimrock and oak canyons. They eat oak berries and acorns. They also eat a plant that grows about a foot high. It is a stalk with a pine cone–shaped cluster of seeds at the top. The bear loves this and it grows all over the country.

I was making an evening call in this type of rough country with a hunter once when we saw a bear coming from a quarter-mile away. He was coming up a rough canyon, moving slow, trying to locate us. It was a big black with a white muzzle—an old bear. He came up to 200 yards and the hunter shot him in the neck with a hand-loaded 7mm. I don't much like the 7mm but this one did a good job. It went in six inches, hit a bone and killed him.

I had a sow come in one time all bristled up. We never saw her until she was close and she was moving toward us at a dead run. She was a hundred yards out when we first saw her and she was bristled up like a porcupine and ready to tear something apart. She was not a real big bear—maybe 180—but a nice bear for a sow. The hunter decided he wanted her and made a good shot. Sows and young boars come to a call fast. The big boars come slower. Being big I guess they can't move as fast.

The Blue Country where I hunt is some of the roughest country you have ever seen. Most of it is wilderness with very few roads. You can't get a horse into most of it. I usually make a pack-in camp up on top of the mountain and we day hunt from the camp. I went in there one day and counted seventeen head of bear.

Calling is a good way to hunt bear. I think they will always come to the call if they have not been fooled before. Bears are smart though, like coyote. Fool them once or twice and they won't play the game. They will either ignore the call or run the opposite way. I have seen lots of them do just that.

Maxwell finds most of his bear in rough country. He makes a dry camp in rough wilderness areas and day hunts from the camp. *Photo U.S. Forest Service.*

14

The Raccoon

Description

The raccoon is a heavy-bodied critter with short legs. A teenage coon will weigh about twelve pounds while a fat old boar may weigh three times that. An adult animal measures about three feet from nose to tip of tail. The body fur is coarse and will range from very dark to a light grizzled gray. His familiar black face mask has earned him the name of wood's bandit in some areas. The ten-inch tail is ringed with alternating bands of dirty white and black, earning him another nickname, ringtail.

Range

The raccoon is steadily increasing his range, possibly because of land development in the western United States and Canada. The omnivorous coon moves into newly developed agricultural areas and makes a home near this windfall of food. Permanent water, a critical element in coon habitat, will increase the attractiveness of the area. Predator control projects in Montana, Wyoming, Utah and Idaho have also encouraged coon expansion. When the larger predators disappear, a place is made for more coons. The coon is an adaptable critter. He will often be found within the city limits of large cities. Many city garbage dumps host a respectable coon population.

Food

The raccoon is not a fussy eater. Garbage dump coons might spend their entire lives eating nothing but the goodies found at the dump. Where he lives determines what he eats. Waterway coons—those that live along streams and rivers and along lakeshores or marshes—will probably make their living catching and eating crawfish, frogs and minnows. Even though the food has just been removed from the water, the coon will usually wash it thoroughly before eating. He seems to lose a great deal of his fastidiousness, however, when he finds a ripe piece of carrion along the bank. He will dive into a rotting carp with a gusto that is a wonder to watch.

The coon will also take fruits and vegetables in season. His fondness for corn, melons and other produce has caused hard feelings with many a farmer. The coon will often balance this agricultural diet with eggs and poultry. He will also eat wild fruits and berries, often going on eating sprees that turn his stocky body into a lard barrel. The stored fat will see the critter through the approaching winter.

The raccoon is not a fussy eater. He makes a pretense of cleanliness if he is around water but will eat garbage and carrion with gusto. *Photo U.S. Forest Service.*

Raccoon will use denning trees year after year if they are not disturbed. Young coon leave the den to hunt when they are about two months old. *Photo U.S. Forest Service.*

Hibernation

The coon is not a true hibernator. He will become inactive in cold weather when food is scarce and may spend a part of the winter in a hollow tree. But if the winter weather warms slightly the coon will leave the den to hunt for food. When the next storm hits he hightails it back to the tree. If no trees are available the coon will choose a hollow log, a cave or an abandoned badger burrow. In lower altitudes, or warmer climate, the raccoon stays active the year round.

Habits

Raccoons breed in midwinter, usually February and March, in the colder climates. In the warmer climates they may breed year round. The three to six young are born in the limb of a hollow tree, or in a ground substitute, about two months after breeding. Male coons are polygamous and will do a lot of travelling during the breeding season. I once shot a called coon in the high desert country north of the Verde River. He showed up several miles away from the nearest water. I was doubly surprised to see the coon answer the coyote call. He showed up at three o'clock on a sunny afternoon. Most coons are night feeders and will answer a daytime call infrequently.

The coon kits are born blind and will remain sightless for the first three weeks. The female is a good mother. She will stay with the litter for almost a full year, or until she is ready to have another litter. The young coon are weaned when they are two months old and are hunting shortly after that. In areas where semi-hibernation occurs, the female will den with the young while the boar seeks separate quarters.

The coon is a good swimmer. He climbs trees about as well as any animal around. The tree climbing may be for food if the tree is a persimmon tree, but it is most often for protection. An adult coon has few enemies. Large boars have been known to top 50 pounds and he is all fight. Most larger predators would sooner find a supper that is less cranky.

Harmful Effects

The raccoon is not an agricultural pest in most of its range. In certain areas they can do great damage. Some parts of the Midwest have allowed coons to overpopulate because of short-sighted conservation practices. States that have banned the use of the leghold trap are particularly troubled. Coons in overpopulated areas can wipe out a corn crop overnight. They are also pests in fruit orchards and gardens. The raccoon can also be a serious predator of domestic poultry.

Value as a Fur Bearer

The raccoon pelt is a staple of the fur industry. Prices will fluctuate, as will the price for all furs, from year to year. Raccoon fur will prime about November and will remain prime through February in most of his range. Many callers keep the coon carcass for Sunday dinner. The meat is dark and moist. Depression babies born in the hardwood hills of the Missouri Ozarks gummed the tasty coon meat before their first tooth appeared. I speak from experience.

Skinning

Raccoon are usually fat and greasy. You should always skin the critter out of doors. If the skinning must be done indoors choose a spot that will be easy to clean. Most coons are skinned open. Slit the inside of the rear legs from foot to foot going through the anal opening. Split the tail on the underside and take out the bone, then cut the hide loose at the heel of each hind foot. Make another cut from foot to foot on the underside of the front legs and cut the hide loose from the heel of each front foot. Make a final cut from the anal opening up the belly to the underside of the chin. Tie the carcass to a comfortable working height and remove the skin.

Some fur buyers prefer to buy coon that has been case-skinned. If that is the case (no pun intended), skin the critter the same as you would skin a coyote or a fox.

Fleshing

Pull the hide onto a stretcher or a fleshing beam. If the coon has been open-skinned, tack the hide onto a flat piece of board or the side of a shed. Use a fleshing knife or a scraper to remove all of the fat and meat particles. Wipe the hide down with paper towels or sawdust to remove residual oil. Wash the hide in warm water and liquid detergent if necessary.

Drying

If the hide is skinned open it can be nailed to a flat board with the fur side in. Place the hide in a shady spot where it is protected from the sun and from any flies that may be about. When the hide is dried it will be very stiff. Remove it from the board and store in a cool dry place until it is ready to market.

Case-skinned coon are handled in much the same way as other case-skinned animals. Pull the hide onto the stretcher with the flesh side out and nail the rear of the hide to the board. Nail the spread tail onto the board so that it is tightly stretched. Place the nails about an inch apart so the tail will dry evenly. Pull the hind legs down on the stomach side of the board and nail into place then run a tapered wedge-shaped board between the hide and the stretcher to create extra tension. When the hide is dry, the board can be removed and enough slack will be left to remove the hide from the stretcher. Push up the center of the stomach skin to make a U-shaped inspection window. This will make it easy for the fur buyer to grade the hide. Coon skins are sold hair side in and the window lets the buyer see the hip fur.

Nail the lower lip to the stretching boars. Let the front leg skins hang. Do not allow the front legs to hang against the stomach hide, however, as these areas will not dry properly and will probably cause souring and fur slip. Lean the stretcher at an angle so that the front legs skin hangs free. When the pelt has dried thoroughly remove it from the board and hang it in a cool and well-ventilated storage area.

Stretchers

If you call a good number of coon in a season you will likely need stretchers in three sizes; small, medium and large. Make the medium stretcher 40 inches long, 9 inches wide at the base, and 6½ inches at the shoulders. Go down 12 inches from the point to get the shoulder measurement. Add an inch to the measurements for a large coon and subtract an inch for a small coon. Make the stretcher from solid stock. A four-foot piece of one-by-twelve does a good job.

Coon Scouting

As a rule coons will not be found far from water. Tracks can easily be found in the muddy dirt at the water's edge, and they disappear into the water for several hundred feet. The coon is hunting the shallow water next to shore for crawfish and other water dwellers. If the tracks are fresh you can bet the coon will be denned close by and will likely answer a call if the area is visited at night.

Rear coon tracks are about three to four inches long and somewhat resemble the configuration of the human foot. The rear is narrow and the front is wider and shows toe marks. The coon travels at a rolling lope which causes the front

Raccoon can be located along waterways by checking the trees with a light on dark nights. *Photo U.S. Forest Service.*

and rear prints to appear as pairs. The prints of a running coon are usually altered; that is, they do not show the imprint of the entire foot. Coon droppings are distinctive and will usually show crawfish shells or vegetable matter. Many areas of high coon concentration will show well-defined trails leading from the stream to the bed grounds.

The coon is found in limited numbers in the marginal habitat of the desert Southwest. The best place to look for him is along permanent waterways in wooded areas. The raccoon seems to prefer mature stands of cottonwood and sycamore.

I was on a mid-winter hunt along Wet Beaver Creek in Central Arizona one night when I happened to shine a light into a stand of cottonwoods. The trees lit up like Christmas trees. A family of coons had taken up residence along that stretch of creek. The raccoon is the only critter Arizonians are allowed to hunt at night. I used my Burnham long-range coon call (Model B-1) to play them a song. In no time I had coons all around me and I left the stand with two big boars swung over my shoulders.

Coon Calls

Coon calls are made by a number of companies but my favorite of the crowd is the Burnham call. It is made to resemble the distress call of a water bird. It took me about two hours of practice to get my call to produce the right sound. The tongue must be fluttered while the call is blown to produce a trilling sound. Any mouth call can be made to trill, it should be noted, but the medium-pitched reed in the Burnham B-1 is tuned to work best in this way. The sound produced is deadly on coon. Don't be surprised if you attract a call-wise coyote or fox to the call also. The trill is a new sound to them and they have an appetite for water birds. When you have mastered the trill, learn to vary the volume of the call. This will change the pitch of the sound and produce a trilling scream. A few hours' practice will educate your tongue to this new task. The practice will pay off when you take the call on the hunt.

Calling Technique

Scout your calling stand in the daytime. Find an area that shows evidence of coon activity and determine exactly where you will set up for the call. You may want to mark the location with a plastic pennant. The terrain often looks differently at night and the marker will make it easier to find the spot. Park your vehicle a few hundred yards from the spot and use a flashlight to find your way to the stand. Wear dark clothing of a soft material. Do not wear rayons, nylons or any other material that will make a sound when scraped by brush. If there is a moon wear camo clothing or stay in the shadows. Raccoons are not spooky coming to the call but coyotes are. If you are not careful you might scare off a hungry coyote that is trying to beat the coon to its supper.

Make a lot of noise with the call when you first start blowing. Keep the beam of the finding light high so that a soft halo of peripheral light surrounds you for about fifty yards. If a set of eyes are located, reduce the volume of the call. If the wind is with you, or if you use a masking scent, the coon will mosey around the light periphery for a few minutes and then amble in. Don't be surprised if he tries to sit in your lap.

I blow a series of six or seven calls on the triller and then rest my mouth while I look for eyes. If a set shows up I ease off on the tube and work him in with low volume. If no eyes appear I will maintain the call-and-pause series for about fifteen minutes. I call it quits then if no customers are in sight.

Callers who live near lakes or marshes may want to try water calling. Use a boat to patrol the bank and make a stand about every half a mile. Work your

George Oakey of Flagstaff holds a night-called coon. We used the Burnham coon call to bring him out of the rocky cliffs above a little used landfill. *Photo Gerry Blair.*

Coons come best during the hungry season of late winter. They have used up their fat and are ready for a handout. *Photo U.S. Forest Service.*

finding light so that as much of the bank as possible is lighted. I like to keep the boat about fifty feet out from the shore. I also like to use a shotgun for this type of hunting. Much of the time the critter will be seen in the thick brush of the shoreline and will offer only a fast shot.

Some callers also hunt coon on moonlit nights using no artificial light. The critters are spotted and shot by moonlight. The raccoon seems to eat equally well during the dark and full phases of the moon. One December night south of Flagstaff, I was calling a little-used garbage dump and had my big butt buried in about six inches of cold wet snow. The combination of snow and moonlight caused the tall ponderosa pines to cast deep black shadows. Two minutes of work on the call brought a hump-backed figure out of the depths of the dump. Before he came close enough to shoot, I sighted four more of the loping forms. I had three shots in my 1100 magnum and spent them wisely. When the smoke cleared I had three fat garbage-eating raccoons scattered in the snow.

If night calling is totally illegal in your state do not despair. Coons are mainly night feeders and they are more easily called at night, but they can also be called in the daytime. They do not come as readily, and I do not feel that they will come as far, but they will come. I have already mentioned the daytime coon I shot hunting the Mazatal Wilderness Area. Daytime callers, I feel, must set up closer to the coon's bed grounds. His chance of success is increased if the call is made soon after daylight or shortly before dark.

Coon calling is made to order for bowhunters. The critters will come extremely close and will not spook out of the county if an arrow fletching grazes their back. Use broadheads as the blunts do not have the muscle to put away a coon. If you are night hunting mark the shaft with a thin strip of reflecting tape. This will make it easier to find your arrow if you happen to miss.

Raccoons are not as hard to kill as other predators. They present a big blocky target and usually come to close range. A good shot with a .22 rimfire can kill a lot of coons if he picks his shots; a .22 rimfire magnum will do the job a bit better. I like the H&R Model 700 which comes equipped with a five-shot clip. I have a 4x power Weaver over the barrel and find the advantage of five quick shots quite an asset. An optional ten-shot clip also is available, but I have had poor luck with the ten-shotter. Both of the ones I owned jammed after the first shot. Five fast shots, I figure, are better than one fast shot and nine slow ones.

The .222 loaded down is also a good coon gun. Use Murry Burnham's load described in the chapter on weapons. It will put the coon away without taking off his coat. Any of the .224's loaded down should do a good job.

The shotgun is also a logical choice for nighttime coon calling. Use either No. 4 birdshot, No. 4 buckshot, or any load between. Use caution, however, that the coon stays a respectable distance away. I took an excitable friend calling once and loaned him my Model 1100 while I used the .22 mag. I put a big boar into his lap two minutes into the first call. He fired the magnum buck point blank at the hungry coon; it was five minutes before the rain of hair stopped. After demolishing the coon the tightly packed buckshot had dug a hole almost large enough to bury the bits of hide and hair we were able to find.

Coons will come to the call better in the hungry season, usually late January and February. They have used most of their summer fat by this time and are hunting seriously. If you decide to hunt them later in the year, during early and mid-summer, contact local farmers. They will be happy to let you call their cornfields, nut groves and fruit orchards. The furs will be worthless but you will be doing a farmer a favor by removing some of his surplus pests. He will probably remember the favor when hunting season rolls around.

15

The Javelina

The javelina is not a predator but I have included him in this book because they frequently come to a well-blown predator call. Many times they will come as a sounder, running around the hidden caller with their little piggy eyes flashing, their tusks gnashing and the coarse gray hair on their backs raised to full attention. I have abandoned otherwise good varmint calling areas to get away from these pesky pigs.

There are a couple of other things that javelina are not: They are not pigs, not even close relatives as some writers report. A wildlife worker with the Arizona Game and Fish Department put it this way: "Peccaries are not much more related to pigs than cats are to catfish."

Peccaries are also not the vicious killers described in lore and legend. This is not to say that they can't and won't hurt you, they can and will. The attack usually occurs when the critter is cornered and you are blocking the only way out. Most reported javelina attacks are nothing more than an incident in which a sounder of very frightened peccaries runs toward a very frightened hunter in an attempt to leave the area. I have never been bitten by a javelina but have come close a couple of times. The first occurred when my brave but foolish German shorthair decided to take on a big boar in Bloody Basin. When I saw that old Jubal was in danger of being skinned alive I waded in to pull him off. The pig decided I wanted a piece of the action and was glad to oblige. He made one pass at my arm with those snapping tusks as I reached for the dog's collar. He missed and I didn't. Jubal, by this time, was glad to be pulled off. We left to hunt quail while the beady-eyed boar bragged on his muscle in loud woofs.

The second experience came when I caught an inquisitive sow in a leghold trap set for fox. She was held by a right hind leg and everytime I tried to reach for the trap to release her she made a lightning pass at my hand with those razor sharp tusks. I removed a piece of rope from my backpack, put a noose on the end of a limb, and let my partner choke the critter down while I did it a favor.

Range

The collared peccary is found in parts of Arizona, Texas, New Mexico and points south. This critter is a salt-and-pepper gray with an apparent white collar that travels across the chest from shoulder to shoulder. The collared peccary will average about twenty-two inches in height and may be three feet long from the tip of his snout to his tailless rump. A big one will weigh about forty pounds. You can disregard most of the stories of hunter-killed javelina weighing more than sixty pounds. The Tucson branch of the Arizona Game Protective Association ran a big pig contest a few years back. The biggest one they weighed tipped the scales at thirty-eight pounds minus his innards. The biggest documented pig

Javelina are peaceable most of the time but can get mean fast if they feel threatened. *Photo Gerry Blair.*

in Arizona came from the area around Klondike a few years back. The critter weighed a bit more than fifty pounds. Hunters and fishermen are notoriously poor judges of weight and this seems particularly true in the case of the javelina. I was hunting with a buddy on the San Carlos Reservation one spring when he bagged his first javelina. He judged it to weigh seventy pounds field-dressed. He weighed the pig when we went through Globe and found the critter had shrunk to thirty-one pounds. "I guess I figured anything that ugly had to be big," he admitted sheepishly.

The second peccary is the white-lipped peccary that lives almost entirely south of the U.S.-Mexican border. Old white lips is a bigger pig. He is slightly darker in color than the collared and does not have the white collar. His lips are a pale gray.

Habits

Javelinas seem to live mostly in the life zone biologists have labeled the Upper Sonoran Desert. The high parts of this zone are characterized by mixed pinion and juniper trees. A bit lower the trees yield to chaparral. The lowest part of the zone is arid and will grow cactus and other water-efficient plants such as the mesquite and Palo Verde trees. Areas with a good concentration of prickly pear seem to suit the pigs best. They will eat the sweet fruit in season, shred the thorn-studded sections for pulp and moisture, and dig out the tasty roots. The range will be shared by desert mule deer, desert bighorn sheep, feral burros and a host of predators.

Lions probably take important numbers of javelina. The javelina habit of denning in caves and abandoned mine shafts makes it easy for the lion. He blocks the entrance and takes his pick as the groceries run by. Coyote and bobcat also take javelina but are probably more of a threat to the young than the adult pigs. It is doubtful they would be willing to tackle a critter that may outweigh them double or triple, particularly when a part of that weight is long, sharp tusks. A medium-sized desert hog can lick a dog without working up a sweat. He would probably do the same to a coyote.

Food

The javelina is a vegetarian. He eats fruit, roots and pulp of the prickly pear cactus. He also favors a low-growing cactus called the hedgehog. The cactus

A pig hunter surveys good pig country. Fresh feeding sign was found on the prickly pear ridges. The pigs were located at the base of the mountain. Note the caves near the base of the large rock. *Photo Gerry Blair.*

diet is supplemented with other succulents, roots, tubers, mesquite beans, manzanita berries and acorns.

Mating

Javelina mate and have young the year round but the peak production period occurs during the hot summer months. The gestation period may extend for as long as four months. One or two young are usual. More than two means trouble as the sow has only two teats and it is obvious someone is going to be on short rations.

Territorial Inclinations

Most mammals are territorial in their range and the javelina is no exception. Studies by the Arizona Game and Fish Department have showed javelina ranges to vary from 254 to 1,660 acres. The average territory in two widely separated studies presented an average range of a bit more than 700 acres. The herd size and range are probably influenced by the abundance of groceries. Good country produces a small home area. Tough country means the pigs have to travel farther to get enough to eat. The integrity of the herd is usually maintained and uninvited guests are discouraged. There were a few instances recorded in the Arizona study where members of one herd ran away from home and took up residence with a neighboring sounder.

Feeding Habits

Javelina move around when they are hunting groceries or water. At other times they will likely hole up in a cave, a shady thicket or a sand wallow. Most of their feeding activity is done in daylight during winter months; the javelina hair coat is not heavy enough to keep them warm in extreme night temperatures. During the hot months of summer, the javelina are most apt to feed at night. I have had my best luck hunting them in early morning and late evening. They are moving to and from the bed grounds at this time and are easier to spot. Most javelina I have known are interrmittent feeders. They will browse a while and then bed down for an hour's rest. They are almost impossible to see when they are bedded; their black stubby outline blends perfectly with the dark shadows cast by the chaparral.

Hunting Techniques

Javelina are spread throughout the Southwest with most of them in Texas. Arizona is second especially in the country south of the Mogollon Rim. New Mexico has the least; much of that state is simply too high to support important numbers of the little pigs. There are also good numbers in many of the Mexican states such as Sonora and Sinaloa.

I would begin a javelina hunt by scouting for sign. The tracks will be seen in sand washes, along ridge trails and among prickly pear patches. The tracks are small and somewhat resemble the track of a deer fawn. The track of the front and rear foot will register as pairs with the hind foot hitting just behind the front. The critter has a short stride, usually around eight inches. Peccary droppings are slender black tubes that will show what the critter has been eating. They will seldom be seen, however (I suspect that some critter, maybe the javelina himself, eats the droppings shortly after they are deposited).

A feeding herd of javelina will leave other sign. Look for dug-up places around the roots of the prickly pear: The segments of the cactus will often be shredded. A cow or a deer that takes a bite of cactus will usually take out a clean cut half circle. Javelina will shred the cactus and will usually leave parts of the inner skeleton visible. If there are hedgehog cactus about, the javelina will use a sharp tusk to slit the sausage-shaped cactus from top to bottom. He will then eat from the inside out, leaving nothing but the skin and spines. The few spines that the javelina ingests do not seem to bother him. If fresh javelina sign is found you can bet that the critters will not be far away, probably less than a mile. If you think they may be bedded, look for them along brushy sand washes or along bluffs that might have caves to shelter them from the sun. If you feel the javelina are still feeding, find a high spot and uses glasses or a spotting scope to locate the herd.

Most of the hunter's work is done when a javelina herd is spotted. They are not smart in the same sense that a coyote or a whitetail buck is smart, and he has about the poorest eyesight of any critter around. His sense of hearing is a bit better than average. I was glassing a herd of javelina from a mile away one spring when I saw a truckload of hunters pull in below me. They were curious about my activities. One of them slammed the car door when they left the truck and I saw one of the javelina stand at attention and look their way. Just then one of the hunters coughed. The whole sounder sold out.

The main strength of a javelina is his nose. Any hunter who gets upwind from a sounder of pigs has just sold the farm. The herd will either steal off quietly or stamp wildly with a great gnashing of tusks. Either way they will not be seen again soon. This keen sense of smell can be somewhat neutralized by using a masking scent such as skunk musk.

Hunters with sharp noses can turn the table on javelina by smelling them. The critters have a gland above the base of the tail that emits a characteristically skunky odor. I am a non-smoker and can smell a herd of javelina from several hundred feet if the wind is right. The musk can also be noticed in caves recently used by javelina.

Calling Hogs

Javelina are not predictable in their response to a varmint call. I blew at a sounder of pigs once until I got trombone lip and never attracted a customer. Another time I played the dying rabbit blues for a small herd and sent them running, clear into the next zip code. Another time I had an adult and a sub-adult run across the road in front of my boy's bright orange International Scout. I poked the Circe call out the window and played a few bars. The adult skidded to a stop and charged the scout. She made two full circles around the vehicle, about ten feet out, huffing and puffing all the way. When she left I called her back with one blast on the tube. She repeated her performance and left again. I called her back a third time. Finally I tired of the game and it's a good thing I did. I have a hunch that the sow would not have quit.

On another trip a friend and I sighted a running herd of hogs from my pickup. The critters had apparently had a recent bad experience with traffic; they were three hundred yards and two canyons away and still running. I stopped the truck and blew enthusiastically into a long-range Burnham. The last three hogs in the herd skidded to a stop, turned on a dime, and headed back. The country was rough and it took them almost five minutes to work their way back to the truck. The three of them paused twenty feet out and I took their photograph. At the click of the camera shutter they broke for the canyon again.

Most of my luck in calling hogs has been in brushy canyons where the lack of long-range visibility makes regular hunting difficult. Stay high when you make your stand as this will make it easier to spot incoming customers. I don't hide as carefully for hogs as I do the predators; their poor eyesight makes it unnecessary. Watch the wind, however, and do not make unneeded noise. Blow the call as you would for a varmint—loud blasts lasting twenty to thirty seconds for the series followed by a minute or so of silence. The pigs will usually announce their presence by loud grunts. When they are upset they have a tendency to grunt every time their feet hit the ground. The entire sounder usually responds. Don't be surprised if you are surrounded by a noisy herd, all with their back hair upraised and all gnashing their teeth viciously. This can be quite unnerving to a neophyte caller. I took a college friend on a photography expedition

The bad end of a pig. The critter's sharp tusks are used mostly when he roots. They can inflict bad wounds on folks or critters who want to mess around. *Photo Gerry Blair.*

once and was lucky enough to bring a sounder close on the first stand. As the herd charged in my friend charged out, abandoning his camera and his self-respect. The pigs left in the opposite direction.

If you scatter a herd of pigs while you are sill hunting they can often be called back using the varmint call. This seems to work best if the javelina are not exactly sure why they spooked. Find a place where you will be inconspicuous and still have vision. Blow a very short series of squeals to stop the pigs. When they stop, lower the volume of the call and wheedle them in with low moaning sounds. If they are not badly spooked, one or two of the sounder, usually the biggest boars, will return to see if one of their girl friends has a problem.

The most difficult part of pig hunting, in my opinion, is locating the pigs. The most effective way to do this is to be in javelina habitat at sunup and work the hillsides with a good pair of glasses or a spotting scope. Use good optics. You may be able to look through a bad set of glasses for a minute or two, but for constant searching you need something that will not create eye strain. I use a set of Bausch & Lomb 7x35 Zephyrs. They are light and the optics are sharp enough to show an apple on a tree almost a mile away. My spotting scope is the Bushnell Sentry II with a 20x eyepiece. Stay away from anything stronger than a 20x. It is not usually needed and will create problems in the form of heat waves and distortion. Even the 20x will pick up heat waves if you use it late in the day. Morning viewing is the best as it is cool then and the heat waves are not noticeable. Also, this is the time when the pigs are most apt to be on the move.

When a herd of pigs, or a single pig, is spotted he is likely to be wearing your tag within the next hour. Pigs feed slowly and will not ordinarily spook without provocation. Get the wind in your face and use what cover is available to make a stalk. If the country is too open to get close, find a hiding place close to the sounder and call them in with the tube.

Pig Guns

Most hunters go afield over-gunned for javelina. They try and use their deer gun on the pigs and it seldom works satisfactorily. Even a big pig, at fifty pounds on the cloven hoof, is half as big as a small deer. A medium loaded .30-06 will spread meat and hair into several zip codes. Even the lightweights such as the .243 and the 6mm are sometimes too much gun for pig. The .222 and the .223 are about right in my opinion. I sometimes use the .22-250 if I am hunting country where I am apt to get cross-canyon shots. Use a hollowpoint or a spitzer point in

Bill Mulleneaux of Safford, Arizona, with a 35-pound boar he called and bagged with a handgun. *Photo Gerry Blair.*

something around 50 grains. I push mine out of the muzzle at about 3,500 fps, aiming for the chest cavity if I possibly can. A hit here will put the critter's lights out fast and will not ruin much meat. Unless you have a strong stomach do not shoot into the paunch. A gut-shot pig will gag a buzzard, and field-dressing that pig will be one of the most traumatic events of your life. Eating the pig will be another. The odor seems to permeate the meat and every bite will remind you of your poor shooting. I also avoid head shots. The pig has a small brain located just above the eye. A hit here will put him down fast but the head will likely be ruined for taxidermy purposes.

Pistols and Pigs

Handgunning for hogs can be exciting sport. After twenty-five years in police work, my favorite is the .357 magnum. I load a jacketed softnose 158-grainer for pigs. The jacketed bullet will penetrate the shoulder bone before expanding if such a shot is offered. The main thing to remember is to take your time for a good shot because you will likely get only one. Let the pigs come as close as they will and use a two-handed grip with the arms braced across your drawn-up knees. Use the factory partridge sights if you have to. My long association with partridge sights has deeply prejudiced me against them. You will do much better on hogs, and all other game, if you will invest in a low-power scope sight.

Skinning

A pig will taste better if he is skinned immediately. I skin mine before I gut him as this keeps a lot of hair off the meat. The hair contains musk and will cause the meat to taste strong. Begin by making a slit down the inside of each hind leg from the gambrel to the vent. The carcass should be suspended for ease in skinning. Tube-skin the carcass as you would any other critter. Skin to the head and cut the short neck bone leaving the head in the hide. Make a slit down the belly from the inside of the hips to just past the rib cage and remove the entrails but do not be concerned with saving them. They are strong in a javelina and will disappoint you. When the skinning and gutting is complete, cover the carcass with a cheesecloth bag and pack it out. The quicker the meat cools the better it will taste.

If you intend to take the hide to the taxidermists, protect it from the sun and make the trip as soon as possible. If you do not want a head mount you might consider having the hide tanned into leather. Javelina hide is thin and strong. The small pits made by the hair roots create an interesting texture. A pair of gloves made from javelina leather are soft and pliable and they will last for years.

Second Opinion

Dick Beeler has been calling predators for twenty-five years. He started in Indiana on red fox and raccoon then moved to Arizona and participated in the World Championship Predator Calling Contests held in Chandler. He took third in 1962, his first contest, and came back in 1963 to win the world championship. He did the same in 1964. Dick lives in central Arizona and does much of his calling in the chaparral of the high desert. He is a licensed guide.

Dick Beeler
I would hate to guess how many hogs I have called, and most have come uninvited. I call for predators and the pigs come as volunteers. I have called several hundred javelina in the twenty years I have called in Arizona. If a javelina is in hearing distance I think he will answer the call most of the time but sometimes they will go the other way. I have seen a herd split and half of them run to the call and the other half run the opposite way. If there are small pigs in the bunch and you make a squeal the adults will come running. They figure something is messing with one of the babies and they come to help.

I have called and killed ten pigs using a handgun and have shot five with a bow and arrow. I prefer the handgun — pigs die hard with the bow. I was archery hunting one year and called in a half dozen hogs. I picked the biggest and put a broadhead through his ribs. The arrow went clean through the pig and hit a rock on the other side. That pig didn't even know he had been shot. I had five arrows and every one of them went through the pig and broke on a rock. The other pigs were getting hostile. I had two of them put me up on a stump and I had to use the bow to slap them across the snout. The pig I had shot was still on his feet but he was a sick pig. I finally ran the other pigs off and managed to find one of my shafts. I used my pocketknife to sharpen the point and shot the pig again with that. I finally killed him but it was one tough job and he was the worst-tasting pig I ever tried to eat. Every pig I ever killed with a bow died hard and every one tasted terrible. I have killed ten pigs with a handgun and they died fast and tasted great.

If you are handgunning for hogs use the biggest gun you can shoot accurately. I use a .44 magnum. My load is 17 grains of 2400 in a .44 special case. It is a very accurate load and does the job well.

I use a Circe tube with a cottontail reed to call them. It is a bit higher-

Dick Beeler has called and killed ten javelina with a handgun. He is shown here with a pair of pigs taken on a hunt south of Payson, Arizona. *Photo courtesy Dick Beeler.*

pitched than the jackrabbit and I like it better for coyote. The pigs might come just as fast to other calls.

I don't think a pig gets call-smart like a coyote. If they are fooled several times in a row they might, but most of the time they come just as good the third time as they do the first. I'll tell you the truth, I am convinced I could take a varmint call and a bow and wipe out an entire sounder – the pigs are that easy to fool. The bow is silent and doesn't spook them like a gun would. One shot with a gun and you are out of business. The bow is quiet and the pigs can't figure it out. They just keep coming at you.

If I am calling pigs and want them in close, I will put the call away when they are a hundred yards out and whuff them in. The pigs talk to each other with this whuffing. It is a quick release of air, kind of like a gruff cough. The pigs hear the whuff and they think I am another pig and come close. Sometimes too close. I have had them try to crawl in my lap or put me up a tree. I think a lot of these tales about charging pigs is just a case of the pig running off and the hunter being in his way. When you are calling though, and have a pig at arm's length, it is not the time to be gambling. I climb a tree and give them the right of way.

Most javelina I have called came full bore, whuffing and clacking their tusks. Some you will never see as they will stay in the brush. You can hear them and smell them but they won't come into the open. If a pig intends to answer the call he will show up in fifteen minutes. If you don't see, hear or smell one by then you might as well move on.

If I am hunting pigs I try and locate a sounder before I make a call. Pigs are a herd animal and run long routes. It doesn't do any good to call unless they are in hearing distance. I will set off across good pig country looking for sign, tracks or digging. If I find fresh sign I hide and make a call. Another way to hunt is to be out at sunup and use binoculars to search the sunny side of the hills. If I spot a feeding herd I get close enough for a shot or get in close enough to call them to me. If the wind is right they will come right on in and give me a whale of a shot.

I blow for pigs just like I do for coyotes. I use the same call and blow the same routine. I blow a hard series for thirty seconds and pause till I get my breath. Then I blow another series. I tried Ed Scerry's technique (blow fifteen seconds, pause, blow fifteen seconds and pause for two minutes) but it didn't work as well for me. I blow longer and don't pause as long.

I have my best luck calling pigs if I sight them first. I might sight a herd just driving down the road. I might glass them up or I might just walk into the middle of them. If they aren't spooked they will answer the call. I haven't had much luck breaking up a herd and calling back the stragglers, and I have a hard time getting them in if they are spooked.

A hunter after pigs will probably have his best luck calling early and late. Most pig country is warm during the day, even in the winter. Pigs will shade up in the heat of the day and will feed when it is cool. That is the best time to spot them and the best time to call. Most of the called pigs I have shot were boars. Every herd, it seems to me, has two or three pigs that are the fighters. The main part of the herd will stand off and watch the action while the fighters come in to kick you around a bit.

I think any hunter can get a pig to come to a call if he gets into pig country and calls so the pigs can hear him. Find a place to sit where you have a good view. Skunk musk might help but I have called a lot of pigs without it. Make your call and stand by for action.

The white line that gives the collared peccary his name is clearly visible on this boar. *Photo Gerry Blair.*

16

Other Volunteers

A predator call will bring a surprising variety of critters, some of which are not particularly welcome. Some will come to the call often and others will come only occasionally. This chapter will deal with those animals who come to the call unexpectedly.

Deer

Deer will come to the call frequently if you are calling good deer country, especially in the spring and early summer. A hoarse-toned call such as the Circe Jackrabbit seems to work best on deer. Perhaps it sounds the most like a fawn in trouble. Does are the most frequent respondents. They usually come to within a hundred feet, take a close look, and leave. I have had deer come uncomfortably close and stamp their feet nervously. Deer response seems to be best early in the morning and late in the evening but they also come well at night. I have often called deer to the camera and have been able to get excellent shots.

I was coyote calling alone one winter when I called in a whole herd of mulies. I had finished the call and was preparing to leave when I heard a startled snort just on the other side of my hiding bush. I walked quickly around and saw a very nice buck with ten or twelve does. They had walked to within a few feet of my hiding bush. I knew that the deer were in the rut then and speculated that the buck had responded to learn if some varmint was hurting one of his does. Another time I was calling thick junipers with my son when we called in about a dozen deer. There were two small forked-horn bucks in the bunch. They stopped about a hundred yards out and looked us over.

I used a varmint call to bring this nice three point out of a jackpine thicket. It was Gerry Jr.'s first deer and he downed him with one shot. *Photo Gerry Blair.*

Whitetail deer seem to answer the call best of all. This critter likes a lot of heavy brush and steep country in this part of the West. I have called both bucks and does. I have never shot a called deer, as they usually appear before and after season. I do believe, however, that calling would be effective for whitetails. Many times their habitat is too thick to permit more conventional methods.

A national park is an excellent area to camera-call deer and other critters. If I am calling close to headquarters I always announce my presence to the ranger. I have called some really big mulies on the north rim of the Grand Canyon National Park. They are not hunted there, of course, and have a chance to grow really big. They are also less wild than deer in unprotected areas.

I have rigged my 35mm camera a special way for photo-calling. The camera and lens are mounted on an old gun stock. A cable release is attached to the trigger area so I can aim and fire as I would with a gun. It is much faster and much steadier. Depending on the country I may use a 300mm telephoto lens or a 135mm telephoto lens. In thick country the 300 is too much lens as the critters often are too close. I use Tri-X film if I am shooting black and white. The 400 ASA lets me choose a fast shutter speed to compensate for camera shake. I stay away from the fast films in color. Kodak makes a 400 ASA color film in both slides and negatives but both are too grainy for my purposes. I normally shoot KMA25, a film so fine-grained that it permits 11 x 14 enlargements from the 35mm format. If I am doubtful about light conditions I may substitute KMA64. It is about one stop faster and still delivers sufficient resolution for enlargements.

Most deer will investigate the predator call if they are not spooked. I called this doe on the California Coast. *Photo Gerry Blair.*

Ringtail seldom come to day calls. This one came out of the rocks 15 feet from my camera. The large eyes and ears help this small predator locate his groceries on the darkest nights. *Photo Gerry Blair.*

Ringtail

This elusive critter of the southwestern United States, Mexico and Central America is sometimes called the ringtail cat. This is somewhat misleading as the ringtail is a relative of the raccoon family. He is cat-like in appearance, however, and in many of his habits. He is a night hunter and a day sleeper. His explosive bark can sometimes be heard in the rocky rim country of the Southwest as he hunts for birds and mice. He will also eat fruits, lizards and grasshoppers. The ringtail, or cacomistle, as he is sometimes called, also has a taste for chicken. Poultry farmers suffer heavy losses in ringtail country.

The ringtail is a sleek, slender animal that is usually a bit more than two feet long, half of which is tail. The body fur is short and grayish-buff on the sides, grading to a cream on the belly and a darker gray on the back. The tail is decorated with alternating bands of black and white. A big bull of a ringtail will weigh a bit under three pounds. The face is foxlike and is dominated by the huge round eyes. The feet are furred and equipped with razor-sharp claws. The claws are partially retractable.

216

The female ringtail has her young in the early summer. Three or four one-ounce kits are normal. They are born blind and will suckle for the first three weeks of life. They grow fast and will be night hunting with momma in a couple of months. Captive ringtails have lived to be fourteen years of age.

I have called a number of ringtail to the camera on night-calling trips. They usually come closer and seem unafraid. I have had my best luck calling the upper limits of the Sonoran Desert, at about 5,000- or 6,000-feet elevations. The ringtails will not come far to the call. They are short-legged critters and not equipped for long distance hikes. The eyes look like moons in the artificial light. Ringtail will usually come slow and will highpoint to inspect the source of the noise. You may see a head peeking over the top of a large rock or the head and a slender neck perched gracefully on a low limb.

I have called one ringtail in the daytime. I was set up in a brushy basin above Camp Verde, Arizona, calling for cats. The elevation was about 5,500 feet, perfect for the lush growth of pinion and juniper that covered the sloped. There was a water catchment at the bottom. I was using one of the lip squeakers marketed by Murry Burnham, hoping to tempt a cat or a gray fox from the canyon bottom. The ringtail appeared suddenly to my right, exposing half its body over the top of a jumble of rocks. I took my camera from the backpack and took a number of excellent photographs. When he left the critter slid back into the boulder pile. I had set up the stand less than fifty feet from his bedroom.

The Flyers

Flying birds of every kind will come to the predator call at one time or another. Hawks are the most common. I call in about as many red-tail hawks as I do fur bearers. They are a protected species and therefore exist in amazing numbers. They are efficient hunters and will take a staggering toll of small game such as quail, cottontail rabbits and tree squirrels. The hawks usually come to the call within the first two minutes of noise. Most hawks will fly as near the call as they can and perch close by. I have had red-tails light in the very bush or tree I was calling from.

I have called eagles, both bald and golden, on a few occasions. Eagles are not abundant in this state and that may account for their lack of response. The eagles that have responded to my calls have never landed. They soar and circle a hundred feet above until they satisfy their curiosity.

Crows and ravens are probably the most common birds a caller attracts. These intelligent opportunists will come in singles, pairs and flocks to investigate

Eagles seldom light at the call but will often circle overhead until they are convinced a 200-pound rabbit is out of their class. *Photo Bureau of Land Management.*

the excitement. They will hover over the hiding tree with a loud swishing of wings, cawing continually. I am glad to see them. Crow response indicates to me that the area has not been heavily called. If it had the crows would have been educated. Crow presence, particularly if they caw, adds to the calling stand because coyotes and other predators trust the crow's judgment. If the crow is there, the coyote knows it can't be too dangerous for him.

Many small birds not ordinarily classed as predators will come to the call. I have had gangs of the bad-mannered pinion jays light in every available tree around me and profane the air with their raucous calls. Other jays also will come, and so will many of the woodpeckers. I have had yellow-shafted flickers look me over almost eyeball to eyeball. The peewees, such as the white-breasted nuthatch and the pygmy nuthatch, will crawl limbs all around my face. I sometimes use the lip squeaker in an attempt to attract the birds to the camera.

Skunks

I have never called a skunk in the daytime. The few I have called at night have been real nuisances. We have all four varieties of skunk in Arizona—the striped, the hooded, the hognosed and the spotted—and in some areas of the state they are plentiful. The striped skunk is the most common. I was calling for coon one dark night along the Beaver Creek watershed when a striped skunk moseyed in to check out the noise. I did everything I could to discourage the visit —shining the light directly in his eyes, tossing small rocks and limbs his way, whispering very uncomplimentary descriptions—but he refused to be discouraged. He seemed intent on crawling on my lap to take a really close look at the piece of plastic that I was eating. I didn't want to get too tough, and for obvious reasons, couldn't shoot the critter. He was too close and besides, Arizona law prohibits shooting any critter at night except the raccoon. I finally backed off and left the canyon to the skunk. I made him pay for his visit, however. I popped an electronic flash unit full in his face at about five feet. Maybe that will teach him.

Owls

Most of the owls come to a call, most often at night. I have also called them on day calls early in the morning. They can be particularly startling at night when they glide by on silent wings, gently brushing a cap or a nose. The large owls, such as the barn owls and great horned owls, are particularly interested in the call. If you are night calling and there are owls about, expect to be surprised by them.

Big Game

I have had most varieties of big game come to the call at one time or another. Most of the time they do not come very close, usually only close enough to check out the source of the noise. But there are exceptions. I had a cow elk almost crawl into the bush with me on an early summer coyote hunt in northern Arizona. I was not fur hunting as the pelts were worthless then. I do not ordinarily call to the gun during the summer but had been requested by the Arizona Game and Fish folks to help thin out a few of the fawn eaters during the peak of the fawning season. The cow came to me on the prod. I suspected she had a calf nearby. The cow refused to run off even after I revealed my 200-pound frame in an attempt to convince her I was definitely not a coyote. I finally left, looking over my shoulder all the while. I am convinced elk come as a protective response since I have called them mainly during the summer when the calves are about. I have also called them in early fall when they are in the rut. Bull elk will come to the call if you set up near a harem. They will not travel far from the harem however, as they seem afraid that some hot-blooded youngster will sneak in to grab a quick bite of the forbidden fruit.

I have had a few antelope come to the varmint call. I used the call one season to help bag a decent antelope. It was the last day of Arizona's three-day season and I had not found the buck I wanted. Shortly after daylight I glassed up a lone buck from about two miles. The critter was feeding in an open area and just behind him was a line of standing juniper. There were pushdowns between us, perfect for a stalk. I could see that the antelope had high horns but could not tell anything about the thickness. It was the last day and I decided to take him.

I was within a half mile of his last position when I blundered into a herd of does. I slid into a pile of pushdowns to wait them out. I hoped they would feed on past without spooking. The herd had a buck, which was not surprising as the Arizona season coincides with the rut. I never got a close look at the buck because he was nervous as hell, but not because of me. He didn't know I was there. He was afraid one of his hard-won sweeties would wander off in the junipers. I wanted a look at him and knew I didn't have much of a chance in the thick pushdowns if I let nature take its course. I always carry a predator call on all of my hunts. I blew one anguished squeal on the tube and that was enough. The buck charged me. He came at what I call the rutting strut. Bouncing with all four feet hitting the ground at once. Every time the feet hit, the buck emitted an explosive grunt. He was a decent buck but nothing to write home about—fifteen, maybe sixteen-inch prongs with fair thickness. I decided not to take him. The other buck I had seen through the scope might be a little larger. The herd buck charged to fifty feet, got a whiff of me and took off. He was running straight to that second buck and I was sure both would spook out of the country. I changed my mind when the little buck was a hundred feet out. The hot-loaded .25-06 100-grainer took him high in the lungs. While I was doing the dirty work I heard a snort. The other buck, the one I had seen originally, was standing about a hundred yards out watching the surgery. I suspect he also came to investigate the call. My buck was a bit smaller. He taped just under sixteen on each horn.

I have called a few desert bighorn sheep. I don't do a lot of calling in sheep country and might have called more if I spent more time there. Most of the time

Desert bighorn sheep also come to the call but seldom come close. *Photo Gerry Blair.*

a sheep will not come close. He will top a ridge and look down disdainfully. I have called the Kofa Mountain Range, the Black Mountain Range and the Castle Dome Mountain Range along the state's western border. I have sighted sheep at all three locations and have taken excellent pictures of called sheep using an 800mm lens. It is not unusual to have sheep come to two hundred yards, about the right distance for the big lens.

On a fur hunt in the central part of the state, I called a big ram to hand-shaking distance. I was calling the rugged Santa Teresa Mountains north of Klondyke. At that time the chaparral-covered hills held good numbers of both fox and bobcat. A little farther down, in the high desert, coyotes were abundant. I was calling from the depths of a squatty juniper on an early morning stand. I put the rising sun at my back to keep it out of my eyes and to put it into the eyes of the customer. Five minutes into the call I heard a rock roll and turned slowly to check it out. The sun was in my eyes of course, but I could see a magnificent bighorn ram less than thirty feet up the hill. I moved a bit to get a better look and the big ram bolted. Other sheep joined him. I never got a count on the herd but suspect it might have been more than a dozen. The sheep, I learned later, were transplanted to the area from the Colorado River.

Other critters will come infrequently. I have called a couple of badger, one porcupine, a hell of a lot of cattle and one bull buffalo. Dogs will often come, particularly if you are calling near houses or a ranch. Once in a while a house cat will answer. If I am a long way from habitation and figure the cat is feral I will give him the same reward I would a coyote. Feral house cats are a problem in most parts of the country. They are ruthless killers of most small game and will take anything up to the size of a cottontail rabbit.

A caller never knows what to expect when he sets out to squeeze the rabbit. He may get nothing. The next call might produce a curious deer. A call a quarter of a mile away might get a mountain lion or a bear. I guess the suspense of the call is one of the things that keeps us calling.

17

Reading Sign

Locating game habitat is the most critical element in successful predator calling. You can't call critters if there are none there to be called. Reading sign is an important skill in locating critter country. I talked about the sign left by each critter in the individual chapters. The treatment there was superficial. This chapter will explore in detail the tracks and droppings left by each of the listed predators. No written material, it should be noted, can make you a good tracker. Most critter tracks will vary in size and somewhat in configuration. The soil or surface which receives the cast will complicate the matter further. The droppings, though often more distinctive than the track, cannot be trusted implicitly. The shape and texture of animal offal will vary with diet.

If all animal tracks were left on level ground in light dust or snow the job of tracking would be much easier; a full foot imprint could be studied and distinctive differences between hind and front feet could be noted. Overlapping, or the lack of it, also would be apparent. The length of the gait would further identify the traveler that left the tracks. Under these conditions even the most inexperienced woodsman could make an identification, but most tracking situations are more difficult. Many times a series of tracks is not available for study. I feel fortunate if I have one complete track. Most of the sign I investigate are partial prints of one foot, and even that portion of a track may be distorted due to alternate freezing and thawing, melting snow or blowing dust. I can often identify the animal, tell his direction of travel, make a good guess on the freshness of the track, determine if it is a front foot track or a hind foot track and decide if the critter was walking or running. If I can find more than one print I can usually tell if it was an adult or sub-adult and if the animal was traveling or hunting. You will be able to do the same if you will read and study the material contained in this chapter but the reading alone will not do the job. You must apply the material to actual tracking problems in the field. Use this knowledge and use your common sense. Experience will teach the rest.

Black Bear

Look for bear tracks along the banks of lakes, ponds and waterways. Away from water the tracks may be seen in the dust of primitive roads, on game trails or almost any place in the snow. The track of the black bear is distinctive in most of his range. If the range of a black bear and a grizzly bear overlaps, some confusion may develop. Size of track is not a reliable identifier. Some grizzlies will leave smaller tracks than some blacks. The best identifier is the placement of the claw marks. The grizzly has much longer claws and the imprint will be a good distance ahead of the toes. This will likely be noticed more on the more heavily clawed front feet.

All bear leave tracks that are somewhat similar in general configuration to a human track. The hind track will be particularly human-like. The pad of the foot will show an elongated triangle fronted by five oval toe prints. The large toe on a bear, unlike human feet, will be on the outside of the foot. The toes will be fronted with five tiny dots made by the non-retractable claws. The front foot of a bear is rounder in appearance, somewhat resembling the imprint of a human who was standing tiptoed. The ball of the foot, the toe marks and the claw marks show. Both bear and humans are plantigrades. That means they walk on the flat of their feet, putting their weight on the entire foot.

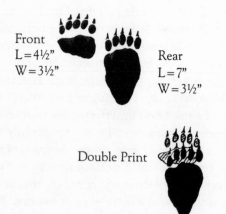

Front
L=4½"
W=3½"

Rear
L=7"
W=3½"

Double Print

Black Bear print

The walking gait of the black bear will show the hind foot imprint slightly forward of the front. The tracks will be on the same side. These two imprints will sometimes overlap, with the hind foot being placed in the exact center of the track left by the front foot. In dust or shallow mud the inside toe may not register, leaving a four-toed track. The rear foot of a bear is considerably larger than the front. Gallop patterns of running bear are distinctive. The hind feet are brought forward of the front feet at every leap.

Black bear use well-established trails. The trail may take them from the bedding area to the feeding area or may wander through an area of good feed. If a fresh track is found, the bear will likely be in the general area, unless a dramatic change in weather or food availability has triggered a migration.

Bear Trees

Most bear have an urge to bite, claw and rub. Trees are mainly the object of this hostile behavior but wooden signs come in for a fair share of attention. Bear trees are usually located at prominent points in a bear's territory and may serve to warn other bear to stay away. In some instances the bear is after a treat. He may tear strips of bark from conifers such as pine, spruce and fir to get at the tasty pulp beneath. Vertical tooth marks are often visible in the de-barked portion. Young bear often climb trees. If that tree happens to be an aspen, the cubs' claws will injure the white bark and cause black scabs to form as the tree heals. The claw marks will remain visible for the life of the tree.

Droppings

Bear scat is distinctive. It is large and is not likely to be confused with the scat of other critters. Bear droppings will vary in size and shape with what the bear eats. If he is on a diet of meat or carrion the scat will likely consist of hair. Vegetarian bear will leave scat that show what he ate and where he had supper. If he dined on ants from a hollow log, the scat will likely contain chunks of rotten wood that went with the ants. If the bear ate a piece of carrion from a lion-killed deer or elk, the scat will show hair and probably traces of the pine needles and leaves the lion used to cover his kill. If the bear fed on nuts or berries the scat will consist of the pulpy residue of that meal.

Bear scat is a reliable indicator of the bear's feed grounds. A feeding bear can deposit a lot of offal in a couple of weeks feeding. These feed grounds will be found mostly in the fall when the fruits, nuts and berries are ripe. The bear will be gorging himself to build enough fat to last through the winter.

Bear scat may take the form of a tube or be in a formless mass. If tubes are formed they will have a diameter of one to one and a half inches. The size of the scat will vary with the size of the bear and with his diet.

A feeding bear will leave other sign. He will overturn rocks to get at the insects that live below. I saw an area once where a bear had overturned every cow pile along a ridge looking for insects. Turkey will do this also. I knew it was a bear in this instance because I found other sign. Anthills may be scooped out, logs will be overturned or torn apart, oak limbs will be torn from trees, and bee trees and bee caves will be attacked.

Bobcat

The bobcat is mostly nocturnal in his hunts and his travels. You will need to depend on your sign-reading skill to detect his presence. The track can be confused with dog tracks or coyote tracks if only a partial track is visible. Cat tracks are more rounded than dog or coyote tracks and will not usually show claw marks. I say not usually because they sometimes do. If a cat is walking on an unstable surface he will extend the claws for a better grip. I have also seen claw marks in cat tracks made in mud and snow. These are usually visible when the cat slips. The claws come out to stop the slide. A sure identifier for cat tracks is the shape of the rear of the pad. If you have a complete track in either dust or snow check for two separate lobes. Cats have two and members of the dog family have only one.

Bobcat tracks will vary in size as do the tracks of other critters. All will be almost round. Look for a track that measures about two to three inches in diameter. The length and width measurements may vary slightly but they will be close. The stride of the cat will also vary with the size of the critter. I have seen tracks with a stride of ten inches; a foot or thirteen inches is probably about average. Unlike members of the dog family, the cat has front and hind feet that are about the same size. Fox, coyote and dog tracks will show a larger print for the front foot. The cat track may show a somewhat smaller ball pad for the hind foot. If the cat is running or trotting the tracks will be about a foot apart. The track left by the front foot will show a wider spread of the toes than the hind foot. If a cat is leaping he may cover more than eight feet at a jump.

Look for cat tracks around waterholes or waterways and along game trails. The sand of brushy canyon bottoms will also show cat travel. Check

Bobcat print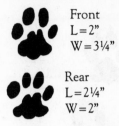

Front
L = 2"
W = 3¼"

Rear
L = 2¼"
W = 2"

Double Print

along drainages. These areas get the most water and will have the most brush. Brush means rodents and that means groceries to the bobcat. I have also seen cat tracks on the points of rocky rims. The critters hunt these areas and will often visit the points to make a scratch or a deposit.

The shape and size of cat droppings will vary with the part of the country and the cat's diet. Here in the Southwest I seldom have a problem in identifying cat scat. It is almost always left in segmented pellets about an inch or two long and with a diameter of about a half inch. The droppings are black and moist when they are fresh. As time passes they harden and lose water. The action of the sun causes the color to change from black to gray and eventually to a chalk white.

In other parts of the country the scat may not be distinctive. In many humid areas, where water conservation is not as important as it is in the Southwest, the scat may or may not be segmented. Unsegmented scat may be difficult to identify, particularly if there are coyotes sharing the same range.

Cat scat, it should be noted, seldom contains vegetable matter. They are primarily meat eaters and their droppings reflect that fact. Look for segmented scat which is mostly hair with perhaps a few small bone fragments. Grass may occasionally be found that the cat has eaten mainly as roughage. Grass is seldom present in most of the cat's range and is not often seen.

Bobcat have scenting areas that they visit on a regular basis. You are likely to find these at the intersection of trails, on rocky points or along drainages. You are apt to find scat from a number of separate visits. These may have been left from the same cat or by a number of cats if the scent post is located at the intersection of two or more territories. You may also see offal from both fox and coyote on top of the cat droppings.

Coyote print

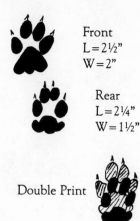

Front
L = 2½"
W = 2"

Rear
L = 2¼"
W = 1½"

Double Print

It is the nature of most cats to make some attempt to cover their droppings. This is often a halfhearted attempt that is made more for the sake of tradition than anything else. Southwestern cats seldom make any attempt. Perhaps the hardness of the soil may have convinced them of the futility of this gesture. Most scratches I have seen here in the Southwest were left by toms during the breeding season. In other parts of the country scratching is more common. If dung is found and it is marked by a scratch you may be certain that it was left by a cat.

Certain areas may have both bobcat and lynx using the same range. As a rule the lynx tracks are larger and may be as large as a small mountain lion. The lynx is a shorter-bodied animal, however, and will have a shorter gait. The lynx is also much lighter than the lion and will not make as deep an impression. In snowy areas the mountain lion's tail will often drag through the snow making the sign unmistakable.

Coyote

If you have seen a dog track you know what a coyote track looks like. There may be trackers around who can tell the subtle differences in the track left by a dog, a wolf and a coyote, but I am not one of them. The large breeds of dog have a track that is much larger than the coyote. Most of the dog tracks we see in the back country are made either by hunting dogs or by a rancher's cow dog. The hunting dogs are usually hounds. They have huge feet and there is no problem in identification. Quail areas will sometimes show tracks left by retrievers. The labs and the shorthairs are also bigger-footed than the coyote and are not difficult to identify. Ranch dogs are another story. They are often mid-size breeds such as the Australian shepherd or the border collie, both breeds with a foot about coyote-sized. I look for horse or man tracks with the critter tracks. If none are found I assume the track was made by a coyote as these dogs are seldom allowed to roam unescorted.

All members of the dog family have a front foot that is larger than the rear. This is particularly evident on the coyote. The length of the prints may be about the same but the width is noticeably different. There is also a difference in the heel pads. If you have a clear track you will be able to see that the heel pad on the rear foot is smaller and of a different shape. If a coyote is walking, the front and rear tracks will be about fifteen inches apart. If he is trotting, the front and rear feet will appear in pairs about four inches apart. The pairs will be noted every fifteen or sixteen inches and the hind prints will be placed forward of the front prints. If a coyote is in a hurry he may leap ten feet at a jump, or about half that if he is in a deep snow.

The diet of the coyote usually makes his scat identifiable. Dog droppings are sometimes similar in shape and size, but the dog does not have to make his living the same way a coyote does. I have had little trouble in the field separating dog and coyote scat. Bobcat droppings will also resemble coyote in a few instances. The contents of the scat will usually make identification easy. The cat is mostly a meat eater and the coyote eats anything, including bobcats. His scat will likely contain a variety of animal and vegetable matter. Seeds, fruits and berries in the scat will eliminate the cat.

What the coyote had for supper will influence the size, shape and texture of his offal. If he is on a diet of pure meat or carrion, the scat will likely be very loose, about the consistency of a thin pudding. If he has gulped down a rabbit, hair and all, the scat is likely to be almost pure hair and be much larger than usual. A diet of juniper berries or manzanita berries may produce a reddish scat that is crumbly with a lot of seeds. Coyotes eating prickly pear will leave scat that is a wine purple with a large quantity of peels and seeds. If there are a large number of javelina in the area you may not notice much in the way of these fruited droppings. The thrifty little pig snuffs them up and runs them through again.

You are most likely to see coyote droppings along trails. Look for high points on the trail where the coyote can let the wind carry the essence of his droppings. The point of intersecting trails is also a favorite toilet for the coyote.

Fox

The fox is another dog. His prints will show much of the characteristics of the coyote prints discussed above with a few notable exceptions. The fox prints, obviously, are smaller. There are also subtle differences between the track of the red and gray fox.

Red Fox

As with other animals the track of the red fox will vary with the size and age of the animal. An average track might measure about two and one half inches long for the front track. The rear print would be a half inch shorter. The foot of the red fox is furred and this foot fur will often show in a deep print. Even shallow prints will be fuzzed by the foot whiskers. The width of the walking trail will be about three or four inches.

The track of the red fox has a distinctive marking that will identify it from the gray fox and from small coyotes. If you have a distinct imprint check for an inverted "V" on the front foot track at the front of the heel mark. This will be seen to a lesser extent in the rear foot track also. In shallow snow or light dust the "V" may show without the rest of the pad showing. This produces a track with the light imprint of the "V," four toes and a fuzzy area caused by foot fur.

Diet will produce a variation in size and looks of red fox droppings. In general they will exhibit all of the variations of the coyote scat. In most instances they will be much smaller.

Front
L = 2½"
W = 2"

Rear
L = 2"
W = 1½"

Double Print

Red Fox print

Gray Fox print Front
L = 1½"
W = 1¼"

 Rear
L = 1¼"
W = 1"

Double Print

Gray Fox

The gray fox track is generally smaller than the red fox and larger than the kit or swift fox. Different-sized individuals cause a grading of tracks that might cause confusion in overlapping range. The gray fox is the only one of his family that climbs a tree readily, so if the tracks lead to the base of a tree and disappear you may be sure it was made by a gray. The front foot is slightly larger than the rear and the foot is not furred. The front track usually shows more distinctly than the rear. This is particularly true in areas where a hard surface permits only a partial print. Grays often have a perfect overlap on the front and rear print; the rear foot will be placed in the exact center of the front print. At times this overlap is slightly imperfect causing a double print that is distinctive.

Gray fox droppings are similar in appearance to coyote droppings but are smaller. In areas where their range overlaps they are likely to be eating about the same things. The scat in these instances will be identical except for size—the larger coyote scat is apparent. Large fox and small coyotes may approach the same size in their scat, however, and size is not a definite indicator.

Like other members of the dog family, the fox will leave his scat at trail junctions, along drainages and at high points in his range. He seeks elevation when evacuating. In flat country with few spectacular features I have seen fox back up to small rocks to make a deposit. They will do the same at anthills and other slightly raised locations.

Javelina

Although the javelina is not closely related to the pig his tracks are almost identical except they are smaller in size than most adult pigs. There is a dewclaw

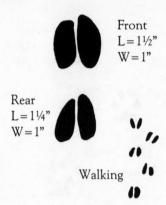

Front
L = 1½"
W = 1"

Collared Peccary (Javelina) print

Rear
L = 1¼"
W = 1"

Walking

on the hind feet that does not show in the tracks. The tracks will be about an inch and a half long by an inch and a quarter wide. I have seen them much smaller. The front foot leaves a slightly larger print. Walking tracks will appear with the front and hind feet tracks closely paired and with about eight inches between the pairs. The tracks will sometimes show an overlap.

Feeding javelina will leave other sign. Most noticeable will be rooting areas around the base of cactus and other plants. The cactus pulp will also be eaten and shredded. Prickly pear cactus is a favorite food. The peccaries will dig at the base of the cactus to get at the spineless roots. They will also take bites from the cactus sections and in season they will eat the fruit.

Javelinas are primarily vegetarian but are not fanatic about it. They eat meat and insects if they are available. Vegetable matter is the main food of the critter, however, and his droppings will be mostly fiber. Look for a cluster of oblong pellets that range in size from one inch to more than three inches in length.

Non-smokers can locate javelina by smell. I have smelled most of the javelina I have encountered before I have seen them. The musky odor is somewhat like that found around an area where cattle congregate and urinate. Javelina leave the spoor in their travels, perhaps as a means of marking feeding trails for other herd members. It will be particularly strong in an area where the critters have been recently startled. Bedding areas in caves and old mine tunnels will also have a strong musky odor.

Look for feeding sign along cactus-covered sidehills. In the winter the pigs will likely feed on the sidehill that gets the morning sun. Both the prickly pear and the hedgehog cactus are favorite foods. Look for tracks along game trails and in the sandy bottoms of dry washes and check the muddy banks of stock tanks and desert streams.

Mountain Lion

The main evidence of the mountain lion is the track. It is large and is usually easy to identify. Some problem in identification may be experienced in the Southwest where the range of the mountain lion and jaguar overlap. The jaguar track is quite similar to the track of a mountain lion but is usually larger.

The front foot of the mountain lion is larger than the rear. If the cat is in a hurry the toes on the front feet tend to spread leaving a wider track. Claws do not ordinarily show but will be visible under the same conditions listed for the bobcat. A lion track made in soft dirt may be three or four inches in width and will be larger in fresh soft snow. The warmth in the cat's foot causes melting which causes an enlargement of the imprint. If the snow is deep the cat's tail will drag. The spread of a mountain lion track will be around eight inches but may vary considerably. A walking lion may leave a foot to a foot and a half between imprints but a trotting lion will leave tracks in pairs and the pairs will be separated by about two feet. Tracks made in soft snow will usually show the drag marks of the feet between imprints.

Mountain lion scat takes about the same variety of form as bobcat droppings. The offal can be segmented in the dry Southwest. It is larger than bobcat droppings with the individual stools sometimes measuring five inches. Many of the droppings will be decorated with scratches. Try and determine which way the lion faced when he scratched as this will usually show his direction of travel. Look for lion sign along game trails, on little-used dusty roads and along the

Mountain Lion print

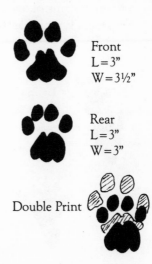

Front
L = 3"
W = 3½"

Rear
L = 3"
W = 3"

Double Print

banks of waterholes. Any area in the mountain lion's range which contains a concentration of deer is also a good place to look for lion sign. Some hunters search out lion by driving the primitive roads in lion country after a light snow. If a lion track is found they either run the cat with dogs or try to trail near enough to bring him in with a call.

Lion also cover uneaten kills with debris. This has been fully discussed already in the chapter dealing with the lion and will not be repeated here.

Raccoon

Like the human and the bear, the raccoon walks plantigrade, placing his weight evenly on his entire foot. The coon is a critter of the water primarily and his tracks will often be found along the muddy shore. The tracks consist of a pad and five toes. The tracks are usually paired with the left hind foot placed adjacent to the right forefoot. The hind track will be the largest and the foretrack will show the widest spread of the toes. Claw marks are usually visible. The hind foot track of a raccoon will measure about 3½ inches in length; the forefoot track will be almost an inch shorter. The paired tracks will be six to twenty inches apart depending on the size of the coon and the style of his gait. Look for coon tracks along waterways and on the banks of lakes and swamps.

Raccoon scat is not as easy to identify as tracks. The offal will range in color from reddish-brown to black. Exposure to the sun will bleach the scat a chalk white. The stools are grainy and irregular in size and may be easily confused with droppings from either skunk or opossum. If the droppings are found on the limb of a tree or on a log it is probable they are from a raccoon.

Front
L = 2¼"
W = 1½"

Rear
L = 3¼"
W = 1½"

Double Print

Raccoon print

18

Skinning Care

There are two techniques for skinning fur bearers—cased and open. Most critters will be case skinned. Simply put, that is when the hind legs of the fur bearer are split from the ankle to the vent and the skin is pulled from the carcass as one would pull a sock from a foot. Open skinning is the technique used on a very few fur bearers. It is always used when the pelt is to be used as a rug mount or for full-form mounting. Open-skinned animals are skinned by making a long cut from the vent to the chin. Other cuts are made from the pad of each foot down the inside of the leg until the belly cut is intersected. Each technique will be described in detail further along in this chapter.

Proper fur care begins before the hunter opens his knife to begin skinning. Hopefully the animal was killed with a cartridge that has not made a mess. Do not drag the critter on the way to the truck as this will damage the fur and reduce the value of the pelt. Dragging will also soil the pelt and cause more work in handling. If you do not intend to skin the animal immediately, place it in the vehicle so that it is protected from dust, mud and sun.

All carcasses should be skinned within a few hours after they are killed. If the weather is warm they should be skinned immediately. Strong stomach acids will cause the inside of the belly to turn a sickly green which is accompanied by a distasteful smell. This condition will make skinning unpleasant and will reduce the value of the pelt. I usually skin as soon as the stand is finished. The critters peel more easily when they are warm. A fox or a bobcat can be skinned in less than ten minutes; older coyotes may take a bit longer. I make it a point to leave the carcass in a location where it will be visible to the flying scavengers. They will make short work of it. Take care that the carcass is not left visible to a public road. There is no need to unnecessarily offend the sensibilities of non-hunters. We have enough problems without inviting trouble.

Case Skinning

Case skinning is the most common technique for pelts that are to be sold. Remember, if you intend to keep the pelt and have it prepared by a taxidermist, this is not the technique to use.

Use a sharp pocketknife and make a cut along the inside of the hind legs. Start the cut at the anal vent and cut in a straight line to the ankle. Slip the point of the knife under the skin and cut from the inside out. This will not damage the fur. Cut a ring around each hind leg above the pad. Pull the hide away from the legs using moderate pressure. It may be necessary to use the point of the knife to free stubborn areas. The hide will come freely on the legs but will become taut around the hip areas. Free the hips and work one hand through the hide just above the tail. Pull the hide back along the tail using the point of the knife to free stubborn areas. You will be able to peel the fur of the tail about two or three inches along the tail bone before it binds up. When this happens take a tail stripper or a pair of round sticks and place one on each side of the tail bone. Grasp these in the left hand pressing them firmly to the bone with the tail fur in front of them. Grab the base of the tail with the free right hand and pull. The tail bone should strip cleanly from the sheath. If problems are encountered use the point of the knife to make a cut along the bottom of the tail extending from the vent to the tail tip. Use pressure and the knife to separate the tailbone from the sheath.

Fasten the critter by a hind foot to a comfortable working height. Use rope or wire, something strong enough to withstand pressure. Grab the hide by the loose portion and pull vigorously, stripping the hide down over the carcass. Use the knife when necessary. The hide will strip easily until the front legs are reached. The hide will be tight around the chest and care must be taken to prevent cutting the hide. Take your time here, alternately pulling and cutting with the knife until you can insert a finger under the base of one of the legs. Use this handhold to exert more pressure and make minor cuts with the knife as needed. Strip each front leg down to the first joint. Some will skin lower on the legs but the fur buyer does not pay extra for the extra skin. Make a circular cut around each front leg and pull the leg fur free.

The hide will tighten again around the neck and skull. A fox, in particular, will be tough at this point. The fox has a small neck and a larger head and it is sometimes quite a task to stretch the neck skin over the skull. Be patient. Exert pressure and use the knife when needed. Use your fingers to feel when the hide has reached the ears. At this point use the knife to cut the ear cartilage away from the skull. Continue pulling and cutting until the eyes are reached. Use extreme care when working around the throat because of a large blood vessel on each side of the throat. If this is punctured the blood will gush out and soil the fur. If this does happen take the critter down and tie the rope to the loose fur and suspend the carcass with the head up. Gravity will keep the blood in the body cavity.

Cut the eyeholes free. Take the black rims around the eyeball with the fur. This can be done by keeping the knife close to the skull and working carefully. Continue stripping and cutting to the lips. Take the black rim of meat with the fur, cutting it from the skull. If the animal is not freshly dead the teeth will likely be locked together, making it difficult to use the knife. Pry the jaws apart and insert a stick to hold the jaws apart; skinning will be easier. Cut the tip of the nose off with the fur and the skinning job is finished. The hide will be hair side in. I reverse the hide so the hair is out until I am home and ready to resume work. This will prevent dirt and debris soiling the wet hide. Place the folded fur into a plastic bag to keep it away from flies or dirt. Place it in a cool place until you are ready to handle it.

Special Problems

Called and shot critters often bleed from the nose which creates a problem in skinning. As the hide is pulled over the head, the blood is transferred to the fur. I solve this potential problem by tying a plastic bag over the head to catch the dripping blood. When the animal has been skinned down to the front legs I take the carcass down and retie it with the head up, then I take the plastic bag from the head and wipe off blood around the face using paper towels. The animal is then tied head up so gravity will keep the blood within the chest cavity.

Another problem often encountered is a bloody front leg. This wound also creates a problem in soiling the fur as the hide is pulled over it. Take an axe or hatchet and cut the leg off at the wound. This will protect the fur of the leg as it is skinned.

Fleas and Flies

Many predators will host an amazing variety of vermin. I shot a female coyote south of Winslow, Arizona, one trip that carried enough fleas to pull a wagon. Some fur handlers advise leaving the hide out overnight in the cold to allow the fleas to migrate but I have found this does not work. I have hung skinned hides outside for days in sub-zero temperatures and found fleas on the hides. I have never experienced any problems with fleas and therefore pay little attention to them. I do know that these fleas are capable of transmitting bubonic plague. Recent studies here in northern Arizona have indicated that a good number of the coyotes host fleas that have feasted on a plague-infested host. I also know that these critter fleas seldom munch on humans. I have never been bitten, neither has any trapper or caller to my knowledge. This doesn't mean that I won't be bitten tomorrow; it simply means that it is very unlikely to happen and I choose to spend my time worrying about more important things. If you are turned off by fleas there are a couple of precautions that can be taken to minimize any danger.

Many callers carry a large green plastic sack on their hunts. When a critter is bagged they slip the carcass into the sack and give a few enthusiastic squirts of Black Flag into the sack. The end is then tied to trap the insecticide. After a half hour or so of fumigating, the carcass is removed and skinned. Most of the fleas are either dead or too sick to worry about migrating.

Another technique is spraying the hind legs and feet of the suspended carcass with insecticide. About the only place the skinner touches the fur is in this area. When skinning progresses past the rear the skinner is handling the inside of the skin and encounters few fleas.

Some skinners also wear gloves during skinning. You will find it difficult to skin if the gloves are heavy, so try the thin latex gloves sold in grocery stores for dishwashing. They protect but still allow the delicate sense of feel needed to skin a critter.

Most of the critters that have given me fleas did so as I was transporting them to the truck. Do not throw the carcass across your shoulders. If you are too far from the truck to carry it comfortably in your hands, it would be well to skin it immediately and place the hide in a plastic bag.

Flies can also be a problem early in the calling season. Protect the unskinned carcass from blow flies if it is not to be skinned immediately. After skinning, the hide needs the same protection. If flies do manage to lay their eggs on the hide brush them off using a stiff brush.

Open Skinning

Open skinning is always done if you intend to have the hide tanned by a taxidermist. It also is done for fatty critters such as raccoon, badger, beaver and bear. In recent times, fur buyers in certain parts of the country have expressed a preference to cased rather than open skinning. It is best to make local inquiries to determine local preference.

To skin an animal in the open—or block—technique, lay it flat on its back and make a knife cut on the outside of each hind leg. Slip the point of the knife inside the skin at the vent and make a straight cut to the foot pad. Do the same on the inside of the front legs, cutting from the foot pad to the center of the chest. The lines will meet at the center of the chest. Now go back to the vent and make a straight cut that extends from the anal vent straight up the belly to the bottom of the chin. Handle the tail exactly as you would in case skinning. It is now a simple matter to pull and cut the skin away from the carcass. If you intend to have taxidermy work done on the hide it is important to leave the footpads and claws attached to the hide. If you will have the hide to the taxidermist in a day or two, you may want to leave the last joint of the leg in the hide. Skin down to the ankle joint and cut between the bones. The taxidermist will be glad to finish the job. If it will be several days before the taxidermist sees the hide, skin out the foot, peeling and cutting as needed. You will find it difficult to cut off the claws. Use a pair of medium-sized diagonal cutters to make the job easier. When skinning is finished apply a light layer of salt to the wet side of the hide. Fold one time so that one half of the fleshy side covers the other. Roll the hide into a ball and store in a cool and dry place until it is to be taken to the taxidermist.

Selling Wet

A number of fur buyers will be willing to buy hides that have not been fleshed, stretched and dried. If there is such a buyer in your area, simply turn the hide hair-side out and roll it into a compact ball. Place the hide in a plastic bag and make it airtight. Place the bagged hide in your freezer and keep it there until the day of the sale. Take it from the freezer on the morning of the sale and give it a few hours to thaw. This will save a lot of work in fur handling but will likely reduce the price the buyer is willing to pay. Instructions on fur handling will be covered in the next chapter.

19

Care of Pelts

Fur buyers handle hundreds of raw hides in the course of a season. Usually they can tell at a glance if the hides have been correctly handled. The better job you do in preparing the hide for market, the deeper the buyer will reach into his wallet. He will pay top dollar for prime, well-handled fur. Every mistake you make in the preparation of the pelt will cost you money. The buyers are in the habit of writing big numbers on the check when I take my fur to market. They know my collection will be prime and well-handled and rightly so. I had good teachers and I listened well. Here are some of the techniques you can use to earn the respect of the fur buyer.

Washing

There was a time when I would wash a pelt at the least provocation. If I saw a spot of blood or a speck of mud I threw the hide into the washtub without a second thought. It didn't take me long to learn I was working for nothing. Many of the more experienced fur handlers never washed a hide and their fur looked about as good as mine and brought the same price. I learned there were better and quicker alternatives to washing in most cases. I still wash a hide once in a while, but it takes a really filthy fur to get me motivated.

Critters killed in areas with a lot of loose dirt will have the fine dust throughout the fur. Many times they will take regular dust baths in an attempt to discourage some of the vermin they pack around. I don't worry about this kind of dirt until the hide is dried and ready to take off the stretcher. At that point I use a stiff-bristled brush to take most of it out. If the hide does not look good after brushing I may use a vacuum cleaner to suck out the stubborn stuff. If you have access to an air compresser, the air hose will do a fine job of removing accumulated dust.

Critters taken in wet weather can also be a problem. Mud often clings to the fur in tiny balls. Unless there are large gobs of mud I don't bother to wash. The mud will dry and then can be removed with the stiff-bristled brush.

Predator callers have a problem with blood. I do not worry about the blood if it is a spot smaller than a silver dollar. I let it dry and use the brush to take it out. If a light brown stain is left, it usually doesn't matter on most critters. Coyote, bobcat and fox all have brown areas and the stain will likely not be noticed. If the blood stain is large, you will likely be money ahead if you take the time to wash.

If the soiled spot is not large you may find it easier and faster to wash that area before skinning the critter. If this is not possible skin the animal and take the pelt directly to the sink or a pail of cool or lukewarm water. Turn the pelt with the fur side out and immerse it completely in the water and add a squirt or two of liquid detergent. Work up a lather and work the suds through the fur. When it is well soaped, empty the water and rinse. Continue rinsing until the last rinse water remains clear. Take the hide from the pail and hold it by the nose. Use your free hand to strip out the water, working from the nose to the tail. When you have removed all of the water you can in this manner give the hide a few vigorous shakes and dry it further. Slip the hide over the stretcher with the fur side out for drying. Do not nail it down as this is not necessary at this point. Place the hide in a shady location away from flies. The drying will be hastened if the hide is placed where the wind can blow on it.

The Big Stink

Although you are not liable to call many skunks you may need to know how to clean a skunk so that the fur buyer won't have to hold his nose when he reaches for his billfold. You may shoot a skunk occasionally or you may shoot a predator that has had a recent experience with a skunk. Unless the musk is removed, the fur buyer may find he has urgent business in the back of the shop when you come to sell your fur. To clean a skunk, immerse the dead animal in a small can of gasoline. The musk has a petroleum base and will be dissolved by the gas. When the fur is well saturated, remove the animal and shake off the excess gasoline. Lay the carcass in a shady place until the gas evaporates. Skin in the ordinary manner. If the odor of gas remains wash the pelt in warm water and liquid detergent.

If the critter you want to clean is a skunky-smelling cat or fox, it will be best if you skin the animal before dipping it in the gas. Turn the hide fur side out and saturate the hide with the gasoline. Dry and wash in warm water and soap. The water wash will remove all traces of gasoline and leave a hide that looks and smells good.

Pine Pitch

Critters taken from pine country may have gobs of pine pitch balled in the fur. Do not try to pull the ball of pitch loose from the hair because the hair will come with the pitch and leave a gap in the fur. The gap will cost you as much money as if you had left the pitch in.

The pitch can usually be removed if it is first thinned with turpentine. Saturate a paper towel with the turpentine and lay it over the pitch ball. The turpentine will soften the pitch and you will be able to work it loose. A little more turpentine applied directly to the spot will remove the few remaining traces of pitch.

Fleshing

The term fleshing may be somewhat misleading. There is always a little flesh left on the hide from skinning but the main object of the fleshing operation is removing the layer of fat that lies between the critter and his hide. If this fat, and the small chunks of meat, are not removed the hide will not dry properly. Too much fat or flesh left on the hide also will cause decay. When this occurs, the hide holding the hair at that spot softens and the hair will fall out.

You will need some way to hold the hide stationary while it is fleshed. A piece of two-by-four board five feet long will do the job if you flesh only a few skins in the course of a season. Round off one end of the board and sand smooth, then plane and sand away all sharp edges. Nail the board to a sturdy support. Now slip the pelt with the hair side in over the board and nail the nose to the rounded end. You will have a work surface a bit less that four inches. Flesh this area and rotate the hide so that a new portion is aligned on the working surface. Continue until the entire hide is fleshed. A larger board will provide more work surface and make the fleshing go faster. You may want to cut down a five-foot piece of one-by-twelve for large animals such as coyote and bobcat. I cut mine to about the same size and shape as a small coyote stretcher.

Burrs, pitch pockets and hair mats must be removed before fleshing. If they are not, the fleshing knife is likely to catch on them and tear an ugly hole in the hide.

To flesh, start at the head of the animal and work the fleshing tool from the head to the tail. A fleshing knife can be any dull scraper but every fur handler has his own idea about the best knife to use. A putty knife might do the job if the sharp edge is dulled and the corners rounded. Some may use a foot-long piece of thin iron which has handles fitted to each end. Most companies which advertise in trapping magazines such as *Fur Fish and Game* offer factory-made fleshing knifes at a moderate cost. Whatever you use, the edge that contacts the hide should not be sharp. Considerable pressure is needed to remove the fat and a sharp flesher is apt to take off chunks of hide and fur at the same time.

There will be areas on the hide the fleshing knife will not reach. The section between the nose and the back of the ears is one such area. Take a sharp pocket-knife to these locations and cut away the flesh and fat. Use caution around the ears. You will find hunks of meat and glands recessed among the folds of the ears. Take your time and remove all of this. If you don't, the small strips of flesh will taint and cause hair slippage.

Use the knife on any part of the hide that cannot be reached with the flesher. It is possible to over-flesh. Don't go down so deep with the flesher that the roots of the hair are disturbed. Good fleshing knives should take off the excess fat but leave the inside of the hide with an even creamy color.

Salt

Some fur handlers use salt as a substitute for proper fleshing. Don't leave enough meat on the hide to feed the local baseball team and try to compensate by pouring on a dime's worth of salt. It doesn't work. Most fur buyers are not enthusiastic about furs that have been over-salted. The salt causes fast drying on the surface but may actually retard the drying of the interior of the hide. Every pass with the salt shaker may cost you money. I use salt only inside the tail because it is usually not tacked flat and is apt to curl during drying, allowing contact between two pieces of hide. If this area is not salted the hide-to-hide contact retards drying and may cause slippage.

Sewing Holey Hides

A well-fleshed hide with no cuts or tears is ready for stretching but hides with holes must be repaired first. Use a white thread of heavy stock and a large needle and work from the flesh side of the pelt. Start by pushing all of the protruding hair back to the fur side of the pelt. If you have problems getting the hair back, wet the area slightly as this will cause the hair to stick together. This should relieve the problem. Pinch the two sides of the tear together and align the sides. Run the threaded needle through both edges about a quarter of an inch from one end of the tear. Sew only the meaty part of the flesh. Do not extend the stitch so that it gathers fur on the opposite side of the tear. Cut the thread leaving enough on each end to tie a square knot. Move down about an eighth of an inch and make another stitch and continue until the opening has been closed. When the pelt dries the repairs will not be visible and should not detract from the value of the pelt.

Forced-Air Drying

Extended periods of wet and humid weather will slow the fur drying process. A recirculating fan can be used to speed up the drying. Turn on the fan as soon as the hides are placed on the stretcher. The exposed fleshy side of the pelt will dry quickly from the action of the moving air. Leave the blower on when the hides are turned fur side out. This will assist in the final drying and will fluff the fur to make more attractive pelts.

The size of the fan needed will depend on the size of the room and the number of pelts. My own preference is a fan with eighteen-inch blades and a three-speed switch.

Stretching

The stretching board allows the green pelt to dry into a shape which takes advantage of the critter's size. Some animals have loose skin which will stretch out almost twice the size of the original animal. If the pelt was allowed to dry without discipline it would shrivel and shrink to a small and unattractive size.

Small fur bearers can be stretched on the wire stretchers available from trapping supply houses. The wire stretchers are also made in sizes to accommodate bobcat and coyote. The advantages of the wire stretchers are moderate cost and ease of use. If you are likely to process only a few furs a season, the wire stretcher might be your best bet.

Many fur handlers are convinced that the wood stretcher permits a more exact fit of skin to stretcher. This extra care, they feel, is rewarded when the fur buyer reaches for his checkbook. There is no doubt in my mind that the wood stretcher produces a more attractive finished hide. The mouth and the hind legs are nailed into position and the stretched hide shows every part of the fur to the best advantage. One drawback to the wood stretcher is cost: You will pay three times as much for the wood as you do for the wire. Another disadvantage is time: It takes longer to dry a hide using wood stretchers.

Two types of wood stretchers are available to the fur handler. One is a piece of solid board cut from one-inch stock. The board is cut to closely approximate the shape and size desired in the finished pelt. The second type of wood stretcher consists of two narrow legs of wood joined at one end to make a "V." This type of stretcher is adjustable and has an open space between the legs to permit air circulation. The two-piece stretcher should be used on fur bearers which are fox-sized or larger.

To make a two-piece stretcher that will accept a coyote skin start with a one-by-six piece of pine that is six feet long. Split the piece down the center with a table saw. If none is available have the piece split at the lumber yard. You will have two six-foot pieces of wood each about two and three quarter inches wide. Taper one end of the pieces to obtain a shape that closely resembles the nose of a coyote and sand the taper smooth. Use a hand plane or a wood rasp to taper the outside edges of the legs from nose to back. Sand away all sharp edges. Drive a small nail into the inside tip of one of the tapered legs. Pull out the nail using a pair of pliers and drive it into the corresponding spot on the opposite board. Cut off the nail head with a pair of sidecutters and position the two legs of the stretcher together. The nail will serve as a pivot point for the stretcher.

Cut a piece of one-inch stock to serve as the crosspiece. When the hide is positioned and tacked to the stretcher, the two legs are pulled apart at the tail-end to supply tension to the hide. The tension is maintained by nailing the crosspiece to the two legs at a point below the hide. You may want to use bolts instead of nails on the crosspiece. Drill a hole and bolt the crosspiece to one of the legs. Cut a slot in the other end of the crosspiece and run a bolt through this slot and through a hole drilled in the opposite leg. Attach a thumbscrew and the crosspiece can be tightened into position.

The length and width of the stretcher will depend on the animal for which it is intended. Average dimensions for most predators are listed below.

Species	Length	Hips	Shoulders
Badger	28 in.	10 in.	9.0 in.
Bobcat	33 in.	9 in.	7.5 in.
Coyote	50 in.	12 in.	9.5 in.
Red Fox	28 in.	7 in.	5.5 in.

Species	Length	Hips	Shoulders
Gray Fox	24 in.	7 in.	5.5 in.
Lynx	34 in.	9 in.	7.5 in.
Raccoon	24 in.	9 in.	6.5 in.
Ringtail Cat	18 in.	4 in.	3.0 in.
Wolf	66 in.	13 in.	11.0 in.

Remember, these measurements are for average-sized animals measured from tip of nose to base of tail. Many of the species will have a wide size variation in different parts of their range. What may be an average pelt in one area may be a large in another. These measurements give you a starting point in the construction of the stretchers. Adjust the dimensions to meet the size requirements of the critters in your particular area. Fur buyers grade fur on a number of factors, one of which is size. A pelt that is stretched to its maximum size without over-stretching will bring the best price.

You have skinned the animal, washed it if it needed washing, fleshed the hide and sewn the holes. It is now time to place the hide on the stretcher. Turn the hide fur side in so the air will have a chance to dry the meat side of the pelt. Position the nose so that it fits squarely on the end of the stretcher. Check the eye holes to see that the fur is not off-center. If a wood stretcher is used, nail the center of the nose into position. The center of the nose should rest exactly between the center of the two boards. Place a small nail on the underside of the board to hold the nose in this position. Wriggle the hide until you get it positioned squarely on the board. The eyeholes and the ears should hit the center of the stretcher at the top. The tail should hit the center of the stretcher at the rear. Pull the hide as far to the rear of the stretcher as possible. Use small nails to secure the end of the legs to the boards. At this point only the nose and the rear of the legs are nailed. Stretch the legs of the stretcher apart until the desired shape is obtained. The hide should be taut against the outside length of the stretcher legs. Nail or screw the crosspiece into position so that the tension is maintained. Now nail the outside edges of the rear legs into position on the boards. Finish by stretching and nailing the mouth and lower jaw into position.

Place the stretcher and the hide into an area that has good air circulation. No sun should strike the hide. Watch that the blow flies are not able to crawl into the cavities to deposit eggs. Take bent clotheshanger wire and insert one into the inside of each front leg. This will keep the leg sheaths from falling and touching the belly hide. Leave the fur in this position until a glaze has formed over the entire surface. This may take as little as a few hours or as much as a few days. Drying time will be determined by temperature, humidity and wind. Check the area around the ears and front legs daily as these will be the last areas to dry.

When the hide is about 80 percent dry remove it from the stretcher for turning. Remove the crosspiece to relieve the tension on the hide. Take out all nails using a set of electrician's pliers and slip the fur off the stretcher. You will find it easier to turn the front leg sheaths first. Check them for dryness: If they are totally dry they are apt to split during the turning. It is best to wet a paper towel and moisten the leg sheaths until they are somewhat pliable. Push the end of the sheath back up into the cavity. Take a pair of long nose pliers and reach into the interior of the pelt and insert the nose of the pliers into the leg sheath. Grab on to the leg end you have pushed into the sheath and pull to turn the legs.

To turn the hide, start the nose down inside the mouth cavity. Keep working more and more of the head down inside the cavity. If the hide is very dry and resists turning use the paper towel and water to moisten the skin until it is pliable enough to turn. When the head is turned back inside the mouth cavity, reach inside the hide from the rear, grab the nose, and pull the hide through.

An alternate method of turning the hide involves the use of an old broomstick. Sharpen one end of the stick until a point is obtained. Remove the sharp point by slight sanding. Use the thumb and forefinger to reverse the nose and poke this part into the mouth opening. Stand the broomstick on end with the sharpened point up. Hold the hide upside down and insert the stick into the reversed nose. Now strip the hide on down over the stick.

When the hide has been reversed place it back on the stretcher and go through the same steps as you did originally. Leave the hide on the stretcher with the fur side out until it is completely dry. Check the nose and the base of the ears. When they feel completely stiff to the touch the entire hide will be ready to take from the stretcher. Hang the hide by the nose in a cool and well-ventilated shed away from flies.

Brushing

When the pelts are to be marketed you should give them a good combing with a stiff-bristled brush. I use one of the wire "poodle" brushes available from most pet stores. Use the brush to remove any small tangles. Brush with the grain of the hair, from nose to tail. Now take the brush and go against the grain. This will fluff the fur and make it appear more luxuriant. When the fur has been fluffed, use the brush lightly to bring the belly fur from the sides to the center. Do the same on the back. This will produce a thick ridge of fur along the center of the back and the belly. This should motivate the fur buyer to reach really deep into his bank account.

Folding

Dried pelts should not be folded unless it is necessary to ship them to market. Even then it is better to leave them unfolded if possible. If it is absolutely necessary to fold the hides, fold large hides such as coyote, bobcat or fox one time only, placing the fold in the middle of the skin.

Shipping

Most fur buyers who buy by mail provide shipping tags and instructions to potential customers. The seller is more or less at the buyer's mercy in this instance as he is not there to speak up for his fur or to contest grading. Some companies will keep the customer's fur separated until he has the opportunity to accept or reject the buyer's offer. If you are dealing with a mail-order buyer for the first time it might be well to take advantage of this feature. You may want your furs returned rather than accept a low price. You should make this request to the buyer at the time you ship. Some buyers do this as a matter of course. They will mail you a check which totals their offer for the lot of fur. You will be told that your furs will be held separate for ten days. If you cash the check the deal is struck. If you do not want to accept the offer call or write the buyer and advise him of your decision.

I have found it to be good business to write a letter to the buyer on the day I ship advising that a lot of fur is on the way to him. In the event the fur shipment is delayed in transit it gives the buyer a chance to notify you your furs are lost enroute. Sometimes a speedy tracer will turn them up.

Only completely dry furs should be shipped. Let me put that another way. Do not ship fur through the mail that is not completely dry. Any green (undried) fur in the packet will likely spoil. As it spoils it will taint the entire shipment of fur with the odor of rotten meat. You will probably get your fur, and the stink, back by return mail. If it is absolutely necessary to ship green, and you have the permission of the buyer to do so, disregard the advice against salting. Salt the entire skin-side surface of the fur to prevent spoilage.

Place a tag inside and outside every bundle of fur. If the outside tag is lost, the inner will identify the fur. Tie a shipping tag to the outside of the packet with the name and address of the fur company and your own name and address. You may package the fur in a cardboard box, or they may be sewn into a burlap bag. The bag will work best because the coarse weave of the burlap will allow some air circulation. Do not ship fur in a plastic bag. Any part of the pelt not completely dry will (notice I didn't say might?) spoil in transit and the entire shipment will be contaminated.

You will have three general options in shipping fur. The U.S. Mail, a passenger bus company such as Continental or Greyhound and the United Parcel Service (UPS). The bus is the fastest but it will also cost you the most money. If the packet of fur is lost or damaged in transit you will have quite an adventure in collecting from the bus company.

UPS is probably your best choice for shipment if you have the service available. They are moderately fast and moderately priced. Their claims service for lost or damaged merchandise seems to be prompt and fair.

Freezing Fur

Some hunters never flesh or stretch a pelt. They skin the critter and put the green pelt in the deep freeze to await the arrival of the fur buyer. This saves the hunter a lot of time and work. It seems, however, that the fur buyer would not pay top dollar for an unhandled fur. Somewhere along the line he has to be paid for the extra work of fleshing and stretching. Not all areas have buyers who will purchase green fur. If your area has such a buyer, give him a try. You may learn that you earn almost as much from your green fur as you do from your well-handled fur.

To freeze a fur, turn it hair side out when it is removed from the critter. If it is only to be frozen a short time, roll the hide into a ball and place it in a plastic bag. Squeeze out all available air and seal the bag with freezer tape. Place the name of the critter and the date of the freezing on another piece of tape and stick it to the bag. Place the wrapped skin in the deep freeze and leave it there until the buyer arrives.

Take the bag from the freezer a few hours before the buyer shows up to give it a chance to thaw. Do not attempt to straighten a frozen hide. Let it thaw first. A frozen hide that is forced open will likely split which will bring you a reduced price. Let the hide thaw naturally, take it from the bag and shake it out, and present it to the buyer for grading.

20

Marketing Pelts

Payday comes for the hunter when he sells his fur. Some hunters save their hides and sell them as a collection while others sell the fur every time the buyer comes to town. The amount of the check will be determined by the number of furs taken, the value of the individual furs, the primeness of each fur and the manner in which it was handled. Well-handled prime fur should bring top dollar. Unfortunately, this is not always the case. Where and how the hunter sells his fur often determines if he has a good or a bad year. Selling your fur to the wrong buyer at the wrong time of year can be disastrous. The 1979-80 season is a good example.

I sold a collection of fur in the last week in November. I received an average of $225 for my bobcat, $60 for my coyote and $48 for my gray fox. A week later one of the environmental crazies filed a federal lawsuit challenging our right to export bobcat hides. A sympathetic federal judge granted an injunction which prohibited the export of bobcat hides until a hearing could be held. As most of the market for U.S. furs is through European markets, the price buyers were willing to pay for bobcat dropped to almost nothing. I was offered $75 for a large prime cat that would have brought $300 the week before. I didn't sell. The depressed price of bobcat also affected the price buyers were willing to pay for coyote. Good big coyotes that might have brought $75 the week before were appraised at $25. I didn't sell any coyote at that price either. The only major fur that remained stable throughout the year was fox. Our gray fox started the season at $48 and ended at $45.

Many small-time trappers and callers sold their fur for whatever was offered. A friend who is a longline trapper sent his collection of fur to one of the northwestern fur auctions. He got about average on his fox and cats but his coyotes were a disaster. He averaged under $25 for his collection of more than a hundred coyote hides. I decided that I would not sell a fur at the depressed price and held the fur until season's end. I was fully prepared to hold them through the summer and sell the following season if necessary. Prices took an upswing at the end of the buying season and I was able to sell all of the fur at a decent price. If I had shipped to one of the auctions I would have been paid only about half of what I received for my coyotes locally.

Most fur buyers are honest. As merchants they must buy lower than they sell. The profit keeps them in business. I do not begrudge the buyer his honest profit; he is in a highly speculative business and gambles big money every fur season. If he buys high at the start of the season and prices plummet near the end he may lose his shirt.

You have four options in selling your collection of fur. You may sell to a local buyer, you may sell by mail, you may market your fur through a fur combine or you may put your collection into a fur auction.

Local Buyers

The local man usually gives the small collector the best price for his few furs. He may live in your town and you may know him personally, so to stay in business he must develop a reputation for fairness. If he does not he soon runs out of customers and closes his doors.

The local buyer usually has some experience as a fur handler. He knows local critters and local fur. He will often stock items of interest to fur handlers and hunters. He is available to buy a few furs if you need a few dollars for a tank of gas, and he is available to offer good advice on fur handling. He will point out to you ways to improve your fur handling skills and increase your paycheck. The local buyer will often buy unskinned critters or frozen hides.

Selling by Mail

If the local buyer does not offer what you consider to be a fair price, or if your community does not have a local buyer, you may want to consider selling by mail. Mail selling may have a number of drawbacks. You may lose your shipment in the mail or it may become damaged. This problem may be minimized if the fur is shipped by United Parcel Service. I have found they offer a fast transport at a decent price. If the packet is lost or damaged, UPS has a settlement procedure that will leave you smiling. The U.S. Mail, on the other hand, is slow and loss or damage is not uncommon. Claims against the Postal Service are as slow as the mails. You will likely have an ulcer before you see one cent of Uncle Sam's money. The collection can also be sent by bus. This is usually the fastest way possible to get your packet of fur from one city to another, but there is apt to be a slowdown on in-city delivery. Claims are also a problem. The legal hassle involved would cause Carrie Nation to make a dive for the gin bottle, not to pour it out but to drink it. My best experience mailing fur has been with UPS.

There are other protential problems in selling by mail. You are not there when the fur is graded and have no way of disputing the decision of the grader. He may call a large a medium. He may label some furs as shedders. He may be able to see singeing and rubbing that no one else can notice. Your only protection is to grade the fur yourself prior to shipment. If you do not have this skill, call upon some more knowledgeable fur handler. If the buyer does not come close to this pre-sale grading, tell him you want your fur back.

If you intend to sell by mail check out your intended market as thoroughly as possible. I would suggest selling only to old, established companies. Check magazines such as *Fur Fish and Game*, *Fur Takers of America*, *Voice of the Trapper* and *The Trapper*. Advertisements seen here will usually belong to established companies with a reputation for fairness.

Price lists from mail-order buyers can be deceptive. All of us tend to look at the price paid for the largest and primest hides. We set our sights on that price and are disappointed if our collection sells for less. Most collections that are properly handled will average more to the medium or high-medium quotation. If there are defects such as unprimeness, damage, singeing or rubbing, the price will go lower.

Fur Auctions

Fur auctions are held several times during the season at widely separated locations. With a number of buyers competing for the same lot of fur you have a good chance of getting a fair price for your fur. This is true of national auctions with a good number of money men present. Small local auctions with only two or three bidders will not pay as well.

One of the largest of the current fur auctions is the Dominion Soudack Fur Auction held in Winnipeg, Manitoba. More than a hundred foreign and domestic buyers competed for the fur sold there last year. This auction regularly pays the seller top money for his prime fur. Check the previously mentioned trapping magazines for auction dates.

Many auctions are held in the continental United States during the fur season. These auctions may be sponsored by a group of fur sellers or by a buyer's organization. They are also advertised in trapping magazines. Listed will be time, location, and prices paid for each species at the previous month's auction.

If you decide to sell at an auction you may personally deliver your collection of fur or send it by mail. Either way it should arrive at the auction two or three days prior to the first day's sale. You will need to separate your collection into lots. A lot of fur is the total number of one species you ship. If you send thirty coyote, eight gray fox and one bobcat to the auction, the coyote would be one lot, the fox one lot and the lone bobcat one lot. You will be asked to list a minimal acceptable bid. This bid will be the average price paid for each fur in a lot. You may put $45 as the minimum bid you will accept for your lot of coyote. That is $45×30 for a total of $1,350 for the lot. The buyers do not see this figure until the bidding is finished. If no buyer bid that price for your fur then the lot will be returned to you unsold or held for the next month's auction. You may want to put *SELL* as the minimum price you will accept. This indicates that your lot of fur will be sold to the highest bidder. You are assured a sale but will not know the amount until the check arrives in the mail. The auction takes a small percentage of the selling price as its commission.

The advantage of the fur auction is most apparent when you have a large quantity of fur to sell. Even then there must be enough buyers at the sale to induce spirited bidding.

One disadvantage of auction selling is the commission kept by the auctioneer. Another is the cost of taking or sending the fur to market. Another may be a lack of competition. Too few buyers will result in low prices. If this happens you may have to pay shipping charges, auction commission and also endure a low price. You may end up with considerably less than the local buyer would have paid.

Fur Combines

The fur combine is becoming popular with many sellers. More fur is sold by the state units of the Fur Takers of America, for example, than any other organization.

One large fur combine is the Oregon Territorial Council. It is managed and operated by the Fur Takers of America, Oregon Chapter. The organization is trapper-owned and trapper-operated. A single three- or four-day sale may see a quarter of a million dollars in fur change hands.

These sales are operated as auctions. The lots are sold by sealed bids. The buyer walks through the sale area inspecting each lot of fur and making notes on the lots he wants. If his bid is the highest of the bidders, and if it meets the minimum selling price set for the lot, he gets the lot of fur. You must pay a display fee and a percentage of the selling price as auction commission.

Here again, if there are not enough buyers with money, you may get hurt. Check the prices paid at the previous month's auction to learn how well the sale draws buyers.

My best advice on selling is to sell locally if you possibly can. He may pay slightly less than what you would receive at an auction but you will avoid shipping expense and transportation expense. You also avoid the hassle of having your collection lost or damaged in transit.

If you have a lot of fur to sell you may want to take them to one of the fur auctions. You would be cutting out the middle man and you will be there to give your furs the last-minute grooming that will make them look their best. And the fur auctions are fun. You have a chance to mingle with like-minded men. New friendships can be formed and old friendships renewed. The exchange of information will provide you with a new insight into the business and it gives you a chance to compare your pelts with others and perhaps gain a new insight into your own fur-handling skills.

When to Sell

When the fur is sold might make a difference in the number on your paycheck but there is no hard and fast rule because there are too many variables. Early fur sales, as a rule, do not see much new fur. Most of the fur sold is holdover fur from the previous season. Buyers do not usually dip deep into their wallets for holdover fur. You can expect prices to start at slightly less than the end of the previous season.

By mid-season the year's prices will begin to stabilize. There are fresh collections hitting the market and domestic buyers are beginning to build an inventory of fur they have contracted to foreign buyers. Prices continue to harden and good prices will be paid for most species through January and February. This coincides with the prime fur period for most fur and may have something to do with the solid market. Some years the prices peak early and go soft near season's end. At other times fur prices will peak at the last sale of the season. Buyers who have held off buying now have to bid high to fulfill their contractual commitments. Some years the market will be flooded with a particular species and prices will plummet. If this happens, in all probability, there will be a lot of holdover fur to be sold early the next season. Prices for that species may stay low through most of the following season as the holdover fur creates a surplus. Watch the prices paid for fur at the auctions. Most trapping magazines print this information as a service to their readers. You will soon learn the current trend of fur prices. Sell when the price seems right to you.

If you do not have room in your home to safely store a large collection of fur you will be forced to sell your pelts in small lots throughout the season. This may work to your advantage. You receive the entire spectrum of prices from high to low and will end the season with a healthy average.

Fur Grading

A buyer will consider a number of features when he grades your fur. Size will be one grading factor. A big prime fur brings more money than a little prime fur if both are well handled. You will get what your hides are worth if you stretch each pelt to the correct size. Do not overstretch, however. Overstretching thins the hide and the fur and you lose more in quality than you gain in size. To grade for size the buyer measures the pelt (or eyeballs it) for length. This will be from tip of nose to the hips. He will also measure for width, once at the shoulders and once again at the hips. These measurements will place the pelt into a small, medium or large category, or in a subdivision of those categories.

Color

Most of the predators have some color variation. Pelts from the same geographic area may show a radical color range. The bobcat, for example, is dark-colored through most of his Pacific Coast range. The cat of the Southwest, north central Canada and the northwest United States is much lighter. These cats also have a white spotted underbelly.

The demands of the fashion industry control fur prices. At the present time the light-colored fur is fashionable. The lighter cats are in demand and bring premium prices, much higher than their darker-colored cousins. The same can be said of the coyote. He has a color range that grades from light silver to auburn. The lighter skins bring the best price. Fashion, of course, is a fickle standard. Color preferences may change from season to season.

Quality

To determine quality the buyer checks the length and thickness of the underfur, the length and thickness of the guard hair, and the overall gloss of the pelt. Fur taken from certain geographic areas rate consistently high in quality. Fur of the same species taken a hundred miles away might score consistently low. Diet, habitat, cover and temperature are determining factors in producing high quality fur.

Quality grading is mostly an eyeball judgment. The buyer considers the overall appearance of the pelt to rate the eye appeal. You will get the best quality rating if the fur is properly handled. If bobcats are selling for several hundred dollars each it might pay to wash every skin. Color is a critical factor in cat grading. If the washing lightens the fur color you may get $50 more for the hide. This is good wages for the hour or so it will take to wash the hide. The washing may also take out flaws such as blood stains. Washing also brightens cat fur and gives it a gloss that is sure to earn quality points.

Always give your pelts a last minute grooming before you hand them to the buyer. Furs develop a crushed look when they are stored or shipped. If cowlicks develop, use the poodle brush to comb them out and fluff the fur. It will look thicker and bring a better price.

Damage

Most fur damage can be repaired, but this should be done before the fur is sold. Bullet holes and skinning cuts should be sewed. Pine pitch snarls can be dissolved with turpentine. Bloodstains can be rinsed out with cold water. Burrs can be removed by first soaking them in mineral or baby oil. Other defects cannot be repaired but can be avoided. Meat chunks left after skinning can taint the hide and cause hair slip. Fat on the hide can do the same. Even a hide that is properly skinned and fleshed can develop hair slippage if it is dried in a poorly ventilated, warm room. Salt on the hide may cause problems. A hide that is removed from the stretcher too quickly shrinks and wrinkles. If the drying board is an incorrect dimension or shape, the finished hide will dry to an irregular and unattractive shape. If a hide is overstretched the fur will be thin and quality points will be lost.

Prime Fur

Prime fur is that which is taken in the winter when cold weather causes the fur to thicken and the hide to thin. Primeness refers to the condition of the hide and not the fur. When a hide is prime the inside will display a rich creamy color which remains when the hide is dry. An unprime hide will show a bluish color on the inside when it is skinned. When it dries the blue fades to an ugly grey.

At certain times of the year the hide may be prime but the fur is degrading. Some animals rub the hip area in the spring to rid themselves of the thick winter coat. This is called rubbing and will be most noted in coyote and fox. As the summer sun becomes warmer the guard hair on many predators begins to curl. This is a condition called singeing. Either rubbing or singeing will degrade the fur radically. It is better to put away the rabbit and the gun when any of these conditions are noted. Leave the critter for the next season when the fur will be prime and you will earn a fair reward for your labor.

21

Record Keeping

Hunters hunt because they want to be afield among the animals. You may try to avoid the keeping of records because it will take you inside and steal time from the hunt. But if you want to be an efficient hunter a certain amount of record keeping is necessary.

Tax Records

Any money you realize from the hunting and selling of fur is subject to federal income tax. Your state may want a few furs also. To prevent paying more than your fair share, you are allowed certain deductions, usually expenses you have incurred in the pursuit of the game. To support these expenses you must keep certain records. The fur buyer may be required by law to furnish a list of monies paid to fur sellers. This may give the tax men the amount of money you made from the sale of fur. Unless proper records are available you will be expected to pay tax on the total paycheck.

Vehicle

The vehicle that you use in the pursuit of fur can be a major part of your expenses. The vehicle may be a four-wheeler, a snowmobile, a motorcycle or the family sedan. I have a friend who claims his horse. He uses the critter to reach inaccessible calling locations. He also uses the horse part of the year for pleasure. He prorates the expense of keeping the horse and takes as a deduction only that portion of the horse used for the hunt. You can do the same thing with a vehicle. If you use your truck two months of the year for hunting and ten months for other use, you may deduct one-sixth of your total truck expenses as a tax deduction. If the truck is used totally for the hunt the entire cost will be tax deductible.

The gasoline and oil you use on the hunt are deductible. You may keep a record of hunting miles travelled and take a mileage allowance. You may also keep records of the exact amount spent. Oil changes, tires, lubrication and mechanical repairs may also be claimed. An easy way of keeping these records is to obtain an oil company credit card and charge all hunting expenses to the card. The credit card company will do your bookkeeping for you. Their itemized statements will provide the documentation you need to support your deductions.

The original cost of the vehicle may also be claimed as a tax expense. If the vehicle is used solely for the hunt you may claim the entire purchase price. Usually, on an item such as a vehicle, the purchase price is prorated over a number of years. You are allowed to claim depreciation for the vehicle over each year of its useful life. If the vehicle is used only partly for the hunt you may deduct that percentage of the cost. If your hunting season lasts four months of the year and you use the vehicle exclusively for hunting during that time you can claim that the vehicle was used 33 percent of the time for hunting and 66 percent of the time for other use. If the vehicle was parked at the end of the hunting season and not used for any other purpose, the total costs should be deductible. Do not forget the less obvious costs. Many hunters claim purchase price, gas and oil, tires, maintenance and repairs but will forget the vehicle license fees and insurance.

It should be noted that the IRS will expect you to make a profit from the business of hunting once in a while. If you claim these expenses when you have no substantial hunting income simply to offset the tax on other income, the IRS man will be out to talk to you. A good tax accountant can keep you from getting lost in the maze of tax laws.

Equipment

The equipment you use on the hunt is also tax deductible. Maintain proper receipts to prevent deductions from being disallowed. I keep my sales receipts. If they do not list the nature of the purchase I write it in on the back of the receipt. Packsacks, calls, guns, scrapers, stretchers, knives, snowshoes and camo clothing may all be claimed. The price of this book, as a matter of fact, could be a legitimate deduction, as is money paid for other publications which may increase your knowledge of predator calling or fur handling.

Freight and Postage

Money spent for postage, either letters or packages, and the cost of sending your furs to market are legitimate expenses. If the fur is taken to the market personally you may deduct the cost of the trip.

Fees and Licenses

The money spent for a hunting license or a business permit might be deductible, as are membership fees paid to professional groups such as state and national varmint calling associations. If you attend a state or national convention of the association you may be able to claim all or part of the trip expense.

Sales

Keep a record of the money you earn from the sale of all fur. If you sell subsidiary parts such as urine, castors, scents or claws, note the amount collected, the date of the sale, purchaser and type of article sold. If you hire an accountant to keep your records and prepare your tax statement, his cost is also deductible.

Reports

Many game departments require annual reports from fur takers. The reports will be used to determine the number of fur bearers taken. These figures will be used to maintain the population of each species. None of us wants to hunt a species to extinction or to hunt it to such a low level that its future existence is threatened. Cooperation with wildlife managers will help them do their job and if they do their job well we will have healty populations of critters to hunt for the future. These reports usually ask for number of each species killed, the general location, sex, age, condition and apparent defects.

Your records will also make you a better hunter. I keep a log of all my hunts. I have a ready reference to tell me the stands that have produced over the years. I know what days to hunt and what time of the day is best for each critter. I know when the deer start moving off the mountain. By knowing that I know where the mountain lion will be. I know when the bears will move into the prickly pear and when they hit the oaks. In these and other ways, records make me a more successful hunter.

Index